A Self-Made Surrealist

Beginning with the publication of *Tropic of Cancer* in 1934, Henry Miller's reputation as a writer has been sullied by critics from all sides, and the trend has not abated in recent decades. The emphasis on Miller's use of obscenity has ignored the fact that he wrote numerous essays on his contemporaries and the role of art. In these essays, desire in a wider and more culturally specific sense, rather than hostile obscenity, lays the foundation for Miller's literary project. *A Self-Made Surrealist* sets out to provide a view of Miller different from both earlier vindications of him as sexual liberator and prophet and more contemporary feminist critiques of him as pornographer and male chauvinist. In this re-evaluation of Miller's role as a radical writer, Blinder considers not only notions of obscenity and sexuality, but also the emergence of psychoanalysis, surrealism, automatic writing, and the aesthetics of fascism as they illuminate Miller's more general twentieth-century concerns with politics and mass psychology in relation to art. Blinder also considers the effect on Miller of the theoretical works of Georges Bataille and André Breton, among others, in order to define and explore the social, philosophical, and political contexts of the period.

Caroline Blinder received her Ph.D. in American literature from King's College, London, and is a lecturer in American and English literature, creative writing, critical theory, and film at Southampton University.

European Studies in American Literature and Culture

Edited by Reingard M. Nischik
(*Constance*)

Caroline Blinder

A Self-Made Surrealist

Ideology and Aesthetics
in the Work of
Henry Miller

CAMDEN HOUSE

First published 2000
by Camden House

Camden House is an imprint of Boydell & Brewer Inc.
PO Box 41026, Rochester, NY 14604–4126 USA
and of Boydell & Brewer Limited
PO Box 9, Woodbridge, Suffolk IP12 3DF, UK

ISBN: 1–57113–133–7

Library of Congress Cataloging-in-Publication Data

Blinder, Caroline, 1967–
     A self-made surrealist: ideology and aesthetics in the work of
Henry Miller / Caroline Blinder.
     p.   cm. -- (European studies in American literature and
culture)
     Includes bibliographical references (p.   ) and index.
     ISBN 1–57113–133–7 (alk. paper)
     1. Miller, Henry, 1891-   —Criticism and interpretation.
2. Politics and literature—United States—History—20th century.
3. Art and literature—United States—History—20th century.
4. Miller, Henry, 1891-   —Political and social views.
5. Surrealism (Literature)—United States. 6. Miller, Henry, 1891–
Aesthetics. I. Title. II. Series.
PS3525.I5454Z654   1999
818'.5209--dc21   99–38103
                                                                 CIP

A catalogue record for this title is available from the British Library.

This publication is printed on acid-free paper.
Printed in the United States of America.

Contents

Acknowledgments

A CERTAIN AMOUNT OF ACADEMIC ADVICE has been ignored in the writing of this book. From the university interviews where I was asked whether I "actually liked Henry Miller" to the university presses suggesting I "keep the theory but cut Henry Miller out," a fair number of critics have warned me against writing on him. This gives me all the more reason to thank the people who supported and helped me along the way.

I would like to thank especially, Professor Clive Bush at King's College London for doctoral supervision, Professor Allan Leibowitz and Professor Pete Nichols for excellent advice, my grandmother Mme. Odette Siegel for helping me translate Georges Bataille, and my father James Blinder for numerous first editions. Finally, I could not have completed this work without the kindness and encouragement of my friends, especially Gary Bell, Jeff Hilson, Peter Steffensen, and Dr. Lucy Hartley. I would also like to thank Mr. Henry Tony Miller, Ms. Valentine Miller, and Ms. Barbara Sylvas Miller for giving me permission to study the archives on Henry Miller at the Department of Special Collections at U.C.L.A., and Lars Busekist for his hospitality during my research in Los Angeles.

Finally, an enormous thanks to my best critic and the person who held my hand through this gestational period — Kim of course.

Introduction

> Art teaches nothing, except the significance of life. The great work must inevitably be obscure, except to the very few, to those who like the author himself are initiated into the mysteries. Communication then is secondary: it is perpetuation which is important. For this only one good reader is necessary.
>
> — Henry Miller, "Reflections on Writing"

EVER SINCE THE UNITED STATES PUBLICATION of *Tropic of Cancer* in 1961, Henry Miller has remained, both in the public and academic eye, the bad boy American writer. Polemicized chiefly in terms of sexual politics, the stress upon the sensationalist nature of his obscenity has made it impossible to pigeonhole him into traditional literary classifications, and instead, critics have continuously fought over whether Miller should be read as a prophet of sexual liberation or an advocate of male chauvinism.[1]

This book seeks to address this unbalance by taking as its starting point a range of essays written by Miller, on and influenced by surrealism, during his expatriate years in Paris. Written for small presses and journals, Miller's essays run the gamut from reviews of contemporary art and homages to friends (Brassaï in "The Eye of Paris," 1938), to more philosophical pieces on obscenity and psychoanalysis. While most of these essays were published in Miller's lifetime, critical writing on Miller has nevertheless focused on the *Tropics, Tropic of Cancer* (1934) and *Tropic of Capricorn* (1939), as the prime examples of his literary voice.[2]

From Kate Millet's attack in *Sexual Politics* (1969), Mailer's defense in *The Prisoner of Sex* (1971) to Erica Jong's more recent *The Devil at Large* (1993), the *Tropics* have been used chiefly to delineate a particular notion of male sexuality. Rather than insert Miller into a more complex historical, political, and aesthetic framework, the effect has been to neglect the period in which he actually wrote most of his best material, namely the 1930s and 1940s.[3] Miller circles around a number of key themes in the immediate pre-war and post-war period. Firstly, the fascination with surrealism; an art movement which he felt at liberty to both critique as an outsider in a political sense, and use as an overt inspiration stylistically and thematically in a literary sense. Secondly — linked to the issue of surrealism — that of the unconscious as a metaphor for creativity, and the idea that certain forms of writing can convey the unconscious in fruitful and radical ways. In Miller's fiction, the desire to search for a transcendental mode of writing often took on a surreal format, while in his essays, he engaged in an ongoing quest for an absolute, a fundamental truth from which to examine creative engagement.

In this sense, surrealism becomes a way to examine the stylistics and thematics which emerge both in Miller's fiction and essays. In the 1930s trilogy: *Tropic of Cancer* (1934), *Black Spring* (1938), *Tropic of Capricorn* (1939), a mental topography is mapped out by the first person narrator in which sexuality and desire is the source of libidinous as well as literary creativity. This mental topography, which Miller returns to repeatedly, is also an urban one — an external projection of the imaginary, with the city as the setting for an internal as well as external social drama. These topographies often mix the fictional with the critical and thus raise crucial questions related to literature's position as a politicized art form in the interim and post-war period. How does literature convey a radical voice without resorting to an ultimately romantic and mythical notion of the writer as prophet? And if so; what are the mechanisms suitable for this quest? Miller's reliance on a confessional and mystical voice, as we will see, links his writing to the surrealist notion of modernity as a development downwards towards a form of primitivism rather than onwards towards rationalism. A paradox thus occurs, as Miller's fiction seems to rely on these mechanisms, while the critical essays represent Miller's American sense of individualism as he struggles to negotiate his way around contemporary artistic groupings and their political and aesthetic definitions of radicalism.

The positioning of sexuality and obscenity as a way to radicalize art is something which Miller shares with the surrealists in crucial ways. The issue is, then, not to validate Miller by placing him in "good European company" but to illuminate his use of sexuality and, on a wider level, his concepts of individualism vis-à-vis the increasing politicization of art movements at the time. In order to structure and define this reading of Miller, this study will be guided largely by a historical juncture: the outpouring of critical thought that distinguished European intellectual life in the 1920s, 1930s and 1940s. In addition, this perspective will gauge both the limits of and transgressions against two important moments in history: that of the author as a historical subject of the period between the world wars and that of the survival of the author in a post war environment. The encounter with surrealism encapsulates both Miller's desire to immerse himself in a distinctly European cultural heritage, as well as some of the complex links between a collective notion of avant-garde aesthetics and his own individualistic, literary project. I have largely argued for surrealism's inclusive role within Miller's work in terms of common themes and concerns, but I have also tried not to neglect the complex links between Miller the American individualist and the collective identity of surrealism:

> Surrealism starts out innocently enough as a revolt against the insanity of everyday life. It is expressed marvellously in one of Breton's early pronunciamentoes: "I am resolved to render powerless that hatred of the marvellous which is so rampant among certain people." Naturally he is not referring to concierges alone. He means everybody (who is not living as a poet), from the President of France on down to the chimney-sweep. It is a big order. It is a defy to the whole world practically. But there is no confusion behind the idea. It is clear as a bell.
>
> (Henry Miller, "An Open Letter to Surrealists Everywhere," 1938)

In the opening chapter of his essay: "An Open Letter to Surrealists Everywhere" (1938), Miller looks at the influence of surrealism, automatism, and the political implications of theories based on the "unconscious" through a comparative view of himself and André Breton. Surrealism's recent academic return, in terms of publications and exhibitions, is still missing in many Anglo-American accounts of modernism. Partly due to the focus on iconography and pictorial style, the surrealists' concern with the unconscious as a motivation in narrative terms has so far been neglected in relation to American writers of the same period. In order to rethink Miller's critical work on surrealism, the ways in which concepts of the unconscious were introduced into art in a programmatic way, particularly through automatic writing, will be examined. As an example, one of Miller's unpublished pieces "Last Will and Testament," a nonsensical attempt to write surrealistically inspired in part by André Breton and Paul Eluard's *The Immaculate Conception* (1930), is compared to some of Breton's writing from the same period.[4] Such a comparison becomes an important guide to Miller's use of sexuality, as it allows for an analysis which goes beyond gender as the sole determinant of subjectivity. As the nodal point of three fundamental ideologies within modernism: psychoanalysis, cultural Marxism, and ethnology, surrealism represents a touchstone from which to examine Miller's aesthetics as well as politics.

Chapter 3 examines how these three fields in particular merge within surrealism as the backdrop for a writing in which sexuality is linked to an increasing eroticization of the urban landscape. Miller's attitudes to the feminine are compared to those of Breton, as both align desire with creativity through the image of the woman on the streets. As sexuality moves into the public domain, the urban landscape is both mythologized and eroticized. In particular, Breton's *Nadja* (1928) and *Mad Love* (1938), represent highly Freudian readings of the feminine in terms of an enigmatic hysteria both glorified and feared. Miller's writings show an awareness of the problems inherent in mythologizing, as well as politicizing the unconscious, and are, in many ways, representative of a working through of the paradoxes set up by Walter Benjamin in "The Last Snapshot of the European Intelligentsia" (1929). As both Benjamin and Miller attempt to pry open the cyclical argument of surrealism, the question emerges of how language can represent the universal in terms of the irrational, which in turn is aligned with ideas of femininity and hysteria. In Breton's novels the figure of the sphinx embodies the unconscious as a feminine and creative muse. Just as the unconscious becomes indicative of a welcome illuminatory and universal force, it also opens itself up to misuse; absolving the male artist from the rationale of reason, largely through the positioning of the unconscious in terms of a feminine "other." These issues are crucial for an understanding of the terminology with which these writers create an absolute; whether it is in the form of desire, the unconscious, or the surreal marvellous.

In "The Eye of Paris," Miller's homage to his friend and later biographer the photographer Brassaï, photography is seen as an art form uniquely suited to represent the hidden facets of the urban landscape. Not only is photography representative of a particular form of modernity, but its individualism ensures that "the photograph seems to carry with it the same degree of personality as any other form or expression of art."[5] For Miller, the prostitutes, the workers, and back-alleys in Brassaï's gritty vision of a particular kind of public humanity, are uniquely suited to accompany his own fictional vagabond persona. "A man of the city, he limits himself to that spectacular feast which only such a city as Paris can offer. No phase of cosmopolitan life has escaped his eye. His albums of black and white comprise a vast encyclopedia of the city's architecture, its growth, its history, its origins" (*Wisdom of the Heart*, 180). For Miller, Brassaï's photographs of working people and objects in Paris are the most apt and contemporary representations of modernism, never compromising the integrity of either the photographer or the people photographed.

"The Eye of Paris" links the focus on surrealist aesthetics set out in Chapters 1 and 2 with an examination into the political ramifications of those aesthetics in Chapters 3 and 4. Brassaï's view of the people of Paris is more politicized than similar surreal images from the same period; a representation which shares Benjamin's ideas on objects as both illuminatory and suggestive of proletarian experience. Miller's essay on Brassaï thus stands out as one of the clearest representations of his ability to link his own individualist philosophy with art's ability to represent a width of experience of a social, economic, and historical nature. Miller speaks of Brassaï in terms of the surrealist ability to sign-post the marvellous through the urban landscape, but he also stresses a Benjaminian approach to art in his belief that objects encompass a complex network of relations which must be read within a historical continuum. Few critics have attempted to read Miller's own use of obscenity and sexuality in these politicized, social terms, apart from the French critic and philosopher Georges Bataille.

Bataille may seem an unlikely partner to Miller, both in terms of fictional and critical methodologies, but his essay: "La Morale de Miller" (1946) is one of the first critiques of Miller which reads the issue of obscenity in political *and* aesthetic terms. "La Morale de Miller" was the first in a series of essays on literature for *Critique*, a journal set up partly as an alternative venue to the French existentialist journal *Les Temps Moderne*. Apart from providing one of the only complex perspectives on Miller's use of obscenity, it also synthesizes a crucial issue introduced through the comparison of Miller and the surrealists; namely the impossibility of actually writing outside rational and dialectical definitions of morality. In ways similar to the surrealists, Bataille wanted to dislodge traditional boundaries between the critic and his subject, aiming to represent a totality of radical experience in writing from an aesthetic as well as political point of view. Bataille was particularly interested in the question of what really constitutes evaluative discourse, and his ethnological and sociological work (linked to sexuality in terms of eroticism and heterogeneity) offers a more politicized version of the surrealist quest for the marvellous; crucial for an understanding of the critical and aesthetic connection between sexuality and fascism: the body-politic as a dangerous as well as creative force in 1930s literature.

Chapters 3 and 4 will therefore look closely at how the mixing of political ideology, whether from a leftist perspective in the form of critical Marxist theory or a move towards a fascist aesthetic with its fascination for authoritarianism, incorporates many of the same structural devices. This intrinsic paradox must be taken into account in an examination of the use of desire and its relationship to the body politic in a wider sense. Whether one views the radicalization of sexuality from a leftist or rightist perspective, the overriding concerns are still a deliberate politicization of the individual as artist. What Bataille realized was that Miller's use of sexuality could be read as a concerted effort to align the structures of desire with language itself (not dissimilar to the surrealist project). Bataille reads the unconscious as a sphere from which sexuality emerges in radically new ways, ready to manifest itself not merely as an artistic aesthetic, but also as an image of the disintegration of the modern world. As far as language is concerned, observations on sexuality and eroticism become a way to portray the writer as he struggles to speak, as well as a way to allegorize sexuality in terms of the creative process itself.

The premise that political ideology cannot be divorced from the creative process is crucial for an understanding of Miller. For both Miller and Bataille, the radical and deliberately uncomfortable sensibility in much of their work coexists with their value as important critics in their own right; something which current work seems hesitant to address. Bataille, in particular, is a writer whose current appropriation into poststructuralism has equaled a diffusion of the disconcerting and uneasy political elements in his writing.

The notion that one can attain a truly radical subversive discourse in literature is the key to understanding writing which plays on and uses marginalization as a force. Bataille locates this marginalization within a larger sphere of heterogeneous activity which in ethnological and political terms is deemed sexual, dangerous and death-driven. Similarly, in these terms, many of Miller's more complex elements stem from the connections mentioned above, rather than any straightforward form of male chauvinism. Chapter 3: "The Politics of Violence," deals with these themes in terms of the relationship between the Japanese writer Yukio Mishima, Bataille, and Miller. Miller's "Reflections on the Death of Mishima" (1971), together with Mishima's "Georges Bataille and Divinus Deus" (1968) show a shared interest in the use of sexuality as a radical and often violent manifestation of the individual, in spite of differing cultural backgrounds. Mishima's fictional debut, *Confessions of a Mask* (1949), returns in equal measure to Miller's over-sexed and frustrated literary persona and Bataille's linking of death with pleasure. In terms of fictional representation, Mishima, Miller, and Bataille used the narrative consciousness as expressed by the writer/heroes of their books to demonstrate, in turn, their own absolute commitment to the writer's life as intrinsically rebellious and dangerous.

The fact that these writers share an interest in sexuality as a radical discourse, does not mean that they do not differ in important degrees as to the nature and extent of this "radicalism." For instance, Miller's use of sexuality often emblematizes the uncomfortable sensations of sexuality as a commodity whereas Breton's does not. In this context, Benjamin and Miller converge to some extent in their critique of commodification within the urban landscape and its potentially de-sensitizing force. As far as the urban sensibility of the artist is concerned, the prostitute for Miller — unlike Breton — is, among other things, an embodiment of the overall exploitation which takes place in the urban environment on a constant basis. Miller, in this respect, uses his own version of American individualism as a way to critique what he considers a falsely romanticized version of love within surrealism. For Miller, the surrealists failed to see that desire in itself could not provide a harmonious view of the writer at ease with his unconscious. Alienation in the modern world is always individual rather than collective, and it is this which emerges strongly in the essay on Mishima, and which explains his reluctance to speak of politics in anything but individualized terms.

The premise that it is impossible to speak of the politicization of aesthetics without simultaneously dealing with political aesthetics is a crucial one for the overall project of this book. Fascist aesthetics not only underlie much fiction of the 1920s and 1930s, but must be seen as an important part of the literary avant-garde in general. If surrealism can be read in part as an anxious response to the fascist glorification of mythology (racist and historicist), then those authors on the fringe of surrealism, whose responses to fascism manifested themselves in aesthetic and not simply overtly political terms, must be examined as well. By looking at fascist aesthetics from this broader perspective, fascism becomes another way to signal an anarchical strain, a perspective on writing as dangerous to established notions of what constitutes viable political rhetoric, rather than another more vehement and fanatical strain of nationalism. While the project of surrealist automatic writing assumed the possibility of a language unhindered by bourgeois and capitalist structures, writers like Bataille and Mishima saw no escape from these structures other than via action of a more direct and violent nature than traditional poetics could afford.

Miller's preoccupation with individualism and non-affiliation in a political sense is made all the more complex by these issues. On one hand, Miller's individualism can be seen in opposition to fascism, a remnant of a democratic American ethic, but his rhetoric is often highly authoritarian, his narcissism extreme. On the other hand, Miller strove to get away from what he considered a restrictive commodified world view at home, and his starting point — the truthful representation of the self — is continuously signposted as American and Whitmanesque in its idealization of self-expression. There is no doubt that Miller's admiration for both D. H. Lawrence and Walt Whitman came out of an interest in the poet-writer's quest for a viable ethic of self-creation and an acknowledgment in turn of this ethic's Anglo-Saxon roots. Nevertheless, Miller's expression of self-hood, particularly in terms of sexuality, turns out to be similar to that of Bataille, Mishima, and the surrealists. The sense of divine inspiration as the artist's prerogative, together with the bodily quest turned into a metaphysical one, were things that in Miller's mind belonged to a tradition of marginalized writing regardless of its national roots.

Forced to return to the United States with the advent of the Second World War, Miller's essays became increasingly influenced by his evolving pacifism. By way of conclusion, Chapter 5 examines the issue of pacifism in Miller's 1946 book on Arthur Rimbaud: *Time of the Assassins*, which also illustrates the end of Miller's obsession with European writers and culture. In a series of letters to the academic and literary critic Wallace Fowlie on the writing of *Time of the Assassins*, Miller fuses the aspects of revolt, exile and the relation towards creativity into an analysis of himself through Rimbaud. This practice of writing on the "self" through others — while in a long tradition of introspective literary analysis — foregrounds some of Miller's shortcomings as a critic. In writing from his homeland on a French writer, Miller seems to have lost the peculiar psychic advantage he had had as an expatriate. As Miller stated in 1932 "no longer being an American" still meant being "a foreigner in Paris," and it is this ambiguous position in literary and political terms which Miller needed to be able to write, both as an American writing on Europeans, and as an American written on by Europeans.

As certain themes emerge in more clarity — fascism as a form of transgression aesthetically as well as politically, sexuality and violence as allegories for communication — the overall emphasis will be on the critical force of these ideas irrespective of the nationalities of the writers concerned. The ideas and themes which emerge in these writers' works are therefore partly estimated through the resistance against them and appropriation by others, regardless of national literary traditions. This approach does not claim allegiance to, nor immunity from, any one critical method, but it deliberately incorporates a series of inter-textual dialogues in order to avoid using preferred writers as oracles. Bataille and Benjamin are obvious examples of writers who are currently being used in this way. In fact, Miller's own multifaceted fictional as well as critical persona is partly due to the realization that nothing in literature emanates from one source only.

Miller tried to retain an anti-political, individualistic stance throughout his career, yet at the same time he was fascinated with his contemporaries' attempts to break existing notions of literary merit and groupings. This created an underlying ambiguity in Miller's work. On the one hand, he wanted to be part of an intelligentsia committed to the creation of a new form of literature, and on the other, he wanted to be seen as a provocative outsider: a form of literary anarchist. As a this book will show, Miller cannot be read as representative of one particular male chauvinist sensibility, but must be seen as part of an artistic landscape, of surrealism, of Paris, of post-war Europe as well as of an American tradition of individualism. As far as literary aesthetics and politics were concerned, the representation of external reality through a voyage inward was ultimately Miller's chief project, a project which places him firmly within a tradition where people such as Georges Bataille, Yukio Mishima, and André Breton become fellow travelers rather than mere contemporaries.

Notes

1 "In some mysterious way, Miller has preserved an innocence of the practice of Literature-with-a-capital-L which is almost unique in history. Likewise he has preserved an innocence of heart . . . he writes a muscular, active prose in which something is always going on and which is always under control. True he often likes to ramble and hear his head roar." Kenneth Rexroth, "The Reality of Henry Miller" in *World Outside the Window* (New York: New Directions, 1947), 154–67.

2 Henry Miller, *Tropic of Cancer* (Paris: Obelisk Press, 1934). *Tropic of Capricorn* (Paris: Obelisk Press, 1939).

3 Kate Millet, *Sexual Politics* (New York: Ballantine Books, 1979). All subsequent quotes taken from this edition.

Erica Jong, *The Devil at Large* (London: Chatto and Windus, 1993). All subsequent quotes taken from this edition.

4 Hal Foster's *Compulsive Beauty* (London: MIT Press, 1993) is one notable exception.

5 Henry Miller, "The Eye of Paris" in *Wisdom of the Heart* (New York: New Directions, 1960), 173–87.

1: Henry Miller and Surrealism

IN 1934, ONLY A YEAR AFTER THE PUBLICATION of André Breton's surrealist manifesto on automatic writing, "The Automatic Message," Henry Miller established himself in Paris with *Tropic of Cancer*, the first in a trilogy of "auto-romances." The auto-romance, a mixture of fiction and autobiography in which a version of "Miller" figures as the main protagonist, charts the narrator's day-to-day existence in Paris, his sexual adventures, the people he encounters, where he eats, sleeps, etc. While *Tropic of Cancer* is primarily known for its rendition of the perverse and obscene, for the unashamed fascination Miller expresses for street-life in all its forms, it also provides a romantic vision of the city as a potentially illuminatory force, as the hunting ground for the modern artist's inspiration.

It is no coincidence, then, that Miller's style in the *Tropics* and his chief concern in the essays written during the same period, fall under the spell of surrealism. For Miller, surrealism provided new ways to describe the juxtaposition of fantasy and reality, the use of dreams and visions, and as such became a convenient source for his own concept of radical writing. Representing above all a welcome attempt at writing which sought to use the unconscious as a literary source, surrealism became a springboard for Miller's own descent into the psychology of the writer; a vision of the possibilities for an aesthetic of the self, conceived in radical terms. As Brassaï writes in his portrait of Miller, *Henry Miller: Grandeur Nature* (1975):

> Like the Surrealists and Dadaists, Henry believed that dreams provided fertile soil for writing, and that writing did involve the struggle to bring to the surface that which was unknown, hidden, and unrealized. But he only employed Surrealist techniques when it felt natural and spontaneous to do so, and not because he wanted to be counted as one of their adherents. He thought that "Automatic Writing" was both too deliberate and too aimless. No writer can renounce meaning and significance; even when he is being obscure, the writer must try to remain intelligible.[1]

What Brassaï grasps is largely the main paradox behind Miller's use of surrealism: namely Miller's interest in "the hidden, the unrealized" and how to convey this without losing the search for "meaning and significance." While Brassaï signals the interest in surrealism's use of dreams, he also points out how certain practices — such as automatic writing — significantly complicate what the definition of "meaning and significance" might actually be.[2]

In Miller's case, this particular aspect of his 1930s aesthetic has so far been neglected, and one reason why, is that the re-evaluation of the relation between American twentieth century writers and surrealism has yet to take place. Even now, with the increasing interest in surrealism, most critical studies isolate it as a specifically continental phenomenon, and when extended to American artists from the twenties and thirties it is usually to painters and photographers such as Man Ray. While this neglect in itself merits an analysis of some complexity, it might be linked to an unspoken divorce which still exists between the notion of what constitutes a European politicized aesthetic, compared to an American one. As with many other American writers, Miller's interest in surrealism is seen as antithetical to the overriding view of him as an anti-intellectual, a sort of primitivist enfant terrible within American letters. Even Georges Bataille, who later revised his opinion, considered Miller "a writer removed from reflective thought"; a far cry from his later analysis of Miller's use of obscenity in which the "instinctual" or anti-intellectual removal from "reflective thought" is aligned to romantic and prophetic strands within surrealism.[3] Both critical and admiring of surrealism, Miller formulates a quest for a discursive voice of an individualistic nature which nevertheless aims to incorporate universal issues, and he does this, by stressing how his own position vis-à-vis the movement was that of an interested outsider rather than a devoted follower:

> I was living in Paris . . . we used to say, "let's take the lead." That meant going off the deep end, diving into the unconscious, just obeying your instincts, following your impulses, of the heart, or the guts, or whatever you want to call it. But that's my way of putting it, that isn't really surrealist doctrine; that wouldn't hold water, I'm afraid, with an André Breton. However the French stand-point, the doctrinaire stand-point, didn't mean too much to me. All I cared about was that I found in it another means of expression, an added one, a heightened one, but one to be used very judiciously.[4]

The key phrase here, in terms of Miller's agenda, is the acknowledged quest for a heightened sense of expression. The cautionary tone is partly born out of the belief that in order for his writing to succeed it would have to engage in an intimate appeal to the reader. The confessional tone of voice might not abolish conventional distance between author and reader, but it would hopefully strengthen the portrayal of the main protagonist and narrator. Of *Tropic of Cancer*, Miller said: "I didn't write a piece of fiction: I wrote an autobiographical document, a *human* book," emphasizing what he described as: "the projection of the universal picture of individuation . . . the author's temporal position in time and space."[5] This "universal picture of individuation" is both antithetical to and dependent on the notion of a collective art-form as proposed by the surrealists. It is antithetical in the way that Miller's self-conscious positioning of himself rejects being part of any movement per se, but also similar to the surrealists' desire to project a universal language of the unconscious through a democratization of the creative process.

In order to delineate the idea of a universal language, automatic writing in particular as mentioned by Brassaï, this chapter will focus on two Miller pieces which bear a direct relationship to surrealism. "An Open Letter to Surrealists Everywhere" (1938), and "Last Will and Testament," a short piece of unpublished fiction taken from Miller's Paris Notebooks now housed in the Special Collection division of U.C.L.A. Both pieces deal in different ways with the position of the artist in aesthetic as well as more politicized terms, but they also share an interest in the schism between a collective notion of the artist and his responsibilities, and a more individualistic one. While not a clear cut binary opposition, this problem points to Miller's attempts at relinquishing the political in an attempt to turn inward, a quest for a system of individualist engagement in art which can be seen in his interest in two major writers of the period, the surrealist André Breton and the French philosopher Henri Bergson.

The Automatic Principle

From early on in his writing career, Miller invoked the influence of the philosopher Henri Bergson (1859–1941) as a crucial factor in his writing. Bergson's ideas of the individual as creatively evolving because he is sentient and consciously accumulating experience, rather than born with an innate unconscious language, are particularly evident in Miller's work. It is possible that Miller stumbled on the hugely popular *L'Évolution Créatrice* (1907) in the New York Public Library while in his twenties. It was translated into English in 1911. In *Tropic of Capricorn* (1938) — Miller's account of his early life in New York — he writes: "What was there then in this book which could mean so much to me? I come back to the word creative. I am sure that the whole mystery lies in the realization of the meaning of this word. When I think of the book now and the way in which I approached it, I think of a man going through the rites of initiation."[6] This fascination with creativity as a progressive force ties in to the surrealist effort to capture the forces of the imaginary, but it is the Bergsonian stress on individualism and what Miller calls "metamorphosis without and within" which illustrates some of the major differences between himself and the surrealists.

In "The Automatic Message" (1933), Breton defines automatism as based on the premise that an unhindered flow of words without any conscious elaboration can signal deeper metaphysical and universal truths; in other words, an accurate transcription of the unconscious. According to Breton, our unconscious contains a language unique to itself, a "murmure"; or a murmur, which coexists in the human mind and which, in ordinary circumstances, is drowned out by our rational faculties.

Although formulated by the surrealists as a novel ideal, automatism was clearly influenced by Romantic ideas of the poetic subject's ability to communicate messages from "beyond." Together with the belief in the poet as transcriber and medium of truths, Breton, who had a medical background, used research he had done during the First World War on patients at lunatic asylums where insanity was seen to produce particular forms of hysterical outbursts of an irrational nature. Such medical research, in conjunction with a nineteenth-century fascination with spiritualism — with voices from "the other world" being channeled through mediums — became, in effect, a way to prioritize the poet's ability to echo what the surrealists would call the *marvellous.*

Because of automatism's obvious pre-history, and as way to avoid the accusation that the surrealists were simply aestheticizing Freudian notions of the unconscious, Breton had to find a viable definition of automatism that did not from the onset place itself in a no-man's land which was neither mysticism nor science. The difficulty lay primarily in how to define a fixed poetic framework, in which the writing produced, was not predetermined and yet of creative value. In other words, automatic writing would somehow have to prove that it could survive in spite of the fact that it was nearly impossible to "grasp involuntary verbal representation and fix it on the page without imposing on it any kind of qualitative judgment."[7]

From the onset, Breton knew that automatism would be accused of being simply a ploy designed to endow the mind with unexamined capabilities. "I will not hesitate to say that the history of automatic writing in surrealism has been one of continuing misfortune. But the sly protests of the critics, particularly attentive and aggressive on this point, will not prevent me from acknowledging that for many years I have counted on the torrent of automatic writing to purge, definitively, the literary stables." In order to counter accusations, automatism had to be set up against existing rules of creativity, in order to gather both a meaning and a goal:

> It remains for us to suppress . . . both that which oppresses us in the moral order and that which "physically," as they say, deprives us of a clear view. If only, for instance, we could have these celebrated trees cleared out of the way! The secret of surrealism lies in the fact that we are convinced something is hidden behind them. Now one needs but examine the various methods of doing away with trees to perceive that only one of them remains to us, depending in the final analysis, on our power of voluntary hallucination.[8]

In this passage from 1929, Breton juxtaposes expressions such as "voluntary hallucination" coupled with a methodical "assault on life" in order to prove automatism's place within surrealism as a method for investigating the psyche of the writer, and as eventual proof that a connection does exist between the individual and the cosmos. By using the word method, Breton implies that automatic writing is not simply an activity which stimulates surrealistic writing, but a method based on the individual's capability to immerse himself in a state of hallucinatory empowerment. In freeing the body from external sensations, typically via hypnosis, the emergence of the automatic message is not only enabled, but actually moves us out of "the moral order" to disrupt the conventions and norms of society.

The implication of automatism is that "voluntary hallucination" can dislodge the writer from the traditionally assigned vantage point as word manipulator, as well as avoid the unanswerable question of how the transfiguration from pre-speech unconscious thoughts to actual recognizable words occurs. Underlying such a practice, the possibility of the unexpected is not only presumed, but effectively relied on as a way to break out of rationality. The leap necessitated by this theory is evident in the way it is theoretically espoused as well. Breton can only avoid an actual explanation of the process of automatism — that is to say how language moves from thought to actual writing without interference — by positing that "there are powerful and complex clusters of conceptions that are formulated outside articulated language and reasoned thought" (*What is Surrealism?*, 109). Without this premise, Breton would have to prove the authenticity of automatic writing once it had been written down, an analysis which in turn circumvents what automatism was meant to do, namely to give "free access to the *unmeasurable* region between the conscious and the unconscious" (italics mine). By defining the potential misuse of automatism, Breton apparently proves its existence:

> ... an inevitable delectation (after the fact) in the very terms of the texts obtained, and in particular in the images and symbolic figurations abounding in them, has had a secondary effect of diverting most of their authors from the inattention and indifference which, at least during the production of such texts, must be maintained. This attitude, instinctive in those who are used to appreciating poetic value, has had the vexing consequence of giving the participant an immediate awareness of each part of the message received. (*What is Surrealism?*, 107)

Breton admits that "an inevitable" process of ordering occurs the minute the text has been written, if not before. However, he also insists on "inattention and indifference" as the guiding principle for pure automatism. In effect, this reverses more "romantic" notions of the poet as an exceptional being, since everyone should be able to access the unconscious. According to this premise, automatism questions — as Miller will be seen to do — whether the poet within surrealist praxis still has a distinctive role to play. In other words, can automatism really be a fruitful practice for all? In Miller's case, any theory which places the products of the artist at the forefront, especially if it is at the expense of the poet-writer's role, is necessarily suspect:

> Art is only one of the manifestations of the creative spirit. What every great artist is manifesting in his work is a desire to lead a richer life; his work itself is only a description, an intimation, as it were, of these possibilities. The worst sin that can be committed against the artist is to take him at his word, to see in his work a fulfillment instead of a horizon. (*The Cosmological Eye*, 164)

For Miller the artist is still a visionary, and the desire to search for something above and beyond reality is the crucial denominator in the creative process. As such, one cannot disavow the importance of personality within the creative equation. In direct contrast, automatic writing, rather than authenticated by the artist's conscious desires and personality: "is made dubious, moreover, by the profound modifications of memory and personality involved" (*What is Surrealism?*, 106).

If memory and personality disrupt the automatic message, it is because the writer no longer functions effectively as a pure transmitter. When Breton uses the phrase "motor message" as a description of the automatic process, he turns the writer into a machine. On one hand this is a logical outcome of automatism as a "science" of the unconscious, but it also discredits the writer's moral obligations:

The question it seems to me, which each one must pose for himself is this: which reality is more vital, more life-giving, more valid, more durable — the reality of science or the reality of art? Assuming a divergence between the scientific and the poetic attitudes towards life, is it not clear enough that today the schism has grown impassable?

(*The Cosmological Eye*, 164)

The crux of Miller's argument rests on his absolute belief in a divorce between art and science. In this sense, his critique of surrealism operates from a premise diametrically opposed to that of Breton. After all, the authentication of the unconscious in itself, in terms of surrealism, rests on proving the empirical presence of "those hidden forces" accessible to all who follow the proper procedures. The schism demarcated by Miller in his critique of surrealist practice is thus a crucial element in his quest for an individual art. There can, in other words, be no human art without memory and personality, and in fact, Miller's reliance on memory as a creative force not only refers back to Bergson's definition of memory as a continuous process of becoming, but constitutes the framework for his inability to accept a synthesis of art and science. Thus while Breton sees the awareness of individuality as a contamination of the automatic message, for Miller, "Fear, love, hate, all the varying, contradictory expressions or reactions of the personality, are what compose the very warp and woof of life. You can't pull one of them out without the whole edifice crumbling" (*The Cosmological Eye*, 162).

Miller's stress on "the warp and woof of life" illuminates the problems inherent in Breton's focus on writing to validate more abstract premises about the accessibility of the unconscious. If conscious lived life is removed from the realm of art, in favor of an uncompromising return to the unconscious, rationalism must likewise be negated in the process. And, indeed, this is precisely what Breton does in "The First Manifesto": "I resolved to obtain from myself . . . a monologue spoken as rapidly as possible without any intervention on the part of the critical faculties, a monologue consequently unencumbered by the slightest inhibition." On the one hand, Breton stresses the fact that a personal resolution must necessarily motivate the automatic process but, on the other, it must present itself without any rationalizing intervention. By using the word "consequently," Breton indicates that once this occurs, our consciousness will fail to exercise its force as an ordering factor. The word inhibition is also crucial as Breton appropriates and subverts the Freudian notion of our consciousness as intrinsically linked to a restricting super-ego, a super-ego which Breton, like Freud, situates outside the unconscious. However, while Freud's compromise between the ego and the super-ego is necessary for social compromise, Breton uses the manifestations of the ego to question the rationality of the super-ego. In some respects, Miller both accepts and questions the "use-value" of the unconscious within this context. While he acknowledges "the release of instinctive life" as fruitful for art in general "the stress on the unconscious forces of man does not necessarily imply the elimination of consciousness. On the contrary it implies the expansion of consciousness" (*What is Surrealism?*, 185). The question then remains of where, in literary terms, this expansion will occur. If it is within the realm of sexuality that the expansive forces of the unconscious attain free reign then it is through a language of the erotic that the marvellous is attained.

The issue of sexuality is deliberately down-played by Breton in his attempts to define automatism as a universal and undifferentiated manifestation of the unconscious. For Miller, however, the issue cannot be circumvented as it ties in to his search for individual freedom and, more importantly, the means with which he attains this as a male writer. What differentiates the two is the fact that for Breton individual freedom is not the highest priority of automatic writing. Automatic writing in this sense represents a break from traditional repressive literary practices, but primarily in aesthetic rather than political terms. Miller's observations on surrealism can point to its problematic status vis-à-vis Freudianism, and its failure in positing the unconscious as a given in a creative sense, but Miller still misreads surrealism's agenda in political terms. What Miller is incapable of realizing is that surrealism is largely driven by concerns deliberately divorced from that of gender, precisely what automatism exemplifies by being deliberately non-gendered.

Breton's manifestoes on automatism deal primarily with a desired radical renewal of the practice of writing and his reluctance to link a discourse of sexual desire with that of communal change is, in this respect, one of the major points of difference between Miller's actual use of surrealist tropes and Breton's ruminations on the subject. It is interesting, that while Miller and the surrealists share a genuine concern with how to present imagination as the central power in the human mind, Miller avoids the one issue where they differ the most, namely the use of obscenity as a way to reactivate the unconscious. While Miller's representation of the locations in which his urban protagonist roams is often described in surrealist terms, the constant stress on the individualism of the artist marks a significant change from the universalist voice of the automatic poet. The use of obscenity as a discourse of the masculine self becomes problematic, precisely because of its narcissism, its constant centering on the self rather than on the collective.[9]

Ironically, Breton's eagerness for automatism to be distinct from traditional Freudian psychoanalytical theory actually aligns itself to Miller's claims that his sexual "confessions" are valid as artistic enterprises rather than therapeutic sessions. Likewise, Miller is against the use of psychoanalysis in any curative sense: "Analysis is not going to bring about a cure of neurosis. Analysis is merely a technique, a metaphysic, . . . to illustrate and explain to us the nature of a malady" (*The Cosmological Eye*, 186). While Freudian psychoanalysis believes in the possibility of finding the key to hidden desires and frustrations, in a curative sense, automatism, as Miller points out, does not want to touch or alter the psychological make-up of the unconscious.

Automatism is a central issue, then, partly because it was seen by Breton to embody a poetic sensibility which had been marginalized within traditional poetic practice, and partly because it relates to the issue of designing a master-plan for a radically new departure into literature. By refusing ready-made meanings and creating the conditions wherein new meaning may manifest itself, automatism slots itself comfortably into the avant-garde's belief in its own radical potential, a perspective which Miller acknowledges even as he is critical of its methods.

Contrary to the automatic premise, Miller does not believe that any one methodology can transcend individual achievements. If "metamorphosis" occurs both from "without and within," then the surrealist stress on an internal, innate language of the unconscious — the necessary premise for all automatism — must be taken up for revision.[10] It is this acute sense of an individualistic voice that causes the schism between Miller and the surrealists, a schism which allies Miller more closely to the Bergsonian ideal that the "creation of self by self is the more complete, the more one reasons on what one does," as opposed to Breton's attempt to circumvent reason by directly tapping into "Psychic automatism in its pure state."[11] While the notion of automatism will cause insurmountable obstacles for the surrealist ethos, Breton insists on linking the definition of surrealism with that of automatism: "Surrealism, n. Psychic automatism in its pure state, by which one proposes to express — verbally, by means of the written word, — the actual functioning of thought. Dictated by thought, in the absence of any control exercised by reason, exempt from aesthetic or moral concern."[12]

"An Open Letter to
Surrealists Everywhere" (1938)

In "An Open Letter to Surrealists Everywhere" (1938), Miller not only critiques the absence of reason within surrealism, but insists that it is an international and long-held aesthetic rather than a uniquely French one. "It is a mistake to speak about Surrealism. There is no such thing: there are only Surrealists. They have existed in the past and they will exist in the future." What Miller is against is "to posit an ism," for to do so, is to deny the fact that surrealism may function as an individual trait, a personal style, rather than a group endeavor. Miller's antagonism towards group endeavors ties in to the politicization which he sees the French surrealists engaged in, deluding themselves into thinking that art-movements carry the potential for revolution, when in reality, individual self-progression is the only viable change. "There is no feasible scheme for universal liberation" as the search for freedom "is fundamentally personal and religious. It has nothing to do with liberty and justice, which are idle words signifying nobody knows precisely what. It has to do with making poetry, or, if you will, with making life a poem. It has to do with the adoption of a creative attitude towards life" (*The Cosmological Eye*, 152–87).

To provide an example, Miller uses the surrealist poet Paul Eluard's ideal of a "fraternity of poets" as an example on this fixation on collectivity. The question for Miller lies not in whether Eluard can create great poetry, but in his adamant pursuit of "liberty and justice," two chimeras which for Miller represent a weak premise for a truly "creative attitude towards life":

> Unlike Paul Eluard I cannot say that the word "fraternization" exalts me. Nor does it seem to me that this idea of brotherhood arises from a poetic conception of life. It is not at all what Lautréamont meant when he said that poetry must be made by all. The brotherhood of man is a permanent delusion common to idealists everywhere in all epochs: it is the reduction of the principle of individuation to the least common denominator of intelligibility. It is what leads the masses to identify themselves with movie stars and megalomaniacs like Hitler and Mussolini. It is what prevents them from reading and appreciating and being influenced by and creating in turn such poetry as Paul Eluard gives us. That Paul Eluard is desperately lonely, that he strives with might and main to establish communication with his fellow-man, I understand and subscribe to with all my heart. But when Paul Eluard goes down into the street . . . he is not making himself understood

and liked for the poet he is. . . . On the contrary, he is establishing communication with his fellow-men by capitulation, by renunciation of his individuality, his high role.
(Query: And why should poetry be made by all? Why?)

(The Cosmological Eye, 152)

Written in 1938, the evocation of Hitler and Mussolini strongly indicates that even the best of political intentions must take the "masses" desire for identification into consideration. Miller even likens the process to the intrinsically commercialized sphere of cinema. While Miller's interest lies partly in a defense of the poet/writer's "high role," it is also a warning of what occurs when art loses its position as a guiding force on a higher intellectual, as well as moral level. Miller does not equate fascist authoritarian leader-figures with the politics of the surrealists, but he sees the institutionalization of politics as driven by "the least common denominator of intelligibility." Miller may in fact have chosen this phrase in response to a line by Breton in "Introduction to a Discourse on the Paucity of Reality," in which Breton affectionately calls his own thought process "this least common denominator of mortals."[13] For Breton this is a complementary term, whereas for Miller, it implies a leveling out of intellectual responsibility, regardless of its political aims.

Miller's rhetoric concerning the a-politicized stance of the surrealists, signals the problems inherent in an individualized ethos vis-à-vis the collective endeavors of the surrealists. In Miller's critique of Eluard, the line that most clearly signals his own convictions is the belief in a street creed of communality: a more localized and less abstract version of the politics of fraternization. Miller's reluctance towards being designated either left-wing or right-wing is partly born out of this desire: to be simply another man on the street; a perspective which was immediately suspect in the eyes of fellow writers of the period. George Orwell's review of *The Cosmological Eye* (1938) including "An Open Letter to Surrealists Everywhere," attests to this attitude:

> Miller refuses to bother about the difference between fascism and communism because "society is made up of individuals." This has come to be a familiar attitude nowadays and it would be a respectable one if it were carried to its logical conclusion which would mean remaining passive in the face of war, revolution fascism or anything else. . . . At bottom Miller's outlook is that of a simple individualist who recognizes no obligations to anyone else — at any rate no obligation to society as a whole. Either one must genuinely keep out of politics, or one must recognize that politics is the science of the possible.[14]

Written in 1946, Orwell's review does not take into account that most of the essays in *The Cosmological Eye* were written before the war, which provides quite a different slant on the issue of fascism versus communism. Orwell recognizes Miller's fidelity to the idea of individualism, but rather than acknowledge the value in Miller's suspicions concerning the aestheticization of politics within the avant-garde, Orwell sees his individualism as a passive, anti-political attitude. In this respect, his attitude is very much that of the "professional" Marxist who does not want "outsiders" dabbling in what he considers "real" political issues. When Orwell speaks of "a familiar attitude nowadays" Miller suddenly represents a broad mass of political indifference rather than a purely personal outlook.

The difficulty of "An Open Letter to Surrealists Everywhere" lies precisely in Miller's constant refusal to position himself in any clear political terms, and yet, he takes it upon himself to criticize the surrealists for their politics. Likewise, a large amount of ignorance accounts for Miller's failure to take into consideration the complex relationship between surrealist aesthetics and the Marxist ideology which it strove to incorporate. Miller's critique of surrealist politics oftentimes appears as a blanket-critique of artists who are publicly politically affiliated; he admits as much by saying: "It seems to me that this struggle for liberty and justice is a confession or admission on the part of all those engaging in such a struggle that they have failed to live their own lives. Let us not deceive ourselves about 'humanitarian impulses' on the part of the great brotherhood" (*The Cosmological Eye*, 157). Among other things, Miller does not consider the on-going debate between surrealism and Soviet Social Realism and he rarely differentiates between individual surrealists, thus leaving himself open to the same criticism which he directed against the movement, namely focusing too much on group activity and dogma, rather than individual accomplishments.

Miller's defense against such accusations is to turn his focus on the surrealists into a general critique of twentieth-century malaise — partly born out of a loss of belief in the individual — but heightened by the tendency to look towards the unconscious for paradigmatic solutions. Forming a direct link between the loss of individualism and an increased use of Freudian aesthetics, Miller laments: "the exploration of the Unconscious which is now under way, is a confession of the bankruptcy of the spirit" (*The Cosmological Eye*, 170). In giving a spiritual determinant a monetary value, "the bankruptcy of the spirit," Miller conveys a very utilitarian belief in the use-value of individualism: a far cry from Breton's denial of individualism in favor of an absolute focus on the unconscious, or as Breton puts it in "The Automatic Message," "the determination of the precise constitution of the subliminal" (*What is Surrealism?*, 100). Nevertheless, as Miller points out, even if the "constitution of the subliminal" could be ascertained, the need for conscious individual elaboration still exists:

> The stress on the Unconscious forces of man does not necessarily imply the elimination of consciousness. On the contrary, it implies the expansion of consciousness. There can be no return to an instinctive life, and in fact, even among primitive men I see no evidence of purely instinctive life. (*The Cosmological Eye*, 189)

Miller touches upon an important point in his analysis of the unconscious, namely the link between the instinctual and the primitive. Once the unconscious is defined in terms of an innate, universal force within man, it allies itself to a theory which proposes a return to the primitive as a lost paradisiacal state wherein man was free from the rationality implicit in consciousness, and indeed, a stifling civilization. As mentioned in the introduction, surrealism's belief in modernity as a movement towards primitivism rather than rationalism can thus conveniently incorporate the idea of the unconscious, although in a different way from that intended by Freud.

Miller's suspicions in this regard can be seen in his use of Freud as well. For Miller, the mental topography of Freud exemplifies not only an artistic aesthetic but also an image of the disintegration of the modern world. This is in stark contrast to the desire for integration which marks the surrealist project, and as such, it represents the struggle between conscious and unconscious forces which constitutes the necessary premise for creativity:

> Freud's contribution to the cause of human enlightenment (as the stupid saying goes) is creative and anarchic. . . . Unable to reconcile himself with the world he turned the world upside down. He created a fiction which helped to pass the time away. Which helped, not to adjust him to the world, but to adjust the world to his own imaginings. His theory of psycho-analysis is a piece of art. . . . The significance of Freud's creation is purely aesthetic. (*The Cosmological Eye*, 168)

Miller's attitude to Freud partly explains his overt hostility to theories based on the unconscious. While he considers Freudian theory emblematic of larger, and crucial disorders in society, Miller's primary interest in Freud is as a case-study for what alternatives man constructs when faced with a world gone mad or "anarchic." According to Miller, the adjustments we make as humans denote a certain aesthetic value in literary rather than scientific terms, and are unfeasible as a methodology for assessing the individual role of the writer within the creative process. The crux of Miller's argument in "An Open Letter to Surrealists Everywhere" lies therefore in his recognition of the explicit connection between the unconscious and artistic creation, and more importantly, its attempts to unite Freudian concepts of a verifiable unconscious with a glorification of the irrational. As mentioned before, automatism's stress on the impersonality of the automatic manifestations, becomes a way to legitimate the words produced in the automatic process rather than the artist from whom they emanate. This de-personalization necessarily de-emphasizes the writer's ability to reason. As Breton puts it, reason is instrumental in "subjecting the works of the spirit to its irrevocable dogmas" thus depriving us "of the mode of expression which harms us the least" (*What is Surrealism*, 26). By equating reason with consciousness and the inhibitions which govern it, Breton warns against reason as yet another legitimation for oppression in general. What Breton does is reverse the Freudian premise. The fact that the instinctual and desire-driven harms our potential as social beings proves precisely for Breton that it is truly a radical means of subverting traditional social structures.

This notion of a radical rearrangement of nature and man-made phenomena is echoed in Miller's own visionary approach, albeit in a different way. Miller also stresses the familiar as strange and marvellous in itself and by focusing on the ordinary as extraordinary sets out to prove the writer's visionary capacity, something which objects in themselves — however mysterious and odd they may seem — cannot provide:

> The Surrealists themselves have demonstrated the possibilities of the marvellous which lie concealed in the commonplace. They have done it by juxtaposition. But the effect of these strange juxtapositions and transpositions of the most unlike things has been to freshen the vision. Nothing more. For the man who is vitally alive it would be unnecessary to rearrange the objects and conditions of the world. The vision precedes the arrangement or rearrangement. . . . The artist is the opposite of the politically minded individual, the opposite of the reformer, the opposite of the idealist. The artist does not tinker with the universe: he recreates it out of his own experience.
>
> (*The Cosmological Eye*, 193)

Miller admires the fact that the "Surrealists themselves have demonstrated the possibilities of the marvellous which lie concealed in the commonplace," but he nevertheless sees it as a "reaction against the crippling, dwarfing harmony imposed by French culture," rather than something intrinsic to the world of the imaginary. "To discredit the world of reality . . . is an act of will, not of fate" (*The Cosmological Eye*,

190). Once again, Miller stresses that the re-creation of individual experience can and should operate without the necessary insertion of political rhetoric. If the goal is to establish communication, as in the case of Paul Eluard, then it must be born out of the artist's individualized and conscious desire rather than any political agenda. In fact it is the conscious recognition of a pure non-partisan desire to communicate which, for Miller, designates the true artist.

In this instance, Miller's use of the word fate designates the reliance within surrealism on chance, intrinsic to the idea of automatism as a spontaneous rather than willed eruption. If will for Miller exemplifies the author's conscious ordering of his material world, then it operates in opposition to the inspirational forces of the unconscious, which Miller equates with a belief in fate. The use of the word fate is crucial here because it implies a pre-determined, inevitable state, probably of an adverse outcome, which is in direct contrast — as is will — to the desired haphazardness of the automatic process. To Miller, Freud is an artist rather than a scientist, and therefore, any approach to the unconscious which is reductively empirical necessarily becomes suspect.

While the schism between science and art can be seen in relation to the differences between automatism and Freudianism, it also explains why Breton prefers the word destiny rather than fate as an explanation for automatism. Destiny implies a great and noble course of events, rather than something potentially ill-fated. In his collaboration with Paul Eluard, *The Immaculate Conception* (1930), Breton designates the poet as: "one who fulfills this magnificent destiny and thinks only of himself, . . . one who inhabits a world without victims, and is not surprised at his adventures here on earth, when people speak of it to him."[15] This type of heroic vitalist figure is particularly manifest in Breton's work; a descendent of an earlier romantic vision of the artist as a messianic as well as pre-ordained figure. By placing the notion of destiny, with the poet as a romantic hero "destined" or foreordained to act out a ritualistic quest, side-by-side with political writings which stress the democratic premise of automatic writing, a strange contradiction emerges. When Breton speaks of the writer in terms of glory and salvation, he refers to a religious and mystical aspect of surrealism, but he also pays tribute to the poet as a romantic and prophetic figure, not unlike Miller's idealization of the artist vis-à-vis the masses intellectually. In fact the heroic vitalist figure could be one way to define Miller's persona in the auto-romances. Amongst other things, *The Immaculate Conception*, which forms the starting point for "Last Will and Testament," is a striking example of how pervasive the romantic notion of the writer as prophet is, even within the context of a twentieth-century avant-garde aesthetic.

Miller's observations on surrealism thus point to the inevitable tug between a nineteenth-century French tradition of poetics and the simultaneous need to view surrealism as a "as a reaction to the crippling harmony of French society." The naive idea that automatism could provide the key for a re-integration of the imagination has to be seen in the context of the surrealists' belief that it had been ignored by a predominantly rationalist philosophical tradition. Thus, while Miller saw the practice of automatic writing as a response to this, in his own work, the refusal to accept ready-made meanings in a surrealist vein nevertheless creates the conditions for Miller's own brand of creativity. Although Miller and Breton differ in ideology, in praxis Miller's attempts to create a fictional universe where time and spatiality are structured around a spontaneous first person narrative voice, aim at the same newness and stress on the imagination as set out differently by Breton. Miller's persona in the *Tropics* prides himself on being in control of the narrative, and yet the lack of traditional narrative continuity, the constant onslaught of an almost manic narrator, creates a pace and spontaneity not far from the rapid and incessant bombardment of images in automatic writing.

"Last Will and Testament"

"Last Will and Testament," from one of Miller's 1930s notebooks, is a short piece devoid of any apparent critical or fictional context. Unpublished, it stands next to the massive amount of writing Miller undertook while working on what was later to become *Tropic of Cancer* and perhaps was intended as part of the book. Written largely as a pastiche, it incorporates the dream-like quality, the erotic imagery, and the irony typical of Miller's work in the *Tropics* and in *Black Spring*, but while the *Tropics* have a more discernible first person narrator, "Last Will and Testament" reads like a transcription of a dream without the philosophizing, polemical tone of a strong central narrator. The passage illustrates Miller's ability to mimic the use of the erotic by the surrealists, and at the same time, it parodies the surreal fascination with the unconscious as a site for creativity:

> The thing to know is if you are crazy or only making literature. To know si l'affaire est dans le sac! That when you turn around there is no shadow behind you or if you're asked for your carte d'identité you

don't have to take off your gloves first. When I open the door I see a
pair of socks lying on the floor of the closet; not to bend down and
touch them with your hands but to quickly kick them about three
inches to the left and rear. The post man wakes up at five thirty punkt;
to know when to write without disturbing him. Everybody is alone,
and it is worse to be alone when you are with people. If you lived on
the same street all your life and there was no time, except at the end,
several years later, when it is too late. Because it snows does not prove
that time elapses.[16]

Miller's notebooks contain copious notes on both James Joyce and
Blaise Cendrars, but while "Last Will and Testament" is highly influenced by a Joycean mimicking of thought processes and Cendrars's use
of collage and montage, the passage above allies itself in particular to
The Immaculate Conception. A straightforward surrealist reading of
"Last Will and Testament" would point to the juxtaposition of seemingly disparate objects and events: the carte d'identité, the gloves, and
so on, but Miller's eschewed vision imparts an almost ritualistic sense of
the writer engaged in gestures and acts whose insignificance seem to
refuse meaning. Thus the references to fetishistic objects, gloves and
socks, become a way to illustrate actions of a disjointed nature by a
fractured narrative voice. This ritualistic aspect figures in similar ways in
The Immaculate Conception, but "Last Will and Testament" presents
itself as a constructed discourse rather than a spontaneous, authentic
representation of the irrational, as does automatic writing. To understand how Miller does this in "The Last Will and Testament" — while
still using the same phraseology and nonsensical sentence structure as
in Breton and Eluard employed in *The Immaculate Conception* — the
actual structure of *The Immaculate Conception* must be considered.

Breton's *The Immaculate Conception* simulates, through writing,
various mental disorders such as schizophrenia and paranoia. As such, it
presents one of the primary themes of surrealism, namely the arbitrari-
ness of the barriers between the normal and abnormal. More importantly, however, *The Immaculate Conception* paves the way for the link
between the erotic and the hysterical subject, something which is even
more obvious in Breton's *Nadja* (1936). Rather than focus on the un-
pleasant, painful aspects of being in the throes of hysteria, the hysterical
subject, usually a woman, is de-personalized to the extent that her
symptoms become her function as well. By setting up the hysterical and
insane subject as a surreal icon, the woman becomes emblematic of a desired link between the irrational, the erotic, and the insane as well as a
conflation between symptom and function. This conflation is evident in

Miller's "Last Will and Testament" as well, in which the female figures as a symptom of the narrator's ambivalent relation to sexuality rather than a three-dimensional character. While "Last Will and Testament" represents this ambivalence in terms of surrealist tropes, Miller's *Tropics* convey the traces of the disembodied woman; the woman whose hysteria becomes her personality as well and whose sexuality becomes commodified in the form of prostitution. In the following section, some of these representations will be delineated and compared to Breton's use of the "hysterical" woman in such narratives as *Nadja* and *Mad Love*.

The use of hysteria as a way to represent the ecstatic, as well as erotic, manifests itself in *The Immaculate Conception* through consistent attempts to integrate the scientific (the simulation of a clinical disorder) with the fictional (the poetic style of Eluard and Breton). At the same time, Breton and Eluard consistently link religious manifestations of absolute devotion and what could be seen as hysterical modes of representation. These rhetorical devices turn *The Immaculate Conception* into a religious parable of the creative process itself; a text where the overt allegorical context and structuring makes it seem far to deliberate to be automatic. To assuage possible confusion, Breton, nevertheless, places the work firmly within the experimental field of automatism:

> The authors particularly wish to stress the sincerity of the present undertaking which consists of submitting the five essays that follow to the consideration of both laymen and specialists. The slightest suggestion of any borrowing from clinical texts or of pastiche, skillful or otherwise, of such texts, would of course be enough to make these pieces both pointless and wholly ineffective. (*The Immaculate Conception*, 47)

In his introduction to the second part of *The Immaculate Conception*, "The Possessions," Breton refuses to define exactly what laymen and specialists he refers to. Does he mean that the text can stand up to close scrutiny by experts on mental disorders or does he mean experts on automatism? Breton and Eluard clearly want to present the texts as their own, linking the effectiveness of the texts to their authenticity. On the other hand, the introduction could also be a tongue in cheek comment on the reader's desire for authenticity, adding a satirical rather than a "sincere" twist.

The Immaculate Conception indicates the birth of surrealism as a sacred event as well as a new era of creativity. In this sense, the semantic context for the deification of the creative process can be read as both religious and sacrilegious; an ambiguity which Eluard and Breton deliberately play on throughout the text. Partly written in defense of disorder and anarchy, the text nevertheless functions in a ritualistic manner, with the various chapters as simulations of disorder as well as stations towards salvation. The complexity of *The Immaculate Conception* thus lies both in its structure and in the way its agenda is couched in religious terminology throughout the book. Consisting of three large movements of continuous prose: "L'Homme," "Les Possessions," "Les Méditations," and a final section of aphorisms, the first section entitled "Man," consists of five texts which chart the movement from gestation and birth to death. What is noticeable, however, is the way in which three of the five texts deal with pre-natal stages; "Conception," "Intra-Uterine life," and "Birth" are all concerned with the satisfaction of the libido in the womb, and the following sections "life" and "death" represent the nostalgia for a lost pre-natal state.

In the second section "The Possessions," psychotic deliriums are written out by Breton and Eluard in an automatic state. The word "Possessions" also refers to demonology, which in this case is secularized, as the authors are inhabited by deliriums of a psychotic rather than religious nature. "Meditations," the last segment before "The Original Judgment," openly refers to the Hegelian concept of meditation used to describe the movement by which consciousness opens itself to the surrounding world and by implication reintegrates the world into its own reality. Thus the text seeks to mediate the immediacy of the automatic experience with the possibilities for this immediacy as a creative springboard for surrealism's attempts to reintegrate the world and present it as radically new.

The short overview provided above indicates the immense planning, both structurally and thematically, which went into the production of *The Immaculate Conception*, proving in some respects the impossibility of automatism as pure unconscious dictation. The title itself adds an ironic twist, as the "conception" is born out of the collaborative efforts of Breton and Eluard, rather than a heaven-sent illumination. Miller's own rendition and pastiche of parts of *The Immaculate Conception* could be seen, then, not as a direct subversion of automatism, but as a sort of alternative version, just as *The Immaculate Conception* can be seen as the surrealist version of the birth of Christianity with a secular twist. Miller's "Last Will and Testament" succeeds in avoiding the more obvious parameters of religious signifiers, but a form of substitution nevertheless takes place, as the creative process becomes nightmarish and eroticized within the context of a surreal aesthetic. The question is, did Miller use surrealism primarily as a license for experimentation or can one actually discern more specific linguistic and stylistic patterns in *The Immaculate Conception* and "Last Will and Testament"?

In "The Original Judgment" a series of alternative proverbs and proposals present themselves in manifesto format. While some of the proverbs appear nonsensical, "Don't drink water," most of them openly preach the advantages of spontaneity, dreaming, and rebellion: "If they come knocking at the door, write your last will and testament with the key," "Don't prepare the words you cry out," "Speak according to the madness which has seduced you," "Let the dawn stir the fire of the rust of your dreams" and so forth, until the last proverb "You have nothing to do before dying" which marks the ending of *The Immaculate Conception*, as well as the life cycle of the creative process from conception to death. Miller's use of nonsensical proverbs in "Last Will and Testament" (the title possibly taken from "If they come knocking at the door, write your last will and testament with the key") seems very similar on a first reading. Then midway in "Last Will and Testament" Miller states: "None of this is sufficiently crazy," an indirect questioning of surrealism's ability to mimic insanity, regardless of its origins. The first line of "Last Will and Testament": "The thing to know is if you are crazy or only making literature," overtly states the connection.

With this premise in mind, *The Immaculate Conception* is in effect as much of a pastiche, as "Last Will and Testament" is of surrealism. Breton's comments in "The Automatic Message" show his awareness of this, but he still insists, as seen in his introduction, that a dividing line can be discerned between imitations of and pure automatism: "Finally, it must be pointed out that numerous pastiches have been recently put into circulation, texts not always easy to distinguish from authentic ones, since all criteria of origin are objectively absent. These few obscurities, these failures, these flounderings, these imitations, now more than ever require, in the interest of the activity we wish to conduct, a complete return to principles" (*The Immaculate Conception*, 102).[17]

In spite of its lack of discernible argumentation, "Last Will and Testament" moves in fictional terms towards Miller's later critique in "An Open Letter to Surrealists Everywhere." Judging from its placement, both in relation to the publication of *The Immaculate Conception*, and in Miller's Paris Notebooks, "Last Will and Testament" marks the beginning rather than the end insinuated in the title. By using the name "Last Will and Testament," Miller retains the reference to *The Immaculate Conception*, and puns on the question of will which he later juxtaposes with fate in "An Open Letter to Surrealists Everywhere." With hindsight, Miller is probably one of the first writers in the early thirties to critique the surrealist movement as something, which to all intensive purposes, could be seen as already dead. Why else call a surrealist pastiche "Last Will and Testament"?

Walter Benjamin's critique of surrealism, "The Last Snapshot of the European Intelligentsia" (1929), refers in similar terms to surrealism as a marker which designates the end of a literary and political tradition rather than a beginning of a working alliance between artists and the proletariat. Indeed, Benjamin pre-empts Miller's critique of surrealist politics by actually specifying the ideological nature of its leftist aesthetic. Focusing on the aesthetic of the "mysterious" or the "marvellous," Benjamin is not against what he calls the "loosening of the self by intoxication," but he is skeptical as to its political benefits:

> To win the energies of intoxication for the revolution — this is the project about which Surrealism circles in all its books and enterprises. . . . Added to this is an inadequate, undialectical conception of the nature of intoxication. The aesthetic of the painter, the poet, *en état de surprise*, of art as the reaction of one surprised, is enmeshed in a number of pernicious romantic prejudices. Any serious exploration of occult, surrealistic . . . phenomena presupposes a dialectical entwinement to which a romantic turn of mind is impervious. For histrionic or fanatical stress on the mysterious side of the mysterious takes us no further; we recognize the mystery only to the degree that we recognize it in the everyday world.[18]

This analysis pre-empts Miller's claim that "the effect of Surrealist juxtapositions and transpositions has been to freshen the vision. Nothing More" (*The Cosmological Eye*, 193). It also stresses, in ways similar to Miller, the impossibility of true vision behind a project based on the artist in a state of surprise; immersed in the automatic process. Absolute reliance on the mysterious, the marvellous in surrealist terms, or the absolute as Miller terms it, is what Benjamin calls an "inadequate, undialectical conception of the nature of intoxication" (*Reflections*, 181).

One could claim, then, that Benjamin and Miller agree that "the vision precedes the arrangement or rearrangement" of an artwork, but this still does not take the role of "the politically minded individual" into account. For Benjamin, it is precisely the politically minded individual on whom the future of art relies. The surrealists have failed in the "impetuous integration" of mystification as the foundation, not only for poetic, but scientific development, which for Benjamin equals a positing of the unconscious in absolute terms: "the belief in a real, separate existence of concepts whether outside or inside things." Automatism thus operates as a transition between "the logical realm of ideas to the magical realm of words," but it cannot provide a quick "transformation of a highly contemplative attitude into revolutionary opposition," something which both Benjamin and Miller consider outside the capacities of the surrealists (*Reflections*, 184).

If surrealism is "the last snapshot" or "testament" of a misguided idealism, born out of a "romantic turn of mind," to use Benjamin's phrase, then it cannot realistically form the basis for both a political and creative aesthetic. The overriding question remains for Benjamin, what have the surrealists left us with in terms of a viable praxis for art? Miller insists that Socialist beliefs invalidate the surrealist aesthetic, and interestingly, Benjamin saw the surrealist flirtation with communism much in the same way.[19] Such criticism, however, does not take away from surrealism's special status as a radical instance of an art which strives to "sabotage" (to borrow Benjamin's term) an intrinsically conservative bourgeois mentality, as well as "revive the sensory powers of man so that he may look upon the world about him with renewed exaltation" (*The Cosmological Eye*, 170).

As Miller and Benjamin decided in different ways how to appropriate and critique various elements of surrealism, the one consistently problematic element turns out to be automatism. Benjamin cites as his "favorite" surrealist text, Louis Aragon's *Paris Peasant* (1928) a text which does not take automatism as its starting point. What *Paris Peasant* foregrounds, is the eroticization of the city in terms of romance, mythology, and its use of the marvellous, issues which influence Benjamin and Miller in different ways. In Miller's case, focusing on the unconscious as a reservoir of sexual desire, not only in Freudian terms, but as something provocative and radical, also becomes a way to side-step the issue of automatism.

Miller's skepticism concerning the possibility of actually entering an alternative state of insanity in the form of a deliberate delirium, points to the larger issue of the authenticity of automatic writing itself. For Miller, the disjointed and absurd tone of parts of *The Immaculate Conception* indicate the writer's mental state vis-à-vis society's rationalizing stance, rather than mere exercises in clinical insanity. And in this sense, while "Last Will and Testament" mimics surrealist word use and sentence structure, its references are less religious and more secular in their insistence on diffusing iconographical value, rather than heightening it. "Last Will and Testament" exemplifies Miller's surrealist influences but his over-riding interest in the writer's role as one of permanent ambivalence is still present. One way to manifest this ambivalence is in terms of sexuality, as the artist himself, rather than desire a complete submersion into the creative process, struggles to retain a sense of self-hood in spite of the precariousness of his own masculinity. "Last Will and Testament" thus provides a combination of cynicism and humor in relation to the complex issue of communication, and in most cases the impossibility of such, among the sexes:

> All that I remember of her is that her dress was cut under her armpits, her breasts were nude, and she said always "later." When they sat on the sofa she said: "I hate birds." And he replied "neither do I." "But that's what I said," she said. "Excuse me then." She replied, "I was mistaken." "It's entirely my fault," he answered. The corpse was lying at their feet, there was a bouquet on it, at the neck.[20]

This exchange differs stylistically from the proverbs listed in "The Original Judgment," and yet the oddly disjointed aspect of the conversation mimics the use of random phrases and discordant images typically found in automatic writing. As a parody of a conversation, the missing links, conveyed grammatically and without indicating who is speaking, refuse any comprehensible logic. This is accentuated by the sense of misunderstanding which underlies and abolishes any possible conclusive aspect to the conversation. The corpse at the couple's feet, wearing a bow, appears as a decorative aspect which in a dead-pan manner refers to the morbid aspect of the conversation and provides a surreal inconclusive ending to it.

In a traditional surrealist vein, the bouquet would function more overtly as an uncanny adornment to death, but here, Miller takes a traditional symbol of love and desire and uses the images' associative value as a gesture towards meaning, while at the same refusing it. While the bouquet traditionally represents a romantic gesture, in this case it also adds to the futility of all lovers' gestures. Because the repressed sense of sexuality is so overwhelming, Miller's parody of a romantic conversation focuses on the ways in which the erotic manifests itself in an inconclusive rather than celebratory manner. The fact that Miller chooses a conversation as a way to portray the frustrating comical aspect of modern romantic endeavors, links surrealism with the issue of how language works. Rather than mimic the automatic process through an attempted transcription of the unconscious, an impossible endeavor in the first place, Miller deliberately formats his "dream" through conversation. Thus while the rhetorical devices in *The Immaculate Conception* are religious and elevated, Miller's use of the misunderstandings implicit in the erotic game, become a way to portray the writer as he struggles to speak clearly and understandably. In comparison, Breton in

Mad Love and *Nadja* uses the obsessive language of eroticism, but usually through the eyes of the male narrator alone and rarely through
conversation. As such, the desired object, the woman, although disturbing, is never really dangerous or instrumental in terms of the actual
rendition of the marvellous, whereas for Miller, she not only propels
the conversation forward in disturbing ways, but does so in "Last Will
and Testament" with a corpse at her feet.

The obsessive quality of surrealist eroticism, typified in most of
Breton's romances by the narrator's incessant quest for a woman he
hardly knows (as in *Nadja* and *Mad Love*), is indicated in "Last Will
and Testament" by the fact that the woman who "always says later" always reappears as well. What she says "later" to is never specified, but
the erotic aspect of her demeanor infers that it is of a sexual nature. At
the end of Miller's "Last Will and Testament" the woman "who always
says later" has become completely eroticized, indicated by her clothing,
which by its design points to her sex:

> "But," she said, "every night I am inspiring your men to fight." That
> did not prevent him from approaching her with a can-opener. Beneath
> the coat of armour she was nude. The under-study got the part. At
> the Ritz a woman was sitting on a shelf looking at a mirror; her breasts
> were exposed. The pattern converged to a dead centre where the legs
> joined. "Later," she said. Then she sat on a hansom and played the
> guitar. He said "I don't like to fight. I want people to love me."[21]

Similar to the ideals of the surrealist romance, in which much of the
imagery heralds back to medieval notions of the heroic poet embarked
on a quest for love, Miller's reversal is ironically gendered, as it is the
woman, not the "knight," who wears the coat of armour. The question
is: what is under the armour? And implicit in this, is also the question
of what roles are being cast in this conversational game where love is
certainly not equal to eroticism. If the chivalric represents repression,
then the armour, a clearly fetishistic device, is also the emblem of a love
not consummated and an encapsulation of sexual frustration. Contrary
to Breton's fiction, the male here represents the emasculated partner
who approaches the woman with a can-opener: a rather ineffective
weapon. The ironic reversal in gender-roles is also accentuated by the
fact that the woman appears to inspire a belligerent attitude, whereas
the man just "wants to be loved." This reversal of stereotypes, com-
bined with the mixing of modern implements and places, the can-
opener and the Ritz, adds to an overall sense of displacement both in
terms of the narrator's role and his sexuality. The unnaturalness is also

heightened by the women exposing themselves in public; an indication that they may be promiscuous but nevertheless in control.

Miller's attitude to exhibitionism in "Last Will and Testament" generally differs from that of the surrealists. While the surrealists strove to integrate the public and private sphere by eroticizing the former, Miller's women emblematize the often uncomfortable sensation of sexuality as an open commodity. The theatrical and artificial rendition of the erotic adds to the sense of a confused relationship between the sexes in "Last Will and Testament" but it also inscribes this relationship in a physical bodily form as opposed to the more romantic stress on love in Breton's narratives.

One could, then, read "Last Will and Testament" partly as a critique of the surrealist view of women as mystical, ephemeral creatures. Such a reading would pre-empt Miller's later de-mystification of sexuality in the *Tropics*. After all, in "Last Will and Testament" the male protagonist ends up alone in bed "waking up with the can-opener in his hand and the suit of armour lying on the floor," a wry comment on the often absurd, if not sad outcome, of sexual relations. This absurdity differs significantly from Breton's romantically heightened sensibility in *Nadja* and *Mad Love*. In terms of eroticism, it more likely that the imagery in "Last Will and Testament" refers to an earlier Breton text, "Introduction to the Discourse on the Paucity of Reality" (1924), written just prior to the publication of the first Surrealist Manifesto. In "Introduction to the Discourse on the Paucity of Reality," the notion of a chivalric romanticism exemplifies how, according to Benjamin, "the Middle Ages was the basis for poetic experience" in surrealism. Miller's knight figure is thus an ironic reversal of the surrealist redeployment of the medieval. In "Introduction to the Discourse on the Paucity of Reality" a small section is entitled "Colloquy of the Suits of Armour." In it, Breton figures as the knight who stands "in the vestibule of the chateau" where "gleaming suits of armour" initiate a reverie consisting of women's voices and his own: "*Woman's voice* — 'Here are some who linger two by two. Have pity for them alone! Suits of armour, gleam more brightly! Lovers, love more and more! Can one being exist for another?'"[22] "Last Will and Testament" mimics this sense of reverie, but more importantly it refuses the romantic question of whether "one being can exist for one another." Instead the chivalric notion of love becomes a laughable myth. In Breton's case, the "Colloquy of the Suits of Armour" is a sincere homage to a Gothic tradition; a tradition in which the strong central male character in pursuit of mysterious truths could be slotted into a romantic gesture of heightened sensibility not unlike that of the ideal surrealist. The Gothic tradition is picked up by Miller, but for another reason. It supports his claim that the surrealists are firmly grounded within a nineteenth-century tradition where the romantic poet as hero becomes a traditional poetic trope rather than a radically modern one. The importance of this tradition can be seen in Breton's "Limits Not Frontiers of Surrealism" (1937), in which the Gothic medieval setting provides the backdrop for an automatic experience:

> *Shall I even confess to you what was the origin of this romance? I waked, one morning . . . from a dream of which all I could recover was that I had thought myself in an ancient castle (a very natural dream for a head filled . . . with Gothic story), and that on the uppermost banister of a great staircase I saw a gigantic hand in armour. In the evening I . . . began to write, without knowing in the least what I intended to say or relate. The work grew . . . in short I was so engrossed with my tale, which I completed in less than two months, that one evening I wrote until my hand and fingers were so weary I could not hold the pen to finish the sentence.*[23]

Apart from the Gothic references, this tale of automatic trance adds a crucial element to the original definitions of automatism as set out in the Manifestoes: namely the use of dreams. Breton even italicizes the event to accentuate its dream-like and transcendent quality. The combination of a dream as catalyst for a reverie, which then puts the writer in an automatic trance, together with the speed with which he finishes the tale, confirms the original definition of automatism. As Breton puts it: "This Account shows that the message obtained, the future model of so many other highly significant in their cumulative effect, must be put to the credit of dreams and of the employment of automatic writing" (*What is Surrealism?*, 157). In "Limits Not Frontiers of Surrealism" dreams become more than mere catalysts for manifestations of the surreal; now they are an important part of "the message obtained."

The stress on dream imagery, albeit part of a increasing interest in Freudian and Jungian dream-theory, also heralds back to a romantic tradition of the poet as dreamer and visionary in a prophetic sense. As mentioned before, Miller's "Last Will and Testament" in this respect owes a great deal to the acknowledged use-value of dreams as a catalyst for creativity. By focusing on the dream-like quality rather than the automatic process by which it is attained, Miller foregrounds the individualistic effort of the creative process, positioning himself as a crucial and active factor in the creative landscape, rather than another automatic entity. Miller never contested the fact that dreams sprang from the unconscious and were indeed a source of creativity, but he also believed that one could not, and should not, displace the role the artist had in ordering his impressions into a coherent structure. In essence, this was Brassaï's point as well. In addition to stressing the artist's "vision" as a guiding force for structuring material, Miller saw disintegration as born out of social circumstances, rather than something inherent in our psychological make-up. This explains why in "An Open Letter to Surrealists Everywhere" Miller equates the curative role of Freudian analysis with surrealism's desire to "resolve the contradictions between the conscious and the unconscious":

> The implication is that the artist sows discord, strife. To try to eradicate the disturbing elements of life by "adjustment" is tantamount to appropriating the artist. Fear, love, hate, all the varying, contradictory expressions or reactions of the personality are what compose the very warp and woof of life. You can't pull one of them out without the whole edifice. (*The Cosmological Eye*, 153)

Whereas Breton focuses on the method and products of automatism, Miller here focuses on the writer who aims to reconcile his innermost feelings with a truthful mode of writing. This emphasis on reconciliation as opposed to alienation is important, as reconciliation on a psychological level does not necessarily imply the abolition of the boundaries between our conscious and unconscious self. The idea of "reconciliation" in terms of individual spiritual progression points to Miller's inheritance of American transcendentalism:

> It's only an effort, at bottom, to return to the original vital source, which is in the solar plexus, or in the Unconscious, or in the stars, if you like. I have used the method here and there, when it came naturally and spontaneously. At least, I hope so. I don't start out by trying to be Surrealistic. Sometimes it comes at the beginning and sometimes as the end — it's always an effort to plough through, to say what can't or won't be said.[24]

In this quote from the 1940s, Miller hesitates in focusing only on the unconscious, just as he later hesitates in only focusing on surrealism as the source of inspired writing. By setting up the unconscious, the solar plexus, or the stars as symbols for an original vital source, he invests the unconscious with a sense of physical, bodily power. Miller's reference to Walt Whitman as "the greatest man American ever produced" also provides us with a crucial reference in "An Open Letter to Surrealists Everywhere." Miller's cosmology in this respect owes a great deal to American notions of an individualized force from within and partly explains his constant use of the body as representative of what is most vital in human nature. Eager to stress that he never deliberately embarked upon a set method, Miller stresses his use of surrealism as "judiciously" spontaneous. The issue is how to dramatize the effort, rather than prove, as in automatic writing, that the means are genuine and authentic. In this context, the fact that "Last Will and Testament" was never published may indicate Miller's fear of being seen as aiming for an experimental style in and for itself. In Miller's notebook concerning an art-exhibition of the "Surindependents," he writes: "At the Surindependents I had a terrific feeling of this desire on the part of the modern man for this unknown uncharted world. I am speaking more particularly of the Surrealist section (the only one worth while, in my opinion)." The image of the modern man in Miller's mind is a surreal one, and desire, rather than intellectual curiosity or political conscience, is the phrase which describes the urge to explore. Miller describes the unconscious as a sort of territory to be explored, as a realm where snippets of information pertaining to the mind of the artist can be gathered up, much like the spoils of a conquest, to be taken "home" and appropriated in usage. Nevertheless, what the surrealists claim to find in the unconscious could just as well be what they set out to look for in the first place. More simply, the surrealists' courage is born out of their desire for enlightenment, rather than their technical abilities as "voluntary hallucinators":

> I want to say, crudely again, that something like this is going on with the elaboration of the doctrine of the Unconscious — that the world as we have known it is being turned inside out, that this unknown realm (really the obverse of the soul) is a fertile field in which these hardy adventurers may explore and chart to their hearts content — to find, of course, that world which they secretly long for . . . (ms. notebooks, 1930–38)

In keeping with his self-willed role as Whitmanesque unlearned American vagabond, Miller puts himself down as being blunt when he is particularly erudite. The surrealists, quite rightly, are not inventing a theory of the unconscious as such. In using the word elaborate, Miller clearly indicates previous models, a Freudian one being the most obvious, and thus a note of irony can be detected in calling them "hardy adventurers" who explore literally to their "heart's content" rather than for the benefit of artistic expression. This implication is accentuated by the fact that what they long for is done in a covert manner, as though they know in their innermost hearts but dare not voice what it is they seek. "There is no doubt about it, Surrealism is the secret language of our time."

While the *Tropics* manifest the search for individual freedom as an American and universal drive, the method with which one attains this freedom is not necessarily universal as well. Going back to his critique of the surrealist movement, Miller states:

> It seems to me that it is a very simple error which the surrealists are guilty of; they are trying to establish an Absolute. They are trying with all the powers of consciousness to usher in the glory of the Unconscious. They believe in the Devil but not in God. They worship the night but refuse to worship the day. They talk of magic but they practice voodooism. They await the miracle, but they do nothing to assist it, to bring about an accouchement. They talk of ushering in a general confusion but they live like the bourgeoisie. A few of them have committed suicide, but none of them has yet assassinated a tyrant. They believe in the revolution but there is no real revolt in them.
>
> (*The Cosmological Eye*, 177)

Once again, Miller's critique of surrealist politics echoes Benjamin. As Benjamin puts it: "But are they (the surrealists) successful in welding this experience of freedom to other revolutionary experience? In short, have they bound revolt to revolution?" (*Reflections*, 189). For Miller, the tendency to posit a new religious mysticism echoes bourgeois cultism and elitism in disturbing ways. As such, surrealism cannot be anything but a political sell-out the moment it refuses to place itself within a viable praxis of change. In this context, "Last Will and Testament" could equally be seen as a parody of Breton's dogmatic humorless "regulations" on how to be a proper surrealist, in the same way that it parodies the heavy-handed rhetoric of "The Original Judgment" by incorporating the proverbs into its own irreverent version of a surrealist text. Miller agrees with Breton that: "the task which the artist implicitly sets himself is to overthrow existing values" but it is nevertheless necessary "to make of the chaos about him an order which is his own."[25] Individualism is a prerogative for any writing that attempts to truly communicate with the reader. But what sort of individualism achieves the ability to communicate? Although Miller never defines his ideal audience, an inverted snobbery is nevertheless implicit in Miller's questioning of the surrealist ethos. In "An Open Letter to Surrealists Everywhere" Miller asks: "How are they (the surrealists) going to make themselves heard and understood if they are going to use a language which is emasculated? Are they writing their beautiful poems for the angels above?" What Miller fears is a literature that has forgotten to speak to the average man, the man on the street who — incidentally — appears as both narrator and audience in the *Tropics*.

For Miller, autobiographical writing fulfilled this criteria. In the transcendental vein of Whitman, the autobiography gains importance as the prototypical example of man creating himself:

> At a certain point in my life I decided that henceforth I would write about myself, my friends, my experiences, what I knew and what I had seen with my own eyes. Anything else, in my opinion, is literature and I am not interested in literature. . . . I learned not to be ashamed of myself, to talk freely about myself, to advertise myself. . . . The greatest man America ever produced was not ashamed to peddle his own book from door to door. (*Tropic of Cancer*, 156)

Miller's pride in his own success, worked for and paid for as he sees it with his own sweat and blood, partly accounts for his antagonism towards organized groups of artists as well as for his determination to remain independent, to believe only in himself. Referring once again to Whitman Miller says: "I am not against leaders per se. . . . But as for myself, I need no leader and no god. I am my own leader and my own god. I make my own bibles. *I believe in myself*— that is my whole credo" (*Tropic of Cancer*, 155).

As a way to "adopt a creative attitude to life" (Miller's phrase) the potential universality of the autobiographical document is perhaps not that far from Breton's vision of automatic writing as a democratized vision of the unconscious. While Miller criticized the surrealists for trying to establish an "Absolute," he too was guilty of the same error in his embrace of an absolutist sense of the self. While Miller rebelled against the Protestant work ethic his German parents had instilled in him, there is a sense that Miller's antagonism towards the automatic voice is caused by the very effortlessness of its production as well as its unreflective qualities. Once the task of finding one's voice no longer requires a monumental effort, the artist's motivation may disappear:

> When I reflect that the task which the artist implicitly sets himself is to overthrow existing values, to make of the chaos about him an order which is his own, to sow strife and ferment so that by the emotional release those who are dead may be restored to life.
>
> (*Tropic of Cancer*, 253)

The process of releasing emotions simultaneously establishes the artist's individuality and his ability to awaken others. Miller places himself here in the position of a revolutionary whose task is to act as a catalyst for literature where creative originality is bound up with a developing sense of the person. Simultaneously, Miller refuses to abide by the old rules of proper narrative form. In order to do this, one must "overthrow existing values" and by cultivating an upheaval of sorts "strife and ferment" life can be restored.

In an ironic reversal, Miller's rhetorical call for a new literary form is couched in expressions which bring to mind political ethics and religious redemption, not unlike that in *The Immaculate Conception*. This is no coincidence. Miller wants to represent himself as a writer on a crusade. If the crusade in surrealist terms consisted of continuous experimentation, devoted to trying to define a pure language beyond reason, Miller's must be seen in the light of the search for continuous self-progression and creation. As shown, the vitalist notion of self-creation as endless projections aligns itself with surrealism's endeavors through automatic writing, but more crucially, it also goes back to the belief of another French philosopher on the aesthetics of the self. In Henri Bergson's work, Miller recognized a theory of the absolute which could reflect the spiritual progression of a narrator, as well as tie in with the conditions of a "rebirth" in transcendental terms.

Henri Bergson
and "Creative Evolution"

For Breton, the attempt to claim a hegemonic role within the creative process on the basis of an immediate relationship between the unconscious and certain linguistic signs took the form of automatism. While Miller was highly critical of the valorization of one discourse over another on the basis of the unconscious alone, his own attempts to center the self could also be read as an ideological maneuver to justify the elitist position of the artist. The question remains, however, whether Miller, although adverse to a mechanically predetermined system of artistic creation, such as automatism, perhaps abided by metaphors of growth and self-generation wherein the notion of an intuitive faculty became simply another hegemonic representation of the self. In automatic writing, the direct access to the unconscious became paradoxically a way to dissolve self-presence all together, as personality was deliberately decentered as the origin of creativity. The answer for Miller, in his quest for a mode of writing which would center the artist and simultaneously bring to the fore the hitherto "uncharted" territory of the unconscious, lay in the intuitive (non-rational) abilities of the self.

Bergson in "Understanding Reality From Within," from *An Introduction to Metaphysics* (1903), espoused the importance of understanding reality from within by intuitive force rather than by logical analysis.

Widely read all over Europe in the 1920s and 1930s, Bergson's popular status as a philosopher who broke with established notions of religious theory made him a natural point of focus for writers who were adamant about remaining anti-establishment. Oddly enough, little has been written on the links between Bergson and the surrealists, in spite of the fact that in trying to subvert the monopoly of the analytical method in philosophy, Bergson pre-empts most of the premises behind automatic writing. Bergson's notion of "The Absolute" together with his theory of "La Durée Réelle" (the notion of continuous time) not only explains some of the ideas behind automatism but also forms a large part of the groundwork on which these theories rely.

For Bergson, the Absolute exists in the interior of things. Only by attributing an interior to a person or an object can one hope to find its absolute qualities. He equates the Absolute with that which is indivisible and whole. It is the effort of imagination which enables us to identify with an object completely. Without this extraordinary effort of imagination a natural detachment from the object in question occurs, one is then forced to observe it from an exterior position and can only hope to attain its relative aspects. The relative is thus the opposite of the Absolute. In writing specifically, true identification with an object is hindered, for example, by the use of symbols. Bergson assumes that the use of symbols implies a translation by the reader, as does the use of description and analysis:

> It follows from this that an absolute could only be given in an intuition, whilst everything else falls within the province of analysis. By intuition is meant the kind of intellectual sympathy by which one places oneself within an object in order to coincide with what is unique in it and consequently inexpressible. Analysis on the contrary, is the operation which reduces the object to elements already known . . . [26]

While intuition is the necessary force for the proper identification and comprehension of the Absolute, it is also inexpressible. Bergson is thus caught between two contradictory claims. By claiming that intuition operates without the use of symbols, which inevitably implies an act of conscious analysis and the use of language, "pure" intuition is indeed incommunicable. The dilemma presented is similar to the inherent dichotomy of automatic writing: how can one represent what is inexpressible in writing without changing it in the process?

Bergson circumvents this question by specifying the object to be identified. The only object which we can hope to ever truly seize from within is our self, but selfhood, rather than a static core, is a life-process of continuous becoming — a *Durée Réelle*. Events may appear disconnected at times but "each of them is borne by the fluid mass of our whole physical existence." In simple terms, the notion of a Durée Réelle proves that experience is a process determined subjectively in the mind rather than chronologically in time and therefore our consciousness is always growing as it absorbs its own sense of the past: "My memory is there, which conveys something of the past into the present. My mental state, as it advances on the road of time, is continually swelling with the duration which it accumulates."[27] Since consciousness cannot by its very nature be identical during two consecutive moments, its sense of continuity lies in the individual's memory. In other words: "consciousness means memory" (*Introduction to Metaphysics*, 183).

This last phrase is crucial to understanding Miller's constant references to past events and his attempts to draw them into the present. In *Black Spring*, for example, the chapters are framed around Miller's dreams and anxious visions of urban life rather than through a plot-driven sense of continuity. Indeed Miller takes as the artist's prerogative the ability to move the narrative in an unforeseen direction without following traditional rules of continuity. "Last Will and Testament" is an extreme example of this but throughout the *Tropics* Miller follows the Bergsonian rule: any writer who wishes to write "authentically" from the self must accept the inner duration of the mind as opposed to chronological time. As inner duration is the sum total of a perpetual mixing of associations, memories, sensations, everything that we absorb in our day to day life, we are always responding, consciously as well as unconsciously, to an incredible amount of sensory information and impressions, all of which are stored and capable of further use. Since we unknowingly perceive the perpetual change which surrounds us, personality which is the sum total of all these perceptions, cannot have a static, non-changing core (*Creative Evolution*, 1–8).

Creative Evolution figures early on in *Tropic of Capricorn* as *the book* which Miller carried while boarding the elevated line at the Brooklyn Bridge after work. On his way home, Miller would have read creation defined in these terms:

> With regard to the moments of our life, of which we are the artisans. Each of them is a kind of creation. And just as the talent of the painter is formed or deformed . . . under the very influence of the works he produces, so each of our states, at the moment of its issue, modifies its personality, being indeed the new form that we are just assuming. It is then right to say that what we do depends on what we are; but it is necessary to add also that we are . . . what we do, and that we are cre-

ating ourselves continually. This creation of self by self is the more
complete, the more one reasons on what one does.

(Creative Evolution, 7)

In essence, dynamics are the very stuff we are made of, and if literature
wishes to represent an absolute truth it must illustrate the dynamical
process. To a large extent, this explains Miller's fascination with the
Bergsonian definition of "creation," a definition which differs from the
automatic premise by adding reason as the necessary ingredient for a
complete creation "of the self by the self." The receiving of impressions
is the very substance of the process in which we remember our past, with
which we form our identity, and with which we plan our future: a convenient proof that the individual still exists within the creative process.

This basic continuum theory legitimizes Miller's continuous return
to the creation of the self as the beginning and end all of literature. In
Tropic of Capricorn, Miller speaks of *Creative Evolution* in terms similar
to his own work, as something which is both modified and created
continuously: "My understanding of the meaning of the book is that
the book itself disappears from sight, that it is chewed alive, digested
and incorporated into the system as flesh and blood which in turn creates new spirit and reshapes the world" (*Tropic of Capricorn,* 221).

"Ideas must be related to living," Miller says and in line with a desired "reshaping of the world" indirectly accuses traditionally accredited
literature with failing in this:

> Up to the present, my idea in collaborating with myself has been to
> get off the gold standard of literature. My idea briefly has been to pre-
> sent a resurrection of the emotions, to depict the conduct of a human
> being in the stratosphere of ideas, that is, in the grip of delirium.
>
> *(Tropic of Capricorn,* 243)

"The collaboration with myself" centres the importance of selfhood but
it also portrays an almost insular approach to the writing process itself.
Miller returns to a surrealist inspired use of terms to describe this process: resurrection, ideas, and delirium are all key phrases in the search for
what Breton (inspired by Rimbaud) calls the derangement of the
senses. This mix of redemptive imagery and narcissistic pre-occupation
with the self becomes a major trope in all of Miller's work. In trying to
strike a constant and fine line between a disbelief in language as ante-
rior to individual personality (as in automatism) and a belief in the intuitive non-rationalizing ability of the writer (as in Bergson) one could
argue that Miller's positioning of himself is more than precarious.
Rather than attempt, then, to place Miller into one or the other cate-

gory, Miller's actual work indicates a crucial awareness of the anxiety inherent in any ideological framework which seeks to authorize and empower writing through the self, while at the same time down-playing such procedures in the first place. Regardless of what aesthetic denominators are used, the risk is always that by trumpeting the qualitative agency of certain procedures, whether one calls them automatic or intuitive, art is sought to be purified according to a difficult and insubstantial notion of what selfhood actually is. For Benjamin in particular, once a metaphysic of writing is set up which disavows a rationalizing stance — as both Breton and Bergson can be seen to do — art becomes dangerously apoliticized:

> If it is the double task of the revolutionary intelligentsia to overthrow the intellectual predominance of the bourgeoisie and to make contact with the proletarian masses, the intelligentsia has failed almost entirely in the second part of this task because it can no longer be performed contemplatively. And yet this has hindered hardly anybody from approaching it again and again as if it could, and calling for proletarian poets, thinkers, artists. (*Reflections*, 191)

Benjamin is willing to concede that our subconscious contains images that work for the benefit of mankind, the main problem for the artist is how to represent the value of the unconscious without, at the same time, circumventing the fact that we traditionally connect judgment with reason. In other words, if rational preoccupation is excluded in the process of automatic writing, what is its value?

Bergson attempts to answer this by offering a qualitative judgment of the Absolute. "In the Absolute we live and move and have our being. The knowledge we posses of it is incomplete no doubt, but not external or relative, it is reality itself." The Absolute is thus a direct and true expression of human reality. If human reality consists of everything in man, the conscious as well as the subconscious, and if our notion of reality according to Bergson is never uncaused, automatic writing, given a cause, also has a meaning. The expression of this meaning is thus as valuable as a meaning generated through logical thought, as long as the writer "reasons on what he does." Writing motivated from the interior is, in other words, as valuable as that motivated from the exterior. As Bergson puts it: "We must appeal to experience — an experience purified, or, in other words, released, where necessary, from the moulds that our intellect has formed in the degree and proportion of the progress of our action on things" (*Creative Evolution*, 210–383).

In Bergson, Miller saw the belief in the individual's experiences as a creative endeavor with an equal status to intellectual pursuits; An idea which for him provided the rational explanation for his own writing which strove to represent external reality through a voyage inwards. Where the surrealists fail, is by not affording the unconscious and the conscious equal value. Once the interior life of man, his unconscious, is glorified and even glamorized, the surrealists run the serious risk of overlooking the value of experience, which for Miller (and Bergson) constitutes the necessary premise for the creation of the self. As Miller states in "An Open Letter to Surrealists Everywhere": "But there is something beyond mind, and that is the whole being of man, which he expresses in action. What is disastrous is the divorce between mind and action. The ultimate can only be expressed in conduct."

In writing about himself, Miller to some extent incorporated the goal of automatic writing: to tap into the unconscious while still remaining faithful to a singular perception which would give both the unconscious and the conscious meaning. Nevertheless, the struggle for individualism rests uneasily within the dogmatic framework of any absolutist aesthetic, regardless of whether it is Bergsonian or surrealist. The stress on the self as a never-ending project represents Miller's fullest accomplishment, in so far as it forms the frame for most of his fiction. Miller can be seen to represent a writer whose interest in psychic life — as a demonstration of the connection between the individual to the cosmos and art with life — in many ways intersects at crucial points with the surrealist ethic of automatism. On the other hand, the fact that Miller's experiences always go on in time, based on growth as an ideal in the Bergsonian vein, means that the unconscious cannot literally be reproduced. In other words, as "Last Will and Testament" shows, Miller's reversal of surrealist tropes indicates his awareness of what the unconscious can be used for, as long as it is allowed to provide an individual vision, rather than a collective truth.

This "all important conflict between the artist and the collectivity," as Miller puts it in "An Open Letter to Surrealists Everywhere," is one which will be further explored. Miller's tentative perspective on the issue of the responsibility of the artist towards others, his own craft, and eventually his own psyche, firmly places him as an individualist first and foremost: "I am fatuous enough to believe that in living my own life in my own way I am more apt to give life to others (though even that is not my chief concern) than I would if I simply followed somebody else's idea of how to live my life and thus become a man among men" (*Tropic of Cancer*, 157). Miller's responses to surrealism show how he both confronted and appropriated the ideology of the unconscious, a necessity really, if he were to give his own twentieth-century version of a complete and truthful autobiography. On the other hand, Miller never claimed to be a "social protest" writer and his attraction to Bergsonian aesthetics concerned itself solely with the spiritualization, rather than politicization, of art. The refusal to commit to any social or political environment is born out of the firm belief that social concerns are both beneath the "liberated" writer and beyond what one person can change, something which may account for why Miller's use and critique of surrealism has fallen by the wayside in later readings of his work. Because Miller focuses on the artist's perceptual abilities as above those of the "masses," his privileging of the artist as inventor of new literary conventions seems crude in comparison to Benjamin's astute political analysis. Nevertheless, Miller's emphasis on the body as locus for intuition, rather than the mind per se, extends itself to how the urban narrator views space and temporality in a distinctly modernist vein. As we will see, Miller's ability to view space as other than a coherent field of experience echoes surrealist practice, and in this sense continues the debate on the applicability of surrealist aesthetics.

If sexuality constitutes an emblematic image of the difficulty of communication among the sexes, as seen in "Last Will and Testament," the ideology of love likewise becomes a way to incorporate wider issues on the role of desire in conjunction with literary creation. In using Paris, as examined in the following chapter, Miller and the surrealists will be seen to share a landscape of the unconscious in which the erotic takes precedence.

Notes

Dates of publication and original title of works in translation are given when known.

[1] Brassaï, *Henry Miller — The Paris Years*, trans. by Timothy Bent (New York: Arcade Publishing, 1995) 155–56. All subsequent quotes from this edition. Originally published as *Henry Miller, grandeur nature* (Paris: Gallimard, 1975).

[2] During those years, Miller wrote a series of essays on surrealist films and artists: "The Golden Age" on Buñuel and Dali's *L'Age d'Or*, "Scenario" an attempted script for a surreal film based on Anaïs Nin's *House of Incest*, "The Eye of Paris" on the photographer Brassaï, and "An Open Letter to Surrealists Everywhere." "The Golden Age," "Scenario," "The Eye of Paris," and

"An Open Letter to Surrealists Everywhere" were first collectively published in *Max and the White Phagocytes* (Paris: Obelisk Press, 1938).

[3] Georges Bataille, *The Absence of Myth*, ed. by Michael Richardson (London: Verso Books, 1994), 95. From Notes in "Initial Postulate," published originally in *Deucalion*, no. 2 (June 1947).

[4] *Writers at Work, the Paris Review Interviews*, ed. by Van Wyck Brooks (London: Secker and Warburg, 1963), 148.

[5] Henry Miller, "An Open Letter to Surrealists Everywhere," in *The Cosmological Eye* (New York: New Directions, 1961), 161. All subsequent quotes from this edition.

[6] Henry Miller, *Tropic of Capricorn* (New York: Grove Press, 1961), 220. All subsequent quotes from this edition.

[7] André Breton, "The Automatic Message" (1933), in *What is Surrealism?*, ed. by Franklin Rosemont (London: Pluto Press, 1978), 97–109. All subsequent quotes from this edition. Originally published as "La Message Automatique" in *Minotaure* (1933).

[8] André Breton, "The First Dali Exhibition," in *What is Surrealism?*, 45. Originally published as a Preface for a 1929 Exhibition catalogue.

[9] The Manifestoes show a curious lack of theorizing on the subject of sex, a sort of coyness accounted for partly by Breton's desire to keep surrealist dogma within the realm of philosophy proper.

[10] In *Tropic of Capricorn*, Miller writes: "In this book by Henri Bergson (*Creative Evolution*), which I came to as naturally as to the dream of the land beyond the boundary, I am again quite alone, again a foreigner, . . . standing on an iron bridge observing a peculiar metamorphosis without and within" (219).

[11] Henri Bergson, *Creative Evolution* (London: Macmillan, 1964), 7. All subsequent quotes from this edition. Originally published as *L'Évolution Créatrice* (Paris: Felix Alcan, 1907).

[12] André Breton, "The First Manifesto," in *Manifestoes of Surrealism*, trans. by Richard Seaver and Helen R. Lane (Ann Arbor: Ann Arbor Press, 1972), 15. All subsequent quotes from this edition. Originally published as *Manifeste du Surréalisme* (Paris: Sagittaire, 1924).

[13] André Breton, "Introduction to the Discourse on the Paucity of Reality" in *What is Surrealism* (London: Pluto Press, 1978), 19. Originally published as a pamphlet in 1927.

[14] George Orwell, "Words and Henry Miller," *Tribune* London, Feb. 22, 1946.

[15] André Breton, *The Immaculate Conception*, trans. by John Graham (London: Atlas Press, 1990), 92. All subsequent quotes from this edition. Originally published as *L'immaculée conception* (Paris: Editions Surréalistes, 1930).

[16] Henry Miller, ms. notebooks, 1930–38. UCLA Special Collections.

[17] The ways in which Miller anticipates post-modern problems of pastiche as an *anti-littérateur* is discussed in Walch. D. Everman's "The Anti-Aesthetic of Henry Miller," in *Critical Essays on Henry Miller*, ed. by Ronald Gottesman (New York: G. K. Hall and Co., 1992), 329–37.

[18] Walter Benjamin, "The Last Snapshot of the European Intelligentsia," in *Reflections*, ed. by Peter Demetz (New York: Schocken Books, 1978), 189. All subsequent quotes from this edition.

[19] Benjamin categorically states: "Surrealism has come ever closer to the Communist answer. And that means pessimism all along the line. Absolutely. Mistrust in the face of literature, mistrust in the fate of humanity, mistrust in the fate of freedom, but three times mistrust in all reconciliation: between classes, between nations, between individuals" (*Reflections*, 191).

[20] Henry Miller, ms. notebooks, 1930–38. UCLA Special Collections.

[21] Ibid.

[22] André Breton, "Colloquy of the Suits of Armour" in "Introduction to the 'Discourse on the Paucity of Reality.'"

[23] André Breton, "Limits not Frontiers of Surrealism" in *What is Surrealism?* Originally published in the Nouvelle Revue Francaise, Feb. 1937.

[24] *The Durrell — Miller Letters 1935–80*, ed. by Ian S. MacNiven (London: Faber and Faber, 1988), 16.

[25] Henry Miller, *Tropic of Cancer* (New York: Grove Press, 1961), 253. All subsequent quotes from this edition.

[26] Henri Bergson, "Philosophical Intuition," in *The Creative Mind — An Introduction to Metaphysics* (New York: Citadel Press, 1992), 107–29. All subsequent quotes taken from this edition. Originally published in 1903.

[27] Henri Bergson, *Creative Evolution*, trans. by Arthur Mitchell (London: Macmillan, 1911), 3. All subsequent quotes taken from this edition.

2: Representations of
the Urban Landscape

IN THE PREVIOUS CHAPTER the discussion of the aesthetic procedures used by Henry Miller in his criticism, and use of surrealism in his fiction, focused largely on the narrative voice. This chapter will examine in more detail the use of location and setting in Miller's fiction, as well as in a number of critical essays. Extracts from *Tropic of Cancer* and *Tropic of Capricorn* are compared to André Breton's narratives in order to define the surrealist romance and what it meant in regard to representations of gender, both in aesthetic and political terms. The city, in particular, constitutes a setting for narratives in which the unconscious is represented as a phantasmagoric landscape, a landscape in which surrealist tropes and icons figure in a distinctly modern vision of the urban. Within this context, the issue of sexuality and the portrayal of women within surrealism, still fits awkwardly into what could be considered a particularly "masculine" mode of writing. Many prominent writers on surrealism including Anne Balakian, Dawn Ades, Rosalyn Krauss, and Mary Ann Caws, have sought to balance the scales by signaling the existence of female artists within the surrealist canon.[1] Nevertheless, the way in which women are represented in the surrealist narratives is crucial for an understanding of the masculine search for identity. In following the premise that surrealism strives to represent the unconscious and the irrational, the representation of women will be seen as couched in a terminology which refers to both in a complex manner.

It may be tempting, in this respect, to condemn the masculine trajectories present in Miller's, as well as Breton's, work from a feminist perspective, but it is important to remember that both writers subverted and at times glorified an aesthetic created well before the advent of more dogmatic feminist approaches.

In the *Tropics*, the dream-landscape introduced in "Last Will and Testament" becomes a more discernibly urban one. As Miller's representations of his inner life are linked to the settings of his sexual and social vagabonding, eroticism and social politics also become increasingly interrelated and the stand for individualism, witnessed in "Last Will and Testament," becomes complicated by the narrator's reliance on women within the urban environment. This is not to say that

Miller's, nor the surrealists' goal for that matter, was to illuminate gender roles. Rather, the use of the erotic becomes a way to portray a particular vision of creativity and the ways in which it operates in a specifically urban context. "Last Will and Testament" used gender as a way to eroticize a humorous parodic intent, in the *Tropics* and *Black Spring*, women become emblematic of forces at work in the urban landscape — forces which are difficult to control. Through a visual style that owes a great deal to photography, the feminine is also linked to notions of aura and the marvellous; both concepts which incorporate an aesthetic treatment of the unconscious as a way to address psychic conflict as well as social contradiction. Miller's essay on the Hungarian photographer Brassaï, "The Eye of Paris," and his piece on the writer Anaïs Nin, "Un Etre Etoilique," will, in this context, be considered as examples of Miller's desire to define and question various modes of creativity within the context of the urban landscape.

In addition, Louis Aragon, whose *Paris Peasant* (1926) lay the foundations for Benjamin's work on the Paris arcades, becomes a crucial point of comparison. Benjamin's work on the shifting perspectives of the city and the artist is represented in the form of philosophical and critical essays, whereas Aragon, like Breton, uses a more romantic form of writing in his descriptions. Similar to the heraldic, medieval tradition signaled in automatic writing, this use of "romance" indicates a very nineteenth-century rhetoric to describe a twentieth-century vision of the artist's role in society. The surrealist romance operates on an erotic and political level highly informed by the interim war period, but as we saw previously, it nevertheless remains a conglomeration of avant-garde aesthetics and nineteenth-century visions of the romantic hero.[2]

Miller's "auto-romances" thus share many of the traits of the surrealist romances, in particular with Breton's *Nadja* (1928). On the one hand, Miller shared the surrealist belief in the importance of desire in the quest for the surreal, a belief which manifested itself in a shared tendency to mythologize the feminine in universal, ephemeral terms. On the other hand, Miller's constant negotiating of his own role, both as narrator and as male, often obstructs the use of sexuality as a convenient search for a surreal absolute. The obsessive sexual activity in the *Tropics* signals, not only a fundamentally different vision of love, but a search which has serious ramifications for the narrator's own precarious identity. The ambivalence of desire signaled in "Last Will and Testament" is foregrounded in the *Tropics* as the narrator's masculinity becomes a social as well as political weapon, in contrast to Breton's primarily ephemeral and distant attitude to love in *Mad Love* and *Nadja*.[3]

While Miller's cynical pose in "Last Will and Testament" manifests the stress on individualism which prompted him to criticize surrealist politics, in the *Tropics*, it also becomes the hallmark of the writer who often finds himself at a loss in the city. In this respect, the psychological sense of exile has both fruitful and harmful consequences. Miller's response to this unease frequently takes the form of a battle against the city's relentless pace and the commercialization of desire in the form of prostitution. While wanting to "spiritualize" the urban environment in ways similar to the surrealists, Miller is also at pains to debunk the mythology of the prostitute as a romanticized figure.

The notion of a specifically modern and urban mythology is thus crucial for an understanding of Miller's relationship to surrealism. In Louis Aragon's work, the city is defined in terms of a modern mythology, and it is through the act of mythologizing that the surrealists and Miller diverge in important ways. In describing the city, Aragon wanted to create a mythology suited to the experiences of the twentieth-century writer. In this context, eroticism was meant to embody the projective surrealist side of the urban environment, that aspect of the city which spoke to the writer in an immediate if not always rational manner. The attempt to define a projective illuminatory creativity, rather than the inverted inward project of automatism with its stress on the unconscious, partly explains Benjamin's affinity with Aragon over the other surrealists.[4]

Benjamin felt it necessary to oppose any theories which might glorify the city as a "pure" representation of modernity. By looking at the city as a modern mythology — a way of life mystified and unchangeable — there would be no viable critiques of it in intellectual and political terms. On the contrary, the risk was that the surrealists, through the act of mythologizing, would "illegitimately" restore coherence in a world of political rift and instability. Benjamin therefore praised Aragon's ability to discard conscious control in favour of a more sensuous fixation on certain objects, women included, but he also critiqued him on the grounds of being overly enamored with his own sensual impressions. "Whereas an impressionistic element remains in Aragon — the mythology — here it is a question of dissolving the 'mythology' into the space of history."[5] "The space of history," in Benjaminian terms, does not eliminate the possibility of a politicized understanding of the surrounding world, but it avoids the temptation to simply substitute old mythologies with modern ones. Benjamin's implicit critique of Aragon continues many of the ideas set out in "The Last Snapshot of the European Intelligentsia," ideas on how to incorporate the surrealist quest for the marvellous without slipping into an extreme and anti-political aestheticism.

Walter Benjamin's analysis of surrealism focuses primarily on the political ramifications of an aesthetic which seeks to critique capitalism as it manifests itself in the urban landscape. What Benjamin ignored was that while the fruits of capitalism — its workers and shops — provided the surrealists with the setting for an aesthetic based on sensual experience rather than intellectual critique, it also provided the backdrop for their eroticized love-affairs. For Aragon, and to a lesser extent Breton, the fact that they confessed to these love-affairs was at the time a radical departure from proper bourgeois conduct in moral as well as social terms. Miller, by taking the love-affairs one step further through a belligerent and graphic promiscuity set the scene for an even more radical departure.

Henry Miller
and the Surrealist Romance

Miller realized, as did the surrealists, that sexuality can be used as a battlefield to fight bourgeois ideas of what constitutes "normality." One example of this is the fact that the family is no longer presented as an ideal construction in any of Miller's narratives. The absence of family frees the male protagonist both from a psychological and economic standpoint and presents us with a "hero" who is always alone, free to roam the erotic landscape both in an active sexual capacity and in geographic terms. However, this proposition goes both ways, for the women in Miller's narratives are always presented as other than mothers or wives. They are usually sexually promiscuous, and if working, then by a trade with no specific location, namely prostitution.

In Miller's case, the imagery used in *Tropic of Cancer* and *Tropic of Capricorn* represents women as over-sexed, symbols of death, and creative muses. The attempt to embrace all of these aspects into one large "truth" is not unlike the scope of the surreal project, but it also provides an indication of why the surrealists failed to give the feminine aspect of the erotic a true face. Similarly, the *Tropics* suffer from simultaneous representations of women as mediators with nature, the unconscious, desire both in present and in future terms, and to complicate matters even further, as the muse who enables the writer to create.

In *Tropic of Cancer*, which places at its centre the male protagonist's search for a voice in exile (the narrative is set in Paris after Miller's arrival in 1930), the role of his ex-wife June (also called Mona/Mara) is crucial, in spite of the fact that she herself is not physically present. Instead, the June/Mona/Mara character becomes the woman whose self-sufficiency forms the catharsis for Miller's necessary removal from America, and by implication, the very reason why he can now write in exile. Miller is not only fixated on her absence, but also financially dependent on the money she never sends from New York. Miller's daily visits to the American Express Office become themselves ironic comments on the male artist's inability to support himself without his wife to look after him:

> She used to say to me, Mona, in her fits of exaltation, "you're a great human being," and though she left me here to perish, though she put beneath my feet a great howling pit of emptiness, the words that lie at the bottom of my soul leap forth and they light the shadows below me. (*Tropic of Cancer*, 250)

Mona's dual role: a confirmation on one hand of Miller's "artistic genius" and on the other as the woman who left him floundering, indicates Miller's insecurity regarding how to place her within his own constructed universe. Mona is allowed to play the femme fatale because she is safely absent, but she is also a necessary constituent of Miller's vision of a world gone mad:

> I saw her looking at me across the table with eyes turned to grief; sorrow spreading inward flattened its nose against her spine. . . . With the wet dawn came the tolling of bells and along the fibers of my nerves the bells played ceaselessly and their tongues pounded in my heart and clanged with iron malice. Strange that the bells should toll so, but stranger still the body bursting, this woman turned to night and her maggot words gnawing through the mattress. (*Tropic of Cancer*, 251)

Miller's use of surreal imagery attains an almost apocalyptic quality, and Mona by proxy becomes a harbinger of death. The physicality of the description aligns her with a corpse but she is also described as a high-priestess whose "tolling of bells" eroticizes the process of creativity, a process which is ultimately situated in the matrimonial bed Miller has left behind. As a figure in conflict with the male sensibility, Mona, in spite of her absence, becomes a formidable opponent both needed and feared by Miller.

In his essay "Narcissism," Norman Mailer sees the relationship between Miller and June/Mona/Mara as the reason for Miller's metamorphosis from "mean calculating street-fucker" to "faithful and tortured young writer":

He shifts from an intelligent and second-rate promoter of bad debts, and some riotous Brooklyn nights, to a faithful and tortured young writer helplessly in love with a Junoesque woman whose maddening lack of centre leads him into an intuition of his own lack of identity. He comes to discover all those modern themes which revolve around the discovery of oneself. Soon he will dive into the pit of recognizing that there may not be a geological foundation in the psyche one can call identity. Like June, he will have to recreate himself each morning, and soon realizes he has been doing it all his life.[6]

Mailer's analysis centers on the importance of Miller's search for identity as an underlying creative force. But oddly enough, he does not consider the possibility that the conflict between Miller and June may constitute a deliberate frame for Miller's tortured persona. In other words, whether Miller really needed to re-create himself each morning is not the whole point. The point is that Miller's use of this conflict — both internally and externally — is implicit in the narrative in Miller's own terms, and hence saves him from recourse to stereotypes of ephemeral and unknowing women. Instead, June's role, although made abstract, nevertheless becomes a cipher for the very strength Miller hopes to attain.

This makes Miller's eroticization of the urban landscape different from the early surrealist romances. A more "Classical Surrealism," to coin a phrase, feminizes the urban landscape as a way to accentuate its mystical as well as erotic qualities; a procedure re-enacted in the land scapes of Aragon and Breton, where the desire to conquer and dominate the city is made possible rather than impossible through the feminization of it in territorial terms. Miller's "love-stories" do this as well, but the project of self-definition and internal struggle nevertheless demands that the setting for this struggle remain indecipherable and unattainable to some extent. Similarly, the June/Mona/Mara character must remain unconquerable in order to function effectively as the inspirational force behind Miller's writing. June's absence in *Tropic of Cancer* thus attains a dual function. On one hand, it constitutes the necessary conditions for what Mailer calls Miller's persona as "tortured young writer," but it also allows Miller to dream of a love free from the matrimonial obligations from which he has escaped. The descriptions of the city in *Tropic of Cancer* become facilitators for an idyllic vision of togetherness which Miller knows is pure fantasy:

We walk down the Rue du Chateau. . . . Walk over the railroad bridge where I used to watch the trains pulling out and feel all sick inside wondering where the hell she could be. Everything soft and enchanting as we walk over the bridge. Smoke coming up between our legs, the tracks creaking, semaphores in our blood. I feel her body close to mine — all mine now — and I stop to rub my hands over the warm velvet. Everything around us is crumbling, crumbling and the warm body under the warm velvet is aching for me. (*Tropic of Cancer*, 19)

Miller knows that this "enchanting" dream cannot last (although it can be recalled and reconstructed in fictional terms) and the city that "crumbles" in amorous acceptance of Miller's desire for Mona, later changes into the setting for sexual exploits of a more violent nature. Similarly, as Miller begins to forget Mona, the women who take her place become more obvious representations of urban decay rather than postcard visions of Parisian love. Situated in New York primarily, *Tropic of Capricorn*, the follow up to *Tropic of Cancer*, charts similar moments of Miller and Mona's love but in all-together different terms. As Miller puts it "I know that we were conjugating the verb love like two mani-acs trying to fuck through an iron gate" (*Tropic of Capricorn*, 236).

Because Miller's exile in Paris represents his flight from the insanity of New York corporate life, as well as from a marriage which was taking its toil emotionally, it is represented in ambiguous terms from the be-ginning. On one hand, it becomes a desired divorce from a restrictive America in creative terms, on the other, an attempted escape from an emotional attachment which he needs in order to write in the first place. Imbedded in this expatriatism lies Miller's urge to explain why he left: a confessional mode of writing designed to gain redemption so that he can start over again, both as reborn writer and man in Europe. Mona's status, as we saw before, is both emasculating in that she draws the locus of inspiration away from Miller's own abilities, but also liber-ating in that it allows him a certain license as he attempts to get over her. Regardless of what perspective Miller chooses, and both *Tropics* swerve continuously from one and the other, their status as straight-forward novels of sexual liberation must be questioned. In this respect, both *Tropic of Capricorn*, which deals with Miller's life with Mona prior to his move to Paris, and *Tropic of Cancer*, provide urban settings for a narrative where separation and love operate in equal measure.

In spite of the complexity underlying Miller's amorous adventures in the city, feminist critiques of Miller often share the proposition that women are simply marginalized in the form of an uncomfortable "other." The fact that these women are represented as having a more complex role, as far as power relations are concerned, is overlooked. Miller's pre-occupation with June/Mona/Mara partly attests to the complex role she takes on in the course of the *Tropics*, as well as the fact that in many respects he never gets a grip on her as a character. This is not to say that Miller affords his ex-wife the chance to liberate herself in more contemporary terms, simply that compared to the surrealists, one cannot accuse Miller of failing to include female emancipation in what was meant to be liberating prose for both genders. In other words, while women may have embodied revolutionary ideas, this does not mean that they automatically became the subject of that revolution as well. In fact one might question whether female empowerment was ever on the surrealist agenda in the first place. If we assume that women were used primarily by the male surrealists to gain access to the surreal, an inherently complex concept in itself, then the ways in which this is represented merit a closer look.

Nadja and June — Two Case-Studies in the Eroticization of the City

In Breton's *Nadja* (1928) the author's relationship with a young girl in the city of Paris is charted through a series of meetings and brief conversations in public places. What fascinates Breton about Nadja, who shows clear signs of mental disturbance, is her absolute disregard for reality: "I have taken Nadja, from the first day to the last, for a free genius, something like one of those spirits of the air which certain magical practices momentarily permit us to entertain but which we can never overcome."[7] Nadja's freedom is intrinsically linked, in spite of her "free genius," to her recognizable admiration for Breton's artistic genius: "As for her, I know that in every sense of the word, she takes me for a god. She thinks of me as the sun" (*Nadja*, 111). Nadja's role is not to disturb the narrator/writer's identity as an artist, but to confirm his vision of what constitutes a muse in a surreal sense. As Breton puts it in *The Second Manifesto* (1930) "the idea of love tends to create a being," and in this case, that being is clearly Nadja.[8] Nadja soon realizes that it is necessary for Breton to appropriate her creatively, to put her in writing if she is to survive. As Nadja implores: "André, André? You will write a novel about me. I'm sure you will. Don't say you won't. Be careful: everything fades, everything vanishes. Something must remain of us. . . . Promise. You have to" (*Nadja*, 100).[9]

The fear of literary annihilation, as voiced by Nadja, nevertheless seems to refer more to Breton's own fears concerning his survival as an author in control. By signaling the mythological structures of the city through Nadja ("a free spirit of the air"), Breton comments on deeper

anxieties concerning writing as preservation as well. If the text constitutes Nadja's identity, then Nadja in turn must survive in order for the
magical traces of the city to remain. The question is: who is most afraid
of being forgotten, Breton or Nadja? If Nadja's freedom is partly located in her madness, then Breton is left as the vulnerable narrator
whose lucidity is his weakness as well. Breton displaces his own anxieties concerning creativity by locating them in Nadja instead, but that
doesn't lessen Nadja's anxiety, for without Breton's use of her creatively, she ceases to exist. Once the writer stops, as he puts it, "understanding Nadja" she is locked away in an insane asylum, leaving Breton
to conclude: "The essential thing is that I do not suppose there can be
much difference for Nadja between the inside of a sanatorium and the
outside" (*Nadja*, 136).

On a basic level, then, *Nadja* portrays a male protagonist seeking his
own identity through a female representational object. To criticize Breton for not placing her as a woman at the forefront obscures the main
issue: the possibility that both *Nadja* and Miller's *Tropics* are designed,
above all, to convey a male writer's attempts at self-representation and
preservation of masculinity. If we assume that an autobiographical
premise underlies the search — in Breton's case for the surreal, in
Miller's for an identity as an artist — then such characters as Nadja and
June gain their right to exist solely through what they can contribute to
the masculine search. What is crucial is not the actual possibility of pos-
sessing a woman, but the ability she has to inspire incessant desire, a necessary prerequisite for the erotic torment of the male protagonist.

Once seen in this light, the intricate games that Breton sets up between himself and Nadja (such as letting chance occurrences decide
where they meet) serve to illustrate the interplay between Nadja as an
object and the writer's desire. Breton describes such a chance encounter as though it were completely natural: "For a change I decided to
take the right sidewalk of the Rue de la Chausée-d'Antin. One of the
first people that I prepare to meet there is Nadja. . . . She advances as if
she didn't want to see me. She seems quite unable to explain her presence here in this street where to forestall further questions, she tells me
she is looking for Dutch chocolate" (*Nadja*, 117). Breton's gaze is
both all-knowing and authoritarian. But in spite of being "prepared" to
meet Nadja, the decoding of events which takes place as he describes
their meeting retains an inexplicable aura. This is indicated by the fact
that Nadja's explanation appears to be an excuse, as if she is doing
something elicit by not following Breton's directives. The gap between
the two, who never really meet in mutual love, is the place where the

marvellous — the recognizably surreal — occurs. Just as the places where they meet become portents of forces beyond their control, so too, does the marvellous signal a momentary loss of memory, a disruption of rationality necessary for the surrealist experience.[10] In this respect, Nadja's ability to perplex Breton, to disrupt his ability to decode the events around him, is crucial. As a woman, she is needed for an objectification of desire but the aim is not necessarily the fulfilment of love. The aim is always an illumination of the male writer: a "solution which is always superior, a solution certainly rigorously fitting and yet somehow in excess of the need."[11]

This "excess" is apparent in Breton's deliberately nonchalant attitude toward love in his romance with Nadja, or rather, what she stands for. While Breton's manifestoes proclaim the importance of re-introducing love into avant-garde aesthetics, his own fiction is curiously devoid of a sense of personal engagement. As far as the romantic aspect is concerned, Breton's desire to be in control via an all-knowing authoritarian gaze seems to supersede any emotional involvement.[12]

This lack of engagement in what is presented as an obsessional love affair (as the title *Mad Love* seems to indicate), explains partly why the outcomes of these love affairs are inconsequential. As in automatic writing, it is not the writing itself, but the re structuring of the self which takes place in the process which is important. In *Nadja*, the meetings between the lovers are always described with a chronological precision which somehow refuses lyricism and yet simultaneously gives each meeting place and time an almost mystical connotation. Similarly, the photographs accompanying the text of fountains, cafes, and churches in Paris are curiously devoid of people or movement, as if the love-affair which takes place there has been frozen and immobilized. It is no coincidence, then, that Breton coins the term "convulsive beauty" in *Mad Love* for that which is "veiled-erotic, fixed-explosive," an indication that in the fixed image of photography lies the hidden erotic. As we will see, Breton's use of Brassaï's photos differs tellingly from Miller's use of Brassaï as illustrator of *his* vision of Paris.

In Breton's romances, sexuality in the form of actual human activity is never shown. Instead, the squares and parks shown in the accompanying photographs are ultra-sensitive zones, places which provide the artist with a sudden onslaught of inspiration which in turn testifies to the city's "explosive" nature, as if things around him were suddenly literally speaking to him. Miller's descriptions of New York and Paris also take on this projective quality, but for Miller, locations have a historicized, oftentimes nostalgic quality, as the writer wanders the city on a quest for inspiration:

> Or wandering along the Seine at night, wandering and wandering, and going mad with the beauty of it, the trees leaning to, the broken images in the water, the rush of the current under the bloody lights of the bridges, the women sleeping in door-ways, sleeping on newspapers, sleeping in the rain; everywhere the musty porches of the cathedrals and beggars and lice and old hags. . . . The Place St. Sulpice, so quiet and deserted, where toward midnight there came every night the woman with the busted umbrella and the crazy veil; every night she slept there on a bench under her torn umbrella . . . and in the morning I'd be sitting there myself, taking a quiet snooze in the sunshine, cursing the goddamned pigeons. (*Tropic of Cancer*, 16–17)

In Breton's case, the purpose of the erotic lay primarily in its projective quality, the ability it had to focus on the city's ephemeral and mystical quality. For Miller, the mystical quality also lies in the city's ability to remind the protagonist of the communality shared by those "down and out in Paris" at any given moment. In this particular passage, Miller aligns himself with the homeless woman, whose "busted umbrella" becomes a marker for the surreal quality of the city, as well as an economic indictment of poverty. Miller may be going "mad" like Nadja with "the beauty of it all" but it is a beauty which goes hand in hand with a sense of Paris as a living organism and not merely a static backdrop for the artist and his muse. Thus, while Miller's description of his own role within the urban landscape mimics Breton's, to some extent, Miller's empathy with those on the periphery of society is markedly different.

Nadja's ability to recognize "those brief intervals which our marvellous stupor grants us" indicates her role as potential medium, a role which operates in a nineteenth-century tradition of women as mediators between the living and the dead, the animate and the inanimate (*Nadja*, 111). The difference is that in the "modern" setting of the surrealist city, women as mediums have moved from the parlor to the street. The move to the street, in Miller's terms, means actually living and sleeping on benches with only an umbrella for shelter. In Breton's Paris, the "real Nadja," according to Breton, "enjoyed being nowhere but in the streets, accessible to interrogation from any human being launched upon some great chimera" (*Nadja*, 113). As a homeless Nadja's availability is unquestioned by Breton, whereas the selfsame availability is accentuated as a form of vulnerability by Miller in his version of the muse "on the street."[13]

In Miller's case, while reminiscent of Breton's romanticization of the female figure, the downtrodden prostitutes and vagrants of Paris and New York nevertheless function primarily as catalysts for the writer's own vision of the city. There, women are necessary means towards a recognition of the city's ephemeral quality; emblematic of the mystical forces that occupy the public spaces of the city in ways similar to the narrator. Thus, the distance necessary for Breton's elevation of Nadja's role into a marker of something which she herself does not, and indeed cannot understand, is not so clear cut in Miller's use of June. On the contrary, June's role depends largely on her ability to intuitively understand those things which Miller himself cannot fathom.

In her essay "Seeing the Surrealist Woman: We Are a Problem," Mary Ann Caws, critical of the way in which these "fictional" women are used, defines this "unknown" feminine contribution as auratic:

> Now the issue is, in a sense, what has aura and what does not. We know, from Walter Benjamin, how crucially important the aura is, and we know, from Breton, that the urgent thing is the mystery of it all — they are on the same frequency, the aura and the strangeness of woman, as long as she remains other. Or at least somewhat other.[14]

Caws assumes that the need to represent women as "others" proves that the surrealist attitude towards women is one of marginalization and estrangement, hence the "We Are a Problem" of the title. Caws does not look into the connection between aura, mystery and surrealism in creative terms. She instead points to three key issues; the Benjaminian notion of aura, the equation of mystery with aura, and the "strangeness of woman." In order to look at how these concepts manifest themselves in surrealist narratives, it is necessary to define the term "aura."

In "The Work of Art in the Age of Mechanical Reproduction," Benjamin describes aura as an object's "most sensitive nucleus — namely, its authenticity," and goes on to say "the Authenticity of a thing is the essence of all that is transmissible." Benjamin uses as an example the mountain which casts a shadow over the person looking at it, once this occurs, the person experiences the aura of that mountain. "Aura" is therefore something which, although tangible from a visual perspective, cannot be grasped or taken with a person. While it is something which makes one understand the mountain better, a transmissible sensation from the object in question to the person viewing it, it is also something which changes according to who experiences it. In other words, an object's aura is transmissible but also ambiguous by nature, and while it authenticates the presence of an object, its "most sensitive nucleus," its uniqueness, will by nature change according to when and by whom it is experienced.[15]

In this sense, Caws is right to equate the notion of aura with mystery. The notion of aura is in itself mysterious because it cannot be defined in any real terms. While Caws questions the use of women as strange and "other," the notion of aura could also be seen as a term appropriately indicative of the ephemeral and mysterious quality embodied in the opposite sex by the surrealists. What Caws does not take into consideration is the major difference in Benjamin's own use of aura in relation to that of the surrealists. On one hand, Benjamin praised the surrealists for moving towards a dialectical — and auratic — relationship between the writer and the world around him, but he also recognized a potential danger in using the auratic nature of objects as a way to mystify the world rather than help it.[16]

Benjamin wanted, above all, to formulate a theory which could get at perception and experience directly, without sacrificing the potential politicization of art at the same time. In order to do this, it was important not to let a mystification of reality detract from a real transformation of that reality. As his goal was always politically-informed, Benjamin stressed the need for the writer's role to be that of an intelligently informed observer. Benjamin was therefore critical of any theory which stressed the writer's capacity to glorify and mythologize the object viewed (as in *Nadja* for example). As far as the issue of auratic experience was concerned, it could only function successfully once a dialectical relationship was established between the object and the artist. The aim was to secularize mystical notions of illumination, in order to both bring it closer to the artist and to historicize the moment of illumination, so that it would eventually "dissolve 'mythology' into the space of history."[17] Without the historical perspective, mythology could too easily slip into another form of worship of the absolute, a critique of surrealism which — albeit from another angle — is similar to Miller's questioning of automatism in "An Open Letter to Surrealists Everywhere." Miller reopens this line of questioning in his homage to Brassaï, an artist for whom the auratic nature of the city is intrinsically linked to a historical and social acknowledgment of the people inhabiting it.

In order to combine a critically-informed historical perspective with an openness to experience on other levels than purely rational ones, Benjamin built a theory of auratic experience based on what he termed "profane illumination." In his version of how the individual integrates himself into the world, the illumination — which in many respects corresponds to the surrealist entry into the marvellous — was seen as worldly, as well as mundane. Benjamin believed that the artist could benefit from turning to such mundane things as buildings and consumer objects, but he also wanted the observer to be cautious in the face of new myths and icons as mere substitutes for old ones.

In *Nadja*, as Benjamin points out, the desired woman is never as important as that which surrounds her. It is precisely her aura, her luminosity which attracts Breton, but it is also the one thing that makes it practically impossible for Breton and Nadja to engage in a reciprocal relationship. As Benjamin puts it: "The lady, in esoteric love, matters least. So, too, for Breton. He is closer to the things that Nadja is close to than to her."[18] As Benjamin points out, the lady herself matters least, precisely because it is what she refers to in the city which in turn determines Breton's love for her. Her role is crucial as the link between the places which Breton haunts because of their aura. The links themselves are accentuated by descriptions which echo the actual names of locations: "We passed the Sphinx-Hotel, Boulevard Magenta. She shows me the luminous sign with the words that made her decide to stay here the night she arrived in Paris" (*Nadja*, 105). Conveniently, the hotel spells out Nadja's role as surrealist medium, not unlike Miller's use of the gargoyle as an indicator of his "vagabond" woman. Both emblems fit into the mythological aspect of surrealist iconography, as the image of the sphinx accentuates the woman's role as mediator as well as catalyst for the surrealist "hero" on a quest to solve a riddle. Nadja's "sphinx-ness" is a hybrid element in itself, but unlike the half woman/half beast in Greek mythology, there is no fear that she will punish those who cannot answer her riddle. It is crucial, in this respect, that Breton never allows her any actual knowledge, and a necessary pre-requisite for her dependence upon Breton's recognition of her. In this sense, Caws is right to point out that the woman remains a form of "other." In fact, while the sphinx provides the riddle, the woman — *as woman* — is there primarily to question the by-passers and "to be interrogated" rather than provide any answers.

In *Paris Peasant*, Aragon connects the metaphysical aspect of places with the appearance of the sphinx as well. A guardian spirit, the sphinx/woman invokes the unconscious thoughts of the writer as he strolls through the city: "Wherever the living pursue particular ambiguous activities, the inanimate may sometimes take on the reflection of their most secret motives: and thus our cities are peopled with unrecognized sphinxes" (*Paris Peasant*, 27). Aragon speaks of the sphinxes as unrecognized, harbingers of a deeper knowledge, but they are always recognizably feminine. If the quest for the surreal is a male prerogative "the ambiguous activities" which form a part of this quest remain un-ashamedly eroticized through a feminization of the process itself.

Although Miller's descriptions of Paris in *Tropic of Cancer* are less ephemeral and more discernibly real, his male quest remains eroticized as well, albeit in a different way than in Breton's *Nadja*. As Miller walks through the "Jardin de Tuileries" he describes "getting an erection looking at the dumb statues" as though the city in itself supplies enough stimuli to make the actual presence of a woman unnecessary (*Tropic of Cancer*, 16). In Miller's case, these solitary erotic reveries present themselves in contrast to his fraught relationship with June (Mona/Mara), and form a welcome respite from the grueling torments of his actual love-affairs. Nevertheless, June remains emphatically Miller's pathway into the marvellous. After living and suffering with her in New York, Miller gains redemption as an illumination described in the form of a metamorphosis. As June's personality dissolves, Miller recognizes what he has been looking for all along; an unexplored re-gion where the irrational and the creative occur simultaneously: "I no longer look into the eyes of the woman I hold in my arms but I swim through, head and arms and legs, and I see that behind the sockets of the eyes there is a region unexplored, the world of futurity, and here there is no logic whatever, just the still germination of events unbroken by night and day, by yesterday and tomorrow" (*Tropic of Capricorn*, 121). The "unexplored region" is June's sex and one of the more obvi-ous instances where one could accuse Miller's focus on female genitalia as being unashamedly sexist. But June also functions in a more complex emblematic way, namely on a wider level as the pathway to Miller's own creative instinct and the one inexhaustible topic which he can cir-cle around — the attempt to understand himself through June.[19]

In Miller's case, this "region unexplored" lies both within June and beyond her, signaling another important difference between Miller's relationship to June and Breton's to Nadja. For Nadja to operate effec-tively as "other," to use Caws's expression, she must retain an indeci-pherable personality. And in order to break with traditional notions of what is normal and sane, it becomes necessary for Breton to represent Nadja as an outcast in ordinary society. For Miller, on the other hand, June is powerful because she contains "the world of futurity." This timeless quality — a sort of feminized version of the Durée Réelle mentioned previously — is something which Miller can only hope to attain "second-hand." June is therefore more than just the intermediary between Miller and the marvellous. Miller may strive to get to the roots of June's enigmatic character but he is never in a position of absolute power. Instead, the female perspective becomes no less than a comment: "on the behaviour of the antlike creature man, viewed from another dimension" (*Tropic of Capricorn*, 256).

Having traced some of the differences and similarities in Miller and Breton's work, we can now see how the entry into the "marvellous" for these male writers depends on the positioning of the woman as intermediary, in textual as well as psychological terms. In Breton's case, this can only be done by keeping Nadja at a distance, a distance accentuated by the descriptions of her as always made up, as though she is an actress *playing* the role of intermediary rather than actual mistress. Breton is attracted to Nadja's use of excessive make-up because it is *out of place*. "Does this mean that what is only slightly permissible in the street but advisable in the theatre is important to me only insofar as it has defied what is forbidden in one case, decreed in the other? Perhaps" (*Nadja*, 65).

By setting himself firmly in control of the narrative mechanisms, Breton can make Nadja's appearance an issue of contemplation rather than anxiety. The comparison with the theatre is perfect in this case. Nadja and Breton are, after all, rehearsing the gestures of lovers rather than seeking to bring their desire to an actual climax. Likewise, Nadja's theatrical gestures accentuate the fact that her role is to move from one place, from one scene to another. As a visitor in the female domain, a domain made theatrical and "unreal," the male protagonist always has the choice of leaving or staying. Miller's constant vagabonding mimics this movement but his inability to function without the mental presence of June differs from Breton's overt distancing from Nadja. In any case, Breton's control of Nadja frees him from the potential entrapment of a bourgeois household in a much more convenient manner than Miller's frantic sexual exploits.

Throughout *Tropic of Cancer*, the threat from the June/Mona/Mara figure is, in addition, economic as well as sexual. Miller's repeated visits to the American Express Office in Paris (in the hope of receiving money from June, albeit financed by her rich American lovers in Miller's paranoid mind), become a series of punctuation devices in the narrative, an opportunity for Miller to remind the reader that he is in fact being supported by a woman. While Miller's acceptance of this situation in part supports his vociferous denial of the social order — his refusal to become a self-supporting member of the community — it also questions his own masculinity. In economic terms, Miller is assigned a feminine role. The anger at being unjustly feminized in financial terms, could be one reason why he persists in aligning June's sexuality with death. June's "sphinx-ness," similar to that of the surrealist muse, seems to convey a problematic desire; partly to return to the womb and partly to escape it:

> I wanted something of the earth which was not of man's doing, something absolutely divorced from the human of which I was surfeited. I wanted something purely terrestrial and absolutely divested of idea. . . . I wanted the dark fecundity of nature, the deep well of the womb, silence, or else the lapping of the black waters of death.
>
> (*Tropic of Capricorn*, 76)

Miller obsessively returns to the image of the womb throughout the *Tropics*. But whereas in *Tropic of Cancer* the womb is primarily a marker for female sexuality, in *Tropic of Capricorn* the womb is always, on a wider level, connected to Miller's persona as an "anti-littérateur," a writer in search of a life divested from "ideas." Miller's version of femininity located in the womb, allows him to represent both a primitive and a nature-driven image of women "as not of this earth," an idea not out of line with what Miller was reading at the time in terms of popular psychoanalysis.[20] Miller, like the surrealists, appropriated the Freudian fascination with Greek mythology and the image of the sphinx as symbolic of the oedipal triangle, a rather crude warning against the dangers of wanting to "return to the womb." On another level, the sphinx also provides an allegorical perspective on the hazards of writing, as Miller strives to "kill" off the bourgeois literary traditions of his forefathers in an "oedipal fashion." The riddle of the sphinx, for both Miller and the surrealists, is about literary origins as well as sexual anxiety, and in this respect the womb becomes the perfect symbol of the female muse — something which, once again, is "not of man's doing."

Miller's desire to return to a pre-natal stage — death-driven rather than procreative — is signaled in the lapping of "the black waters of death" and in the regressive rather than progressive qualities of his sexual relations. Hal Foster's book on surrealism, *Compulsive Beauty*, sees the erotic imagery, and by extension the focus on the muse, as indicative of a return of the repressed in psycho-analytical terms. For Foster, the use of the erotic indicates the surrealists' inability to acknowledge a death drive which is then sublimated and couched in terms of the marvellous and the auratic. To back up his point, Foster uses images of mechanization and sadomasochism within surrealist art to illustrate the regressive and anxiety driven forces behind surrealist eroticism.[21]

Foster's recognition in *Compulsive Beauty* that surrealist art has an ambiguous relationship to its internal impulses and the external signs upon which it projects these impulses, owes a great deal to Benjamin's earlier work on this paradox. The fact that this paradox is at its most visible in the demonic aspect of the sphinx, a threatening as well as guardian figure for the male artist, can be read both as a promise of love in the future, as well as a return to past obsessions. Nevertheless, it would be too easy to slot Miller's obsessive attachment to June into a Freudian pattern, but in itself, such Freudian analysis would not necessarily adequately explain the connections made in a fetishistic sense between buildings, structures, and locations to women in surrealist romances.

In order to illuminate these connections, the eroticization of the city has to be examined from another perspective than as a convenient entry into the marvellous. If the city can be read as a collection of anxious signs to be mastered (the gargoyle, the sphinx, etc.), the fetishistic aspect of love in these narratives can also be seen as critiques of capitalism in a wider sense. Structures, monuments, and objects made feminine (the statues in the "jardin de Tuileries") signify the fascination with the decrepit, the historically determined, as well as the erotic. By reading the ephemeral mystical properties of the urban landscape in this manner, wandering the city becomes a dialectical play, not only between men and women, but in narrative terms between the past and the present as well.

Halfway through *Tropic of Capricorn* Miller presents an "interlude"· "The Land of Fuck" or "The Ovarian Trolley." Interspersed with Miller's ruminations on the nature of sex as an emblem of creativity, Miller launches into various critiques of New York as the hub of commercialized America. But rather than critique the ethics of capitalism methodically in a Marxist vein, Miller's critiques become extensions, rather than digressions, on the issue of sexuality; thus high capitalism is placed within the realm of the physical:[22]

> There is a condition of misery which is irremediable — because its origins are lost in obscurity. Bloomingdale's, for example, can bring about this condition. All department stores are symbols of sickness and emptiness. . . . There is the smell, not of decomposition, but of misalliance. . . . Man, the miserable alchemist has welded together, in a million forms and shapes, substances and essences, which have nothing in common. . . . The ark is so full of bric-a-brac that it has become a stationary building above a subway in which the smell of linoleum prevails and predominates. (*Tropic of Capricorn*, 205)

Miller's accusation of "misalliance" is based on the belief that commercialization intrinsically breaks the natural order. Hence the comparison between the pride of metropolitan living — the department store — and a non-functional ark. What was meant to rescue humanity becomes instead a botched experiment by "the miserable alchemist man." By caricaturing the pretentiousness of surrealist rhetoric, which insists on the mystical properties of the urban landscape, Miller elevates his own abilities as urban savant, and by turning the department store, symbol of progress and prosperity in the 1920s, into a store-house for humanity's refuse, Miller sets himself up as capable of sniffing out its fake, "easy-to-clean" nature. In this vision of the urban, Miller's purpose is not to debunk the auratic nature of the city, but instead firmly situate it within his own critical, rather than romantic, realm of observation. In other words, this is Miller *against* New York City; as opposed to Breton's exuberant embrace of metropolitan Paris.

It might be convenient to conclude that Miller's vision of modernity is primarily negative, whereas Breton was more in thrall to the forces of commercialization which enabled the growth of the city in the first place. But Miller's language is tellingly personalized: the department store makes *him* sick and it is of no consequence to the vast majority of people who have "lost the origins of their misery" anyway. In this sense, Miller's visions of the urban are still auratic; that is to say they speak to him of a deeper malaise indecipherable to most. In other words, Miller's visions are illuminatory on a purely personal rather than collective level. The grand statement: "I am going to die as a City in order to once again become a man" may be nihilistic, but it is also a statement of redemption (*Tropic of Capricorn*, 123). What is crucial is that it is centered on the survival of the artist above all.

Miller politicizes sexual conduct by connecting it with urban commercialization on a larger scale, but this does not mean that he successfully negotiates the issue of gender in more convincing terms than do the surrealists. Miller's use of women as auratic markers may seem less restrictive but the focus is still, above all, on the male writer's emancipation from the restrictive norm of bourgeois behaviour. This is spelled out clearly in the passages where prostitution constitutes a realm of freedom from the monogamy implicit in conventional sexual behaviour. In this respect, Miller has more in common with Aragon's humorous descriptions of brothel visits; a far cry from Breton's dispassionate kisses exchanged with a reluctant Nadja on trains and park-benches. "Let those who are happy throw the first stone," Aragon writes in defense of his regular brothel visits, "they have no need of this atmosphere where I achieve rejuvenation. . . . What do I care if a man, proud of having succeeded in accustoming himself to a single body, is revolted by this pleasure, what do I care if he considers this pleasure of

mine a sort of masturbation? My masturbations are as good as his"
(*Paris Peasant*, 118).

For both Miller and Aragon, the commercialization of sexuality, in
the form of prostitution, becomes an added attraction of urban life, a
way for urban man to enact a fantasy of freedom. This does not mean,
however, that this "fantasy" is not accepted as precisely that — an anti-
dote to the overly romanticized perspective of Breton's urban flaneur.
Nevertheless, to take what might be a stylistic difference amongst
authors and claim it as a socially informed critique is still a large move
in analytical terms. In spite of the complex representations of June,
most women still function as fetishistic objects, objectified through
their sexual value. In this instance, a prostitute is the perfect fetish due
to her monetary value. As Benjamin puts it: "The commodity clearly
provides such an image: as fetish. The arcades which are both house
and stars, provide such an image. And such an image is provided by the
whore, who is seller and commodity in one" (*Reflections*, 171).

Benjamin hesitates in equating the prostitute "who is seller and
commodity in one" with any emancipatory effect. Instead, he seems
more interested in isolating those objects not made obsolete by tech-
nological advances, objects which remain emblems, both alive and objectified. While buildings and structures must be reanimated in order to
be spiritualized, the prostitute is already an animate as well as spiritualized object, the perfect surrealist fetish, without any effort required on
the part of the narrator/writer.

In *Looking Back on Surrealism* (1956), Theodor Adorno makes a
similar point in his critique of surrealist aesthetics. By combining the use
of the erotic with a primarily fetishistic attitude to love, the surrealists
ignore the social and historical ramifications of the images they provide:[23]

> These images are not images of something inward; rather, they are
> fetishes — commodity fetishes — on which something subjective, li-
> bido, was once fixated. . . . The things that happen in these collages,
> the things that are convulsively suspended in them like the tense lines
> of lasciviousness around a mouth, are like the changes that occur in a
> pornographic image at the moment when the voyeur achieves gratifi-
> cation. . . . As a freezing of the moment of awakening Surrealism is
> akin to photography. Surrealism's booty is images, to be sure, but not
> the invariant, a-historical images of the unconscious subject to which
> the conventional view would like to neutralize them; rather they are
> historical images in which the subject's core becomes aware that it is
> something external, an imitation of something historical and social.
>
> (*Notes on Literature*, 89)

Adorno's criticism hinges on a reading of the fetishistic aspect within surrealism as applied towards self-gratification first and foremost. The "lasciviousness" of instant gratification is a more conservative assessment of the commodification process as described originally by Benjamin. In this respect, Adorno echoes Miller's distrust in his "An Open Letter to Surrealists Everywhere" concerning surrealism's absolute claim to the unconscious. While Miller singled out the impossibility of transcribing the unconscious through automatic writing, Adorno focuses on the visual representations, the photographic quality inherent in the so-called: "ahistorical images of the unconscious." Using writing as an example, Adorno suggests that the surrealists know that there can be no such thing as an accurate rendition of the unconscious: "the Surrealists themselves have discovered that people do not free associate the way they, the Surrealists, write, even in psychoanalysis" (*Notes on Literature*, 87). More importantly, Adorno connects the convulsive and explosive quality of the surrealist erotic with photography. By saying that the photographic image is indicative "of a freezing of the moment of awakening," Adorno returns to Benjamin's definition of the auratic experience; the moment where the "veiled-erotic" is "unveiled" and can manifest its full potential. Thus the awakening that the surrealists wish to freeze is in reality another form of "profane illumination." The problem for Adorno is not what they capture in written or visual terms, but that they remain fixated, "suspended," on certain objects. Once these objects comes into focus, the surrealist — like the voyeur — is content to observe without participating.

Ironically, Miller's persona in the *Tropics* falls conveniently into this category, as he spends a great deal of time watching rather than participating. Nevertheless, Miller's critique of Bloomingdale's — although a crude version of Benjamin's "profane illumination" — is still an "auratic" moment: the moment when one sees the essential quality of an object, what lies behind it and its revolutionary potential. Benjamin used his definition of profane illumination as a way to stress the importance of the "intoxicating powers" which exist in the cities. But while Benjamin's "profane illumination" can be associated with Miller's desire to use the urban landscape as a springboard for the artist's "personal illumination," the question of how to use the aura of things is clearly answered in different ways.

"The Eye of Paris" — On Brassaï

In his critique of surrealist aesthetics Adorno made a crucial link by commenting on how "the freezing of the moment of awakening can be seen as akin to photography." While Adorno sought to show the negative — that is to say non-progressive aspect of surrealist practice (hence the freezing) — the issue of photography's connection to "a writing of the urban" is one that Miller picks up on in "The Eye of Paris," his essay on the photographer Brassaï. In 1933, Miller wrote to a friend of his intention to "make a niche for him (Brassaï) in this present book," partly in "honest tribute to this talent" and secondly "because one of the principal themes of my book is the 'street.'"[24] The illustrations Miller obtained from Brassaï never went into *Tropic of Cancer*, as intended, but were incorporated into Miller's *Quiet Days in Clichy* twenty-three years later.[25] In the meantime the two artists became close friends, and "The Eye of Paris" was published in the collected essays, *Wisdom of the Heart* (1941)[26] Although it took Miller over twenty years to actually use Brassaï, the original project, described in the 1933 letter as intended "to convey an impression of the streets of Paris of which the photographs of Paris seem the perfect illustrations," shows Miller's desire to convey a distinctly European image of the city.

In Miller's use of Brassaï, the streets, bars, and dance-halls of Paris are transformed with the desire to show, rather than hide, the erotic aspect of the city. Brassaï's photographs had previously been used in *Nadja*, but usually as ephemeral portraits in grey tones of fountains, statues, squares, and empty parks with an air of secret rendezvous and assignations. Brassaï's Paris, as used by Miller, differs by being one of life and openness. In *Quiet Days in Clichy*, street-scenes of prostitutes waiting for customers, cafes where sailors and women are seen kissing in public, are all designed to conform to a constructed image of "Paris" and "night-life." Nevertheless, as we shall see, Miller's analysis of Brassaï as photographer is quite different from his actual choice of Brassaï photographs. *Quiet Days in Clichy* is a nostalgic look at Miller's bachelor life in Paris; one in which his constant promiscuity has little of the anxiety or surreal quality of the *Tropics*. "When I think about this period, it seems like a stretch in Paradise . . . even though the world was busy digging its own grave, there was still time to enjoy life, to be merry, . . . a period when cunt was in the air" (*Quiet Days in Clichy*, 35). This is the "scene" that Miller wants Brassaï to illustrate, and in turn, Miller's anecdotes will illustrate Brassaï's photographs: "At one corner of the Place Clichy is the Café Wepler, which was for a long pe-

riod my favourite haunt. I have sat there inside and out at all times of
the day. . . . I knew it like a book. The faces of the waiters, the manag-
ers, the cashiers, the whores, the clientele, even the attendants in the
lavatory, are engraved in my memory as if they were illustrations in a
book which I read every day" (*Quiet Days in Clichy*, 8).[27]

By stressing the illustrative quality of Brassaï's images, rather than
the procedural effort, Miller moves away from Adorno's analogy between surrealism and photography, and in the process signals one of
the major differences in how to "read" the use of photographs within
surrealism as a whole. In simple terms, Adorno linked photography and
surrealism because they appeared to stress both the immediacy and
spontaneity attainable through what he called "a moment's awakening." According to Adorno this provided a clear image of surrealism's
limitations as a viable political aesthetic. The overwhelming problem
was that surrealism was unable to show how various modes of representation (photography and writing), in a progressive dialectical sense
could operate between the reader and author, the viewer and photographer. For Miller, on the other hand, photography, rather than
"freezing" communication, re-enacts a series of correspondences made
manifest in memory and writing. Photography becomes a process
wherein the artist can situate himself, precisely because he shares the
photographer's visionary abilities; an ability made valid rather than suspect (or pornographic as Adorno described it) through the recognition
of the marvellous. Miller's "The Eye of Paris" is thus not merely Brassaï's "eye" but Miller's as well. For Miller the key issue is not whether
the writer/photographer *can* assimilate the urban landscape around
him, but *how* one does this successfully. Ultimately the aim is to recognize the emotional impact of the city on the writer and photographer
and not to focus only on the finished image or text.

In similar terms, Brassaï sees Miller's writing as operating from a
premise of endless correspondences: "He multiplied metaphors from a
fear that by itself one wouldn't illuminate every facet of a subject,
couldn't render the subject in its totality. . . . It took me some time to
understand that the author of the *Tropics* never intended images to illuminate a subject; he used the subject to spawn a whole new generation of subjects. . . . By journey's end, who can remember that it all
began with the simple description of one photographer's eyes?" (*Henry
Miller — The Paris Years*, 45). The reason Brassaï cannot "remember
that it all began with the description of one photographer's eyes" is
precisely because it did not. It begins, as Miller points out in "The Eye
of Paris," when: "eye to eye with this man you have the sensation of a

razor operating on your own eyeball" (*Wisdom of the Heart*, 174). This image, stolen from *Un Chien Andalou* is an image of a violent moment of recognition. In cinematic terms, it allowed Buñuel to "cut open" and expose the irrationality of the surreal landscape (interestingly seen through the eyes of a woman), while here, Miller compares it with "a crack in the wall or the panorama of a city." Once again, the city appears as a thematic device with which to link various modes of representation: in this case the allusion to cinema, photography, and writing. Repeating what he did in the *Tropics*, Miller returns the original subject — Brassaï's photographs — back to what really interests him, namely his "own eyeball" and the place where he can locate these personal visions; namely the city.[28]

As we saw earlier, the *Tropics* contained no single perspective from which to situate women in terms of the marvellous. In fact, compared to Breton's eroticization of the urban landscape, Miller's approach was more class and economically-related and in that sense politicized. This is also obvious in Miller's choice of Brassaï as "illustrator" of his "personal" Paris, a choice which imprints a distinctly human and proletarian aspect on the city. While "The Eye of Paris" is about the importance of individual vision within artistic expression, it is also in line with Miller's previous work, a response to surrealist trends. By 1956, Miller would have seen the Brassaï illustrations for *Mad Love* in which the black and white pictures of squares and monuments create a backdrop devoid of people. In this respect, Miller would have noticed the importance of locations rather than people within Breton's vision of the erotic.

A contrast is clearly visible, then, between the selection of Brassaï images in *Quiet Days in Clichy*, and *Nadja* and *Mad Love*. Miller's interest in the human perspective tends to stand out, which is somewhat odd when one considers how the narrative of *Quiet Days in Clichy* centers on the sex life of Miller and his house-mates to the exclusion of all other social commentary. This discrepancy between the illustrations and the story-line is probably due to the fact that the images were intended originally for *Tropic of Cancer*, that is to say, a 1930s story as opposed to one revised and published in 1956. This would support the idea that Miller chose the Brassaï images with a distinctly 1930s surrealist use of photography in mind. According to Brassaï, Miller "especially admired André Breton's *Nadja*. . . . But Miller could also be very hard on the surrealists. . . . Their insanity was a little too clean, he felt; they mobilized all the conscious powers so that they could flesh out the unconscious" (*Henry Miller — The Paris Years*, 155). Brassaï's assessment of Miller is impressively accurate, as we saw in the introduction, considering what he had at stake when it came to a general critique of surrealist aesthetics. The expression "to flesh out the unconscious" is especially apt since the majority of Brassaï locations in *Mad Love* are noticeably empty, ghostly, and dark, indicative of how even buildings, streets and monuments devoid of human activity can represent auratic experiences.

Thus, while Miller's choice of images differs in *Quiet Days in Clichy* from that of Breton's in *Mad Love*, the descriptions of Brassaï's abilities in "The Eye of Paris" use a rhetoric similar to that of the surrealists: "How else are we to explain that a chicken bone, under the optical alchemy of Brassaï, acquires the attributes of the marvellous? . . . The man who looked at a chicken bone transferred his whole personality to it in looking at it; he transmitted to an insignificant phenomenon . . . the experience acquired from looking at millions of other objects" (*Wisdom of the Heart*, 177). The "optical alchemy" Miller describes is not far from Benjamin's "optical unconscious"; the ability, in other words, to take the mundane and recognize its illuminatory potential. Brassaï claimed that Miller did "not intend to let images illuminate his subject," which may have been an accurate assessment of Miller's poetics, but the statement runs contrary to Miller's definitions of the dialectical role of photography vis-à-vis writing. In this respect, Miller saw photographs in terms of a deposit of the marvellous, a way to grasp momentarily at the convulsive beauty in the ordinary:

> Brassaï strikes at the accidental modulations, the illogical syntax, the mythical juxtaposition of things, at that anomalous, sporadic form of growth which a walk through the streets or a glance at a map or a scene in a film conveys to the sleeping portion of the brain. What is most familiar to the eye, what has become stale and commonplace, acquires through the flick of his magic lens the properties of the unique. Just as a thousand diverse types may write automatically and yet only one of them will bear the mark of an André Breton, so a thousand men may photograph the cemetery Monmartre but one of them will stand out triumphantly as Brassaï's.
>
> (*Wisdom of the Heart*, 173)

Miller's "mythical juxtaposition of things" and magical "lens" are not dissimilar to what Adorno called "the invariant, a-historical images of the unconscious subject" in his critique of surrealism. The quote relates to photographic practice — an active endeavor — but Miller nevertheless chooses to define it in relation to the "unconscious subject"; "the sleeping portion of the brain." The claim that the unconscious is constantly absorbing the "properties of things," their "mythical juxtapositions," falls in line with the surrealist definition of automatism. What Miller does is take this version of the unconscious and combine it with an attempted individualization of the creative process. Eventually, only one image out of a thousand "will stand out triumphantly as Brassaï's." In "An Open Letter to Surrealists Everywhere" Miller critiqued the surrealist reliance on an absolutist notion of the unconscious yet here he compares automatic writing, which necessitates direct access to the unconscious, with photography. In his assessment of Miller, Brassaï makes a similar "mistake" and tacitly assumes that Miller was engaged in "dictation by an unseen force." "In the calm after the visitation of the muses, Miller would reread what he had written and find in it a trace of another hand. He was convinced that we create nothing, that writing happens only through us and to us" (*Henry Miller — The Paris Years*, 150).

Not withstanding possible discrepancies between what Miller may have thought Brassaï wanted to hear and what he wrote in his critical essays, the real problem lies in the apparently seamless comparison between photography and automatic writing. In many ways the two practices lie in opposite ends of the surrealist notion of what constitutes creativity. Automatic writing was, as defined by Breton, the attempted rendition of the unconscious through a partly hypnotic state, a state wherein the artist was no longer "in control" of his production. Photography, on the other hand, by nature of the medium (and especially so in the 1920s and 1930s) required deliberation and preparation. Brassaï's night photography was not created through the use of flash but rather with lengthy exposure times, another factor which counteracts the immediacy of the procedure. In other words, it would have been virtually impossible to emulate the automatic process because of the very nature of the apparatus used.

Given this perspective, we must look at Miller's homage to Brassaï from a slightly different angle. Let us assume that Miller is trying to define not the process of creation itself (as automatism attempted), but the final product, that is to say, what the photograph shows. In this case, Brassaï's ability to give "that which is stale and commonplace the properties of the unique" has to be discernible in the finished image and cannot be governed by "the unconscious" alone. The issue is not to what extent the photograph bears the mark of the artist, but the way in which the artist portrays the object being photographed. Behind this idea, lies the belief that photography can in fact reveal the intrinsic properties of things:

> Now and then, in wandering through the streets, suddenly one comes awake, perceives with a strange exultation that he is moving through

an absolutely fresh slice of reality. Everything has the quality of the marvellous — the murky windows, . . . the contours of the houses, the bill-posters, the slumping figures of men and women, . . . the colors of the walls — everything written down in an unfamiliar script. . . . In this condition it happens that one really does see things he had never seen before — not the fantastic, harrowing, hallucinating objects of dream or drug, but the most banal, the most commonplace things, seen as it were for the first time. (*Wisdom of the Heart*, 181)

The idea that the "quality of the marvellous" resides in the everyday enables the urban landscape to take on a revelatory quality, as we have already seen. As in automatic writing, the "unfamiliar script" is conveyed through the ability of the artist as interpreter. But here, the objects are also images — images of reality rather than images of a fantastical or hallucinatory nature. Going back to Brassaï's illustrations for *Nadja* and *Quiet Days in Clichy* respectively, Miller's use of Brassaï is informed, not by a desire to set the city apart as dream-like and "other," but to provide "a slice of reality." The empty squares and glittering images of the Seine at night in *Nadja* thus become the crowded dance halls, the streets with prostitutes in *Quiet Days in Clichy*. "The desire which Brassaï so strongly evinces, a desire not to tamper with the object but to regard it as it is, was this not provoked by a profound humility, a respect and reverence for the object itself?" The paradox is that Brassaï's photographs, whether they be of people in cafes or empty streets at night, seem to minimize the influence of the photographer, couching the emphatic viewpoint in a deliberate detachment. While on the other hand, according to Miller, they portray an immense respect and reverence for the objects and people being photographed: "When I look at these photographs which seem to have been taken at random by a man loath to assert any values except what were inherent in the phenomena, I am impressed by their authority" (*Wisdom of the Heart*, 177). Where the "authority" lies is never completely clear though. As the above quotation indicates, the artist wandering the streets could, in this case, be either the photographer who provides the images or the viewer who simultaneously sees "things he had never seen before." As in Benjamin's "profane illumination" the issue is once again one of assimilation. What interests Miller is the emotional impact of the city, the dialectical nature of the imagery as it speaks to the writer/photographer.

In this respect all phenomena/objects contain inherent values. And the value contained in these objects can ultimately only be born out of the human activity and responses to which they refer. This aligns itself to Benjamin's insistence on aura as an intrinsic quality in all objects as long as they "speak" in some manner to the observer. Miller's perspective on photography can therefore be defined as auratic: "The object and the vision are one. Nothing flourishes after the vital flow is broken, neither the thing seen, not the one who sees it" (*Wisdom of the Heart*, 178). The vital flow is, in other words, what occurs between the artist's image of something, and the sensation we feel upon realizing its hidden qualities. As an example, Miller speaks of Brassaï's photograph of a chair in a Paris park:

> I think of a chair because among all the objects which Brassaï has photographed his chair with the wire legs stands out with a majesty that is singular and disquieting. It is a chair of the lowest denomination, a chair which has been sat on by beggars and by royalty, by little trot-about whores and by queenly opera divas. It is a chair which the municipality rents daily to any and every one who wishes to pay fifty centimes for sitting down in the open air. A chair with little holes in the seat and wire legs, which come to a loop at the bottom. The most unostentatious, the most inexpensive, the most ridiculous chair, if a chair can be ridiculous, which could be devised. Brassaï chose precisely this insignificant chair and, snapping it where he found it, unearthed what there was in it of dignity and veracity. THIS IS A CHAIR.
>
> (*Wisdom of the Heart*, 178)

By claiming that Brassaï is able to capture the essentialist nature of objects, "that which constitutes the uniqueness of an object, the first, the original, the imperishable vision of things" (*Wisdom of the Heart*, 183), Miller makes the object auratic — something which contains an indefinable and yet real property. He also aligns himself with Benjamin's call for a historically informed version of the marvellous, one which allows the marvellous to insert itself into a social context as opposed to a purely mythical one. The chair is auratic because it represents a continuum of proletarian experience from a historical perspective — albeit in an extremely discrete manner. Its position becomes that of an iconic pointer to culture, an object which encompasses a complex network of relations. In this instance, Brassaï becomes the contemplative and intelligent medium, not because of choice, but because he intuitively chose an object whose history is contained in the many references to the people who have used it, to the way it looks, as well as its "outmodedness" and charm. In ways similar to the prostitute in the surrealist romance, the chair can be seen to represent an everyday "object" (or fetish) which in a unique manner is "at home" both outside and inside. From a social perspective, it caters to people regardless of their status, and because it is frequently used, its outward appearance indicates both a sense of dilapidation and timeless beauty. Miller has realized that, through Brassaï's eyes, the chair acquires the ability to represent a width of experience of a social, economic, and historical nature. In the *Manifesto of Surrealism* (1924), Breton acknowledges this historical perspective as well: "The marvellous is not the same in every period of history: it partakes in some obscure way of a sort of general revelation only the fragments which come down to us."[29] This is not to say, that *any* object represented in auratic terms works as a signpost towards the marvellous, but it affords the artist the hope of capturing something — whether it be in writing or visually — whose universality evokes a certain authenticity. Unlike Breton's vision of the marvellous as something ephemeral and divine which "comes down to us," Brassaï situates the marvellous in a park, rented daily by the Parisian municipality. In this context, the word "authority," used by Miller to describe the quality bestowed on objects by Brassaï, is an authority otherwise lost in a world where objects — such as the chair — have no intrinsic value.

The dream of an urban landscape filled with possibilities, where any street provides a unique perspective on the "commonplace," starts out as a distinctly French one for Miller. This is not to say that American urban landscapes do no contain the same illuminatory possibilities but rather, that America seems content to ignore such possibilities. The rant against the American commercialization of life in his critique of Bloomingdale's in New York City was partly against a place where objects had become pure commodities. Brassaï knew that the attraction Miller found in his art was partly based on an idealization of the Parisian landscape vis-à-vis that of New York. But more importantly, he realized that Miller was engaged not in providing a portrait of the ideal city, but the ideal man. The artist Miller wanted to be was, according to Brassaï, the one he described in "The Eye of Paris":

> Trying not to hide behind the subjects and characters one is presenting; foregoing every thumbprint, every trace of the author; resisting all smugness, all embellishment; being but a witness to *what is*. All these represent the opposite pole from which Henry Miller, with what one might even call nostalgia, turned his back. Chance would have it that I be the one whom he thought embodied the expression "submit yourself to the subject." The true subject of "The Eye of Paris" is not me, but his nostalgia for what he is not. By drawing me, he is drawing himself — but *en négatif*. (*Henry Miller — The Paris Years*, 147)

The photographic expression, to be drawn "en négatif" strengthens the analogy between the writer and the photographer. But it also puts a different slant on Miller's need to bestow authority and, by extension, a sense of authenticity on the photographer's ability to provide a "fresh slice of reality." In this respect, Brassaï's modesty is questionable, but he does recognize Miller's need to hide behind other characters and subjects, and in particular Miller's constant anxiety concerning the nature of what it means to be a "witness." The work on and with Brassaï thus extends what may be Miller's grand theme: the issue of how to frame the subject — particularly when it turns out to be oneself — within the urban environment. In this respect, "The Eye of Paris" repeats the *Tropics* and the attempt by the artist to insert himself physically as well as aesthetically into the urban landscape:

> How then am I to refer to these morsels of black and white, how refer to them as photographs or works of art? Here . . . I saw my own sacred body exposed, the body that I have written into every stone, every tree, every monument, park, . . . and dwelling of Paris. I see now that I am leaving behind me a record of Paris. . . . The whole city — every arrondissement, every carrefour, every impasse, every enchanted street. (*Wisdom of the Heart,* 179)

"Un Etre Etoilique" (1938) — On Anais Nin

"The Eye of Paris" sets up another paradigm in support of Miller's quest to define the relationship between the subject and object, city and observer. While the *Tropics* and *Quiet Days in Clichy* place a high value on immediacy in the creative process, they also contain implicit critiques of the temptation to rely on an absolutist notion of the unconscious. As we saw, Miller's romances deal with the feminine in a more political and radical mode than that of Breton. Nevertheless, as Brassaï realized, Miller may have been able to do this because his chief subject always remained the same — namely himself. Miller allows his protagonist, the fictional one as well as the critical one in "The Eye of Paris," to alternate between an eroticized discourse, and a more critical one in relation to urbanization as commodification. This allows Miller to take Benjamin's critique of surrealism as a private, rather than collective, search for meaning at face value.

Walter Matthews, whose book *The Surrealist Mind* (1991) is primarily a defense of surrealism, touches on the notion of self-obsession as a crucial *and* positive part of the surrealist aesthetic. For Matthews, private, inward investigation and not collective politics appears as the surrealist aim:

> It is not overstating the case nor is it a criticism to say that the surrealist mind was self-obsessed. The operation of that mind was concentrated primarily on understanding itself better, on sharpening its perceptions and pushing back its horizons. The surrealist mind devoted itself to verifying its own capabilities with greater precision. . . . More often than not, reading surrealist theoretical writings lets us see the surrealist mind communing with itself instead of seeking new converts.[30]

Accepting that surrealism did not seek to "convert," Matthews *allows* the surrealist project to function as a private exploration rather than a call for universal revolutionary action. In this context, there is nothing "wrong" with the fact that although Nadja and Breton recognized the collective, auratic nature of places and structures in the city, they nevertheless chose not to describe them in such terms. Instead, the auratic nature of public places becomes a catalyst for Breton's intrinsically narcissistic love-affair.

In the *Tropics* and *Nadja*, the idealized observer is always male. Nevertheless, while Miller was roaming the Parisian nightlife with his friend Brassaï he was also working on an homage to another artist — namely his lover and designated muse — Anaïs Nin. "Un Etre Etoilique" is chiefly an essay on Anaïs Nin's diaries. It is one of the very few pieces Miller wrote on a woman artist and it provides us with an insight into what Miller considered an intrinsically feminine voice:

> It is the first female writing I have ever seen: it rearranges the world in terms of female honesty. The result is a language which is ultra-modern and yet which bears no resemblance to any of the masculine experimental processes with which we are familiar. It is precise, abstract, cloudy and unseizable. . . . It is the opium world of woman's physiological being, a sort of cinematic show put on inside the genito-urinary tract. There is not an ounce of man-made culture in it; everything related to the head is cut off.[31]

While Miller claims that Anaïs Nin's writing is radically different from "masculine experimental processes" (i.e. surrealism), he nevertheless defines Nin's writing as similarly sensual rather than dictated by reason. The feminine voice is eroticized by being located "inside the genito-urinary tract"; a physicalization of the creative act which concords with Miller's vision of writing as an erotic activity. Here, the interior of the body is put on show as opposed to the image of the eye being "sliced" open in "The Eye of Paris." By supplying a cinematic reference, the "show" put on by Nin is both urbanized and modernized — something that can be "watched" at one's leisure. While the physicalization centers the body within the text, it also authenticates the format of autobiography (Nin's diaries), the disclosure of the self rarely seen. This is different from "The Eye of Paris" in which the external image of the eye opens up to a surrounding world where nothing is hidden. In "Un Etre Etoilique," the world is an interior one and Miller's affinity with Anais Nin lies in the use of the familiar, the autobiographical as a way to express the "unseizable." "Our age," writes Miller, "is obsessed with a lust for investigating the mysteries of the personality" (*The Cosmological Eye*, 270). The auto-romance thus becomes, in a very Bergsonian vein, the prototypical investigation of the self.

In addition to being representative of the self in creative terms, Miller and Nin's shared interest in the auto-romance was also a way to internalize the urban landscape they shared in Paris. In this respect, Miller's demarcation of Nin's writing as particularly "feminine" inadvertently becomes a demarcation of the auto-romance as a particular mode of writing in which the city figures prominently as "feminine" as well. This use of the city as a marker for sexuality as well as gender is, as we saw in Breton's case, potentially suspect if only seen from a male perspective. Nevertheless in Nin's case, literary critics have allowed her the prerogative to use the city as a poetic macrocosm for her own sexual obsessions and indeed seen this practice as empowering in feminist terms. In Miller's case, of course, such a practice has more often than not been regarded as deeply suspect. In reality, both Miller and Nin could be accused of playing at being urban flaneurs, of flaunting a French tradition of bohemianism which, strictly speaking, they have no claim to. Seen from this perspective, Miller's definition of Nin's particular mode of writing is also a way to justify his own aesthetic tactics. Likewise, Nin's critical analysis of Miller often seems to inadvertently touch on her own literary shortcomings.

While working on her diary, Nin also spent a great deal of her time providing Miller with comments and critical analysis, eventually writing the Preface for *Tropic of Cancer*. As it turns out, while Nin encouraged Miller in public, her private diary entries attest to a more critical perspective, one which turns the tables on Miller's definitions of "feminine" writing by providing a woman's view of a masculinist mode of writing:

> I want to be a strong poet, as strong as Henry and John are in their realism. I want to combat them, to invade and annihilate them. What baffles me about Henry and what attracts me are the flashes of imagination, the flashes of insight, and the flashes of dreams. Fugitive. And the depths. Rub off the German realist . . . and you get a lusty imagist. At moments he can say the most profound or delicate things. But his softness is dangerous, because when he writes he does not write with love, he writes to caricature, to attack, to ridicule, to destroy, to rebel.

He is always against something. Anger incites him. I am always for
something. Anger poisons me. I love, I love, I love.[32]

Nin's chief objective in criticizing Miller is to define her own voice in
the process (as it is for Miller in most of his work on other writers).
What is interesting is the way in which she portrays quite stereotypical
notions of male writing as hard, realistic, and essentially born out of
anger, while her own writing is based on love. The repeated "I love"
glosses over the fact that her comments on Miller are born out of the
same feelings of anger which she saw as the instigating factor in Miller's
work. "I want to combat them, to invade them, and annihilate them,"
she says, clearly frustrated in the face of an established male literary
voice. Brassaï, in his chapter entitled simply "Anaïs," confirms this "literary" tension: "Anaïs began to envision Miller as her antipode: 'Henry
is becoming unreal. Nothing warm and living remains. . . . The inhu-
man transposition of life into memory. He doesn't live in the present.
He always has to remember who he is . . . I want to stay inside untransformed human life'" (*Henry Miller — The Paris Years*, 54). The
reference to "untransformed human life" is a crucial one, on one hand
it goes against the Bergsonian notion of creativity as wholly linked to
change and progression, while on the other, it refers back to the womb
which, as we have seen, Miller regards as a conglomerate image of both
womanhood and creativity. Nin herself supports this image by allowing
her diarist/heroine to be the messenger of secret truths, at times a
"strong poet" and at others a woman governed by her physical desires — in other words — a woman whose biological make-up directly
impinges on her creative output.

The sense of biological determinism, which runs through most of
Nin's oeuvre, is reiterated in much critical work on Nin. Harriet Zinnes
in "Art, the Dream, the Self" stresses a semiotic and binary reading of
Nin's preoccupation with the self, the "relation of that womb (the self,
the subject) to the phallus (the world, the object)." This physicalization
of the more discursive aspects of Nin's writing is, even with the psychoanalytical and feminist slant not unlike Miller's earlier locating of Nin's
writing inside the "genito-urinary tract." Both could be seen as attempts to ground the "unveiling of the self," as Zinnes calls it, or the
auto-romance within the actual physical presence of the writer. By doing so, the more abstract notion of writing as essentially self-creation is
geographically located within the body, just as the writer is painstak-
ingly located within the city. While both Nin and Miller stress their

vagabond existence within the actual city, their respective bodies and sexual desires increasingly become rudimentary "homes."[33]

In Nin's later exposition on the act of writing, *The Novel of the Future* (1968), Nin more explicitly narrows down that part of the body which — together with the womb — is the locus of creativity, namely the unconscious:[34]

> The world of the dream can reveal to us the mythical way in which we re-experience life, and the way our emotion, our inner-motivated drama, acts like a spotlight, choosing only what concerns it . . . if that is the way our emotions live out their dramas or comedies in the unconscious, it must serve a purpose. (*The Novel of the Future*, 27)

Not unlike the surrealists, Nin provides the unconscious with its own irrefutable proof of existence, an almost physical truth. It is this belief in the inherent logic of the unconscious, and its manifestation in dreams, which distinguishes Nin and Miller and which ultimately alters the way in which they view the city. Nin pragmatically states that "in the world of the unconscious there is an inevitability, as logical, as coherent as any found in classical drama," but she fails to define what the logic is (*The Novel of the Future*, 28). Miller does not critique Nin's blind faith in the logic of the unconscious, as with the surrealists, but he does essentialize her "female" writing in terms of a something anti-rational and primitive. This "something" is firmly situated, once again, in the womb:

> Not only, as with the ordinary artist, is there the tyrannical desire to immortalize one's self, but there is also the idea of immortalizing the world in which the diarist lives and has his being. . . . Every one, whether consciously or unconsciously, is trying to recover the luxurious, effortless sense of security which he knew in the womb. Those who are able to realize themselves do actually achieve this state; not by a blind, unconscious yearning for the uterine condition, but by transforming the world in which they live into a veritable womb.
> (*The Cosmological Eye*, 280)

What Miller realizes is crucial; namely that the diary format is no guarantee of realism. It is an attempt to transform the world of the writer; to create the ideal conditions for the writer's rebirth — hence the importance of the womb. But oddly enough Nin is either incapable or strategically disinterested in seeing Miller's auto-romances in such symbolic terms. Because Miller has no interest in creating three-dimensional female characters, Nin sees him as incapable — equally — of providing a three-dimensional view of himself:

> I glanced over what Henry was writing in *Tropic of Capricorn*, and
> there it was, the great anonymous depersonalized world of sex. In-
> stead of investing each woman with a different face, he takes pleasure
> in reducing women to a biological aperture. That is not very interest-
> ing. His depersonalization is turning into an obsession with sex it-
> self . . . (*The Diary of Anais Nin*, 260)

For Nin the obsession with sex skirts the real issue, the attempted rendition of the self. For Miller, however, the sexual encounters could be
read as a frenzied attempt to "descend into the womb," to create the
conditions for a rebirth in symbolic terms. Miller speaks of a "tyrannical
desire to immortalize one's self," whereas Nin often takes it upon herself to speak for women in general. In this respect Nin conveys a more
universal stance which lends itself to a reading of the unconscious as
timeless and universal by nature.

"Un Etre Etoilique" is essentially an homage to Anais Nin which
largely explains why Miller does not want to critique her reliance on the
unconscious in the same terms that he employed against the surrealists.
What Miller can and does do, is compare Nin's childhood diaries with
surrealism. Here Miller stresses, as he did in "An Open Letter to Surrealists Everywhere," that the search for the marvellous remains at the
heart of the matter:

> One thinks inevitably of the manifestoes of the Surrealists, of their un-
> quenchable thirst for the marvellous, and that phrase of Breton's, so
> significant of the dreamer, the visionary: "We should conduct our-
> selves as though we were really in the world!" It may seem absurd to
> couple the utterance of the Surrealists with the writings of a child of
> thirteen, but there is a great deal which they have in common and
> there is also a point of departure which is even more important. The
> pursuit of the marvellous is at bottom nothing but the sure instinct of
> the poet speaking and its manifests itself everywhere in all epochs. . . .
> But this marvellous pursuit of the marvellous, if not understood, can
> also act as a thwarting force, can become a thing of evil, crushing the
> individual in the toils of the Absolute. (*The Cosmological Eye*, 277)

Miller reiterates that the "pursuit of the marvellous" cannot lead any-
where as an absolute value. It must be used as an illuminatory force
rather than an experience to be worshipped in itself. As before, his descriptions of Nin invariably fall into the stereotype of feminine sensuality (among other things he constantly stresses her childlike quality)
versus masculine reasoning. Nevertheless, it is still unclear exactly what
he wants her art to embody. On one hand, he wants that which is tran-
scendent/spiritual, and yet it must also be tangible, real and physical.

Miller re-uses the same parameters here as he did in his critique of the surrealists. The surrealists may have chosen the marvellous, the ephemeral in favour of the "real," but because they have no real interest in progressing as individuals, they cling to an iconography which, far from being truly modern, falls back into nostalgia for the artist as a superior creature. The result is that the artist is divorced from the collective, unable to help it:

> Do we want a closer report between artist and collectivity, or do we want an increasing tension? Do we want art to become more communicative, or do we want it to be more fecundating? Do we want every man to become an artist and thus eliminate art? Unconsciously, I think that every great artist is trying with every might and main to destroy art. By that I mean that he is desperately striving to break down this wall between himself and the rest of humanity. . . . The worst sin that can be committed against the artist is to take him at his word, to see in his work a fulfilment instead of an horizon.
>
> (*The Cosmological Eye*, 167–68)

In this context, the autobiographical document is by nature an example of something permanently unfinished, resting on the progression of the artist as he or she is creating it. There is no possibility for absolute fulfilment, however frustrating this might be, because the artist daily sets him or herself new horizons. Similarly, the use of the urban landscape as a metaphor for the writer's journey allows for a graphic rendition of a life in flux. For Miller the successful rendition of this urban existence relies, then, not on its proximity to the unconscious (as it did for Breton) but on its proximity to the real world. This is partly why Miller admires Brassaï's ability to verify the existence of things. Put simply, it is infinitely easier to convey something like a chair than something as unphotographable as the unconscious. What Nin fails to see in this respect is that Miller's literary project is partly to convey the author's inability to portray himself "truthfully." It is no coincidence, then, given the stress on autobiography as a truthful source for writing, that precisely this became an issue of contention between Miller and Nin:

> Anaïs' conceptions of autobiography . . . In Miller's mind, brought into play a fallacy that made the immediate inscription of actions and facts an illusory act: to commit the events of one day, or even of one hour, to paper takes days if not weeks. Anaïs would therefore never catch up with events, and her diary would never be truly current.
>
> (*Henry Miller — The Paris Years*, 53)

Brassaï's paraphrasing of Nin stresses the importance Miller placed on art as a communicative process per definition: "To break down the wall" between the artist and "the rest of humanity." Total immediacy, although the diary format may appear conducive to this, is impossible, and importantly, does not guarantee any literary "truthfulness."

Miller's gripe with surrealism was born out of the seriousness with which he viewed artistic expression. Indeed the purpose of all art, for Miller, was to create new means for expression, but not at any cost. Miller's individualism did not mean however, that the collective held no interest for him "for after all," Miller would say "the art of telling is only another form of communion."[35] Such a communion takes on a variety of shapes in the decades discussed here, and while the political benefits of a collective notion of the auratic were seen clearly by such people as Adorno and Benjamin, Miller's notion retained an individualistic streak. In this context, Miller's fascination with Brassaï's photographs of working class Parisians slots itself into a Benjaminian version of the auratic, but it also keeps a political distance, largely through an eroticization of the environment in surrealist terms. The fascination with the creation of the self — the auto-romance — was markedly a romance with the city, albeit a very fluid one as seen in Nin's gendered notion of an interior city in the form of the unconscious. The short essay on Nin illustrates both the limitations of Miller's take on gender, and his attempts to link creative expression with the body politic on a wider scale; issues which the two following chapters will examine in more detail. As the Second World War moves closer, Miller's questionable idealization of the womb as a protective feminine sphere cannot be anything but threatened.

Notes

[1] See *Surrealism and Women*, ed. by Mary Ann Caws (Boston: MIT Press, 1991), and Susan Suleiman, *Subversive Intent: Gender, Politics, and the Avant-Garde* (Cambridge: Harvard UP, 1990).

[2] Louis Aragon, *Paris Peasant*, trans. by Simon Watson Taylor, (Boston: Exact Change, 1994). All subsequent quotes taken from this edition. Originally published as *Le Paysan de Paris* (Paris: Gallimard, 1926).

A complete collection of Benjamin's notes and essays on "The Paris Arcades," an unfinished project, are published in German: *Gesammelte Schriften*, ed. by Rolf Tiedemann and Hermann Schweppenhauser. Vol. IV. (Frankfurt: Suhrkamp, 1972–1989). Parts of *Das Passagen-Werk* in translation are collected in: Walter Benjamin, *Charles Baudelaire: A Lyric Poet in the Age of*

High Capitalism (London: Verso, 1983). All subsequent quotes from this edition.

[3] André Breton, *Mad Love* (1937), his most famous story of "L'amour fou" was thus published three years after *Tropic of Cancer* (1934) whereas it is likely Miller would have read Louis Aragon's *Paris Peasant* (1926), Philippe Soupeault's *Last Nights of Paris* (1928), and Breton's *Nadja* (1928) while living in Paris.

[4] Two studies in particular: Susan Buck-Morss, *Walter Benjamin and the Arcades Project* (London: MIT, 1991) and Margaret Cohen, *Profane Illumination* (London: U of California P, 1993) provide an in-depth analysis of Benjamin's relationship to surrealism and politics.

[5] Walter Benjamin, *Gesammelte Schriften*, ed. by Rolf Tiedemann and Herman Schweppenhauser, vol. 4 (Frankfurt: Suhrkamp, 1972–1989), 1014.

[6] Norman Mailer, "Narcissism" (1976), in *Critical Essays on Henry Miller*, ed. by Ronald Gottesman (Macmillan: New York, 1992), 137.

[7] André Breton, *Nadja*, (New York: Grove Press, 1960), 78. All Subsequent quotes from this edition. Originally published as *Nadja* (Paris: Gallimard, 1928).

[8] André Breton, *Second Manifesto of Surrealism* (Ann Arbor: U of Michigan P, 1972).

[9] The published letters between Miller and Anais Nin contain numerous references to Miller's fear that June, his ex-wife, will disapprove of his literary representation of her. Miller was convinced that June would destroy his manuscripts should she find them. Similarly, Miller and Anais Nin fell out on several occasions because she found his descriptions of her deeply chauvinistic. Anais Nin, *Henry and June* (New York: Harcourt Brace Jovanovich, 1986).

[10] Originally a medieval term for a rupture in the natural order of things, the word marvellous can also mean supernatural and/or mystical.

[11] André Breton, *Mad Love*, (London: University of Nebraska Press, 1987), 13. All subsequent quotes from this edition. Originally published as *L'Amour fou* (Paris: Gallimard, 1937).

[12] "Having to consider the question of a woman's sexual temperament would in itself make me unable to continue to love her." André Breton in *Investigating Sex — Surrealist Discussions 1928–1932*, ed. by José Pierre (London: Verso, 1992), 47.

[13] The link between the inanimate and the animate in terms of femininity and commodification is typically represented in the surrealists' fascination with mannequins. The German filmmaker Walter Ruttmann, inspired by surrealism, used stop-frame animation to animate mannequins in shop-windows in *Berlin — Die Symphonie einer Grostadt* (1927).

[14] Mary Ann Caws, "Seeing the Surrealist Woman: We are a Problem," in *Surrealism and Women* (London: MIT Press, 1991), 15.

[15] Walter Benjamin, "The Work of Art in the Age of Mechanical Reproduction" in *Illuminations, Walter Benjamin — Essays and Reflections* (New York: Schocken Books, 1968), 221. All subsequent quotes from this edition.

[16] In itself, the ways in which feminism often equates "otherness" with "difference" is problematic. Caws ignores the possibility that a representation of difference may occur in surrealist practice, without the qualitative judgment implicit in her own use of the word "other."

[17] Walter Benjamin, "Fourier and the Arcades," in *Baudelaire* (London: Verso, 1983), 171. All subsequent quotes from this edition.

[18] Walter Benjamin, "Surrealism — The Last Snapshot of the European Intelligentsia," in *One Way Street* (London: Verso Books, 1985), 229.

[19] Miller's use of the female genitals as a marker for a primitivist notion of universal time could be construed on a wider level as yet another re-writing of Bergson's Durée Réelle; a "space" within sexuality where the intuitive is unhindered by rationality and where, more importantly, creativity can be expressed simultaneously in both spatial and temporal terms.

[20] In similar terms, Jung's "Archetypes and the Collective Unconscious" (1934), introduces the feminine archetype "The Anima." The Anima represents fecundity and birth leading: "straight back to the primitive wonderworld" to a time when "consciousness did not think, but only perceived."

[21] Hal Foster, *Compulsive Beauty* (London: MIT Press, 1993). The title puns on the surrealist expression "convulsive beauty" as coined by Breton in *Mad Love*.

For a wider discussion and introduction concerning Benjamin's work on Paris, Surrealism and Politics see: Susan Buck-Morss, *The Dialectics of Seeing — Walter Benjamin and the Arcades Project* (Cambridge: MIT Press, 1991).

[22] In *Tropic of Cancer*, Miller goes on the prowl with his friend Van Norden but once they have initiated sex with a prostitute, the proceedings turn sour. In this example, the "fantasy," rather than liberating, becomes belligerent and war-like: "the moment the condition is precipitated nobody thinks about anything but peace, about getting it over with. And yet nobody has the courage to lay down his arms, to say, 'I'm fed up with it . . . I'm through" (*Tropic of Cancer*, 142).

[23] Theodor Adorno, *Notes to Literature*, Vol. 1 (New York: Columbia UP, 1991), 89. All subsequent quotes from this edition.

[24] Brassaï, *Henry Miller — The Paris Years*, (New York: Arcade Publishing, 1995), 31. All subsequent quotes from this edition.

[25] Henry Miller, *Quiet Days in Clichy* (Paris: Olympia Press, 1956). All subsequent quotes from this edition.

[26] Henry Miller, *Wisdom of the Heart* (New York: New Directions, 1941).

[27] The reappearance of the "flaneur" in contemporary criticism of both Breton and Benjamin shows the importance of the role of the urban bohemian narrator. Taken originally from Baudelaire, the flaneur represents the world-weary poet on the prowl.

[28] We know Miller was familiar with surrealist films. In 1930, he claims to have attended the premiere of *L'Age d'Or* at Studio 28 in Paris. Miller also wrote a passionate defense of the film, under attack by right-wing groups, which was published by *New Review* (1931).

[29] André Breton, *Manifestoes of Surrealism* (Ann Arbor: U of Michigan P, 1972), 16.

[30] Walter Matthews, *The Surrealist Mind* (Selinsgrove: Susquehanna UP, 1991), 24.

[31] Henry Miller, "Un Etre Etoilique" (1938), in *The Cosmological Eye* (New York: New Directions, 1961), 280. All subsequent quotes from this edition.

[32] Anais Nin, *Henry and June — From the Unexpurgated Diary of Anais Nin* (New York: HBJ, 1986), 50. The writer referred to is John Erskine, whom Anais Nin also knew personally.

[33] Harriet Zinnes, "Art, the Dream, the Self," in *Anais Nin — Literary Perspectives*, ed. by Suzanne Nalbantian (London: Macmillan Press, 1997), 57.

[34] Anais Nin, *The Novel of the Future* (Athens: Swallow Press, 1986) All subsequent quotes from this edition

[35] Henry Miller, *The World of Sex*, (London: Calder and Boyars, 1970), 102.

3: The Politics of Violence

THE BELIEF IN ART'S CAPABILITY to unleash revolutionary and creative energies extended itself, in the previous chapters, from the surrealist fascination with the unconscious to a more general view of the urban landscape as both an erotic and political sphere. As we saw, Henry Miller used the aesthetics of surrealism as an inspirational force as well as a way to situate himself within contemporary arts. For Miller and Breton, the search for creative illumination was paramount, and the city a prime site for experiences of a sensual as well as reflective nature. Benjamin's caution concerning the use of the city in these terms was partly born out of the surrealist tendency to recreate a romanticized myth of the city, rather than strive for actual social change, but his fears were also grounded in the link between the return to, and glorification of, collective forces and the increasing fascination for fascism of the 1920s and 1930s. While Benjamin saw it as his task to point to the possible dangers of mythologizing modernity, other writers sought to take the consequences of their belief in it, and it is through this endeavor that the link between sexuality and politics acquires a more radical and lethal outlook than the eroticism of the surreal romances.

The following chapter will therefore examine some of the political ramifications of the aesthetics outlined so far by using as a starting point the French critic Georges Bataille. Bataille, an early member of the surrealists, and one of the first literary critics to write on Henry Miller, based his fictional and philosophical writings on a sociology of sexuality and politics. His radical view of a literary aesthetic based on transgression, violence, and death is a useful starting point for an attempt to define what violence and "fascist" aesthetics might mean within literature, and in particular, how it is applied in his article from 1946, "La Morale de Miller." To extend the analysis of fascist aesthetics, this section will then go on to examine another link between Miller and Bataille, namely the radical Japanese writer Yukio Mishima; a writer whose extreme violence both politically and in his fiction caught the imagination of Bataille and Miller.

The writers in question share widely differing cultural backgrounds, but they also share an affinity towards a glorification of violence, in Bataille and Mishima's case, and a need to deal with the ramifications of it, in Miller's. It may be tempting to construe this affinity as an indication of an imperial and fascist legacy born out of French, American, and Japanese heritage. Nevertheless, all three writers considered themselves anti-establishment and were ultimately interested in formulating a literary practice wherein violence — on different levels — would become politicized *and* aestheticized.

Like Miller, Bataille took a more critical stance vis-à-vis surrealism's belief in a purely language driven, poetic path towards liberation. By 1929 Breton had proclaimed supreme leadership of the French surrealist movement, and as one of the "original" members Bataille was beginning to move away in search of a less dogmatic approach to the surrealist credo. Breton, in turn, started to reject Bataille on the grounds of espousing an extremist political revolt.[1] In "The Second Surrealist Manifesto" (1930), Breton condemns Bataille for attempting a brand of anarchism claiming to be against all movements and systems per se, an anti-rationalist stance which Breton considers impossible:

> M. Bataille's misfortune is to reason: admittedly, he reasons like someone who "has a fly on his nose," which allies him more closely with the dead than with the living, but *he does reason*. He is trying with the help of the tiny mechanism in him which is not completely out of order, to share his obsessions: this very fact proves that he cannot claim, no matter what he may say, to be opposed to any system, like an unthinking brute.[2]

Breton's accusation of distasteful narcissism is partly a response to Bataille's critique of surrealism's naive belief in its own capacities for revolt. Although Bataille was later to revise his opinion on the relative merits of automatic writing, his initial response was to see surrealism as a solipsistic endeavor, one in which political aims were nothing but a "religious enterprise" concealed "under a feeble revolutionary phraseology" (an opinion not dissimilar to that of Miller in "An Open Letter to Surrealists Everywhere").[3] While the surrealists were engaged in elevating the role of the unconscious, proposing that true revolutionary writing lay in recapturing a subconscious language unhindered by bourgeois or capitalist structures, Bataille saw no escape from these structures other than via direct action, action of a more violent nature than traditional poetics could afford.

This schism between Bataille and the surrealists must be seen in the light of Bataille's stress on the importance of wider social determinants. For Bataille, surrealist concerns were of an inner psychological nature, and although a valid field for investigation, he wanted to investigate how social reality affected the sense of self, without relying solely on the unconscious. In trying to describe the nature of action, conscious as well as unconscious, Bataille formed a series of ideas on the role of literature as an expression of ecstasy in which the obsession with death, or rather the aesthetics of the death-drive, became an explanation for fascism as well. In stressing the importance of the death-drive, Bataille was influenced in particular by Jung's universal archetype which manifests itself by expressing personal and social distress in a violent manner.[4] For Jung "politics should not be regarded causally, as necessary consequences of external conditions, but as decisions precipitated by the collective unconscious" (*The Archetypes of the Collective Unconscious*, 23). For the surrealists, on the other hand, the idea that the death-drive was an integral part of the collective unconscious was sign of moral degeneracy. Bataille's approach, however, cannot be read simply as an antithesis to the "official" surrealist line. Just as automatic, spontaneous inspiration in surrealist terms was not meant to replace God, neither was degradation and death a straightforward replacement for Bataille. Instead, some of the answers to the hostility between Bataille and the surrealists can be found in his concept of the "heterogeneous."

Fascism and the Heterogeneous — Henry Miller and Georges Bataille

For Bataille, the heterogeneous functions largely as a catch-phrase for those elements, anthropologically, psychologically, as well as historically, which oppose all claims to truth by traditional Western philosophy. This definition of the heterogeneous is crucial for several reasons. Firstly, the term links violence, fiction, and theory into a generalized methodology from which to examine the nature of creativity. Secondly, and crucially, it sets up the concept of the heterogeneous artist as a radicalized version of the underground writer; a concept which Bataille then applies to Miller's anarchical protagonist in the *Tropics*.

Together with the notion of the heterogeneous, the exultation of violence and sexuality in a political sense also carries strong fascist connotations in the 1930s. Bataille's critique of fascism "The Psychological Structure of Fascism" (1933) is therefore a potential entry into fascism as a literary as well as political phenomenon in the period. The essay introduces the *idea* of a fascist aesthetic as partly liberating in a creative sense; a theme which on another level contains clues for an understanding of

Miller's obsession with apocalyptic imagery in the 1930s, and his later post-war pacifist views on militarism in connection with Mishima.[5]

To a large extent, the subversion of reason that underlies Bataille's attempts to define the heterogeneous through fascism is impossible, but Bataille's theories nevertheless create a flux of anarchistic creative endeavors, or as Miller puts it in the first page of *Tropic of Cancer*: "a gob of spit in the face of art." This "spit in the face of art," like Bataille's outlook on the theory and use of fascism in the early thirties, makes little sense unless read in the context of the intellectual attitude towards politics and aesthetics at the time. Although the expression "aestheticization of political life" was coined in 1935 by Benjamin in "The Work of Art in the Age of Mechanical Reproduction," theories on the relationship between politics and art were continuously dealt with in the twenties and thirties from varying perspectives. The spectrum ranged from the radicalization by the dadaists in the early twenties to Jung's warnings about the political implications of instinctually-driven masses in such essays as "The Archetypes of the Collective Unconscious" (1934) and "The Concept of the Collective Unconscious" (1936).

Roughly speaking, two main directions emerge from the early essays on the rise and dangers of fascism. Writers such as Herbert Marcuse, Benjamin, and to a certain extent Breton, had a distinctly Marxist approach which viewed fascist politics as enabled by and fed on bourgeois economics and capitalist social structures. Many of the critical essays deal with the issue of production and point to the danger inherent in a society where surplus weapons must be produced and then adequately utilized in order to keep the capitalist status quo; a status quo which also necessitates the elimination of leftist opposition in political as well as artistic terms. Neither Marcuse nor Benjamin insisted upon forcing their analysis into a strict Marxian framework, but they did feel an imperative to show that fascism was not an inherent evil but something that could be avoided if proper political and moral procedures were taken.[6]

In "Theories of German Fascism" (1930), Benjamin makes an emphatic call for "the light that language and reason still afford" to awaken people to action against "the metaphysical abstraction of war." The warning against the possible "abstraction" of war is not dissimilar to that given against automatism, which in absolutist terms posits the unconscious as the "metaphysical" equivalent of some sort of inherent truth. Miller's decision to focus on how art relies on politics — and vice versa — in "An Open Letter to Surrealists Everywhere" is crucial in this respect. While Miller never openly tackled the question of fascism, he shared with his contemporaries an interest in the abstraction of war and violence, from a psychological perspective.[7] Similar to Bataille, Miller's more immediate theoretical ancestors could be seen as Freud and Jung, who also theorized on the dangers of collective instinctual behaviour from the perspective of a "defect" society which does not manage to channel its aggressions or "collective archetypes into productive behavior." Jung's determinism, as we will see, is actually close to the sense of bleak determinism which runs through Bataille's theory on the heterogeneous and in Miller's sometimes apocalyptic visions of the city in the 1930s.[8]

In the same decade that Bataille was working on his concept of the heterogeneous as a violent expulsion of a creative and political nature, Henry Miller was using the urban landscapes in the *Tropics* and *Black Spring* as backdrops for his narrator's aggressive, if not outright violent, adventures in sexual promiscuity. To a large extent, Miller's focus on his own excessive sexual drive, coupled with a nostalgic return to a childhood untainted by sexual politics, were the themes that caught Bataille's attention. In order to understand why it is necessary, however, to take a step back and examine Bataille's actual definition of the term "heterogeneous." The term itself springs from Bataille's theories on a "general economy," a term used to indicate a study of society which incorporates economics into the wider frame of sociology. For Bataille, a "general economy" must take into account the links between collective action, sociology and economics; "the a need to study the system of human production and consumption within a much larger framework."[9] According to Bataille, as long as capitalism refused the often irrational and excessive aspect of collective behavior it would misread human needs: "Humanity exploits given material resources, but by restricting them as it does to a resolution of the immediate difficulties it encounters (a resolution which it has hastily had to define as an ideal), it assigns to the forces it employs an end which they cannot have" (*The Accursed Share*, 21). The utilitarian ideals of capitalism, for comfort and material goods, causes society to strive for homogeneity, stressing economic accumulation which in turn forces people to exist only through their social roles, i.e. as producers and consumers. In order for the continuation of the utilitarian work ethic, society must suppress those forces which hinder the smooth functioning of economic progress and it is these forces which, in a sociological sense, are heterogeneous and which lie at the margin of society in the form of crime, the unemployed, the socially deviant; that is, all those who do not comply with the economic ethic of production and consumption. Within this framework, Miller was seen by Bataille as an obvious example of the heterogeneous anti-establishment writer, the untidy, irrational, unpredictable artist who does not fit capitalism's desire for "efficient" order. The writer, who is a microcosm of the society he or she inhabits, manifests the heterogeneous in excess of an emotional nature, in sexuality, and most importantly in "socially" useless activities, such as poetry, literature, painting, etc.[10]

This definition of the heterogeneous is crucial for an understanding of how Bataille "reads" literature and creativity and why he defines certain writers (Miller amongst them) as heterogeneous. Because the concept of the heterogeneous is inseparable from politics as well as the arts; transgression in fictional terms is always motivated internally, psychologically, as well as externally, politically. The consequence of writing which allows internal and external motivation to interact in this way, without taking society's taboos or norms into consideration, is often violence. Insofar as violence may function as a political *and* literary tool, Bataille's overall project as a literary critic lies in the attempt to trace a cross-cultural lineage of representations of violence, and in a sense, this is what this chapter will do as well. By looking specifically at Bataille, Miller, and Mishima the lineage examined also becomes one of mutual defenses. All three writers share the dubious honor of being literary "outcasts" at home; writers who had nothing to lose, in other words, by mutual praise.

Nevertheless, the idea of the heterogeneous still poses numerous problems in terms of a general literary mode of criticism. For one thing, the question of where to place Bataille within the generic categories of literature and philosophy is still a point of contention. Roland Barthes's introduction to *Story of the Eye* (1963) designates Bataille a Sadean rather than a surrealist writer, and in recent work on Bataille, a majority of critics have cast him as "qualitatively more radical than the surrealists."[11] As mentioned before, Bataille's alliance with the surrealists started in the early twenties where his main interest was to benefit from the aesthetics of the movement, as long as it did not hinder his rather more radical perspective on politics. By the end of the twenties, however, the manifestoes which set out the main tenets of surrealism also contained harsh objections to anyone who did not follow the "party line," as laid out by Breton. After an attack in the *Second Surrealist Manifesto* (1929), Bataille started his own group "Cercle Communist Democratique" to counterbalance the surrealists. In the last and eighth issue of *Documents* (1930) — the movement's journal — Bataille attacked surrealism for exploiting psychoanalysis in order to create a new form of poetics, when in reality they should have been writing for the proletariat. The article "L'esprit Moderne et le Jeu des

Transpositions" (Modern Spirit and the Game of Transpositions) shows how Bataille considered the "transposition" of psychoanalytical theory into a poetic form of automatism, as not only politically futile, but nothing more than a "game."[12]

In spite of this, the artistic aims of the surrealists, to shock and promote the ecstatic forces of dream-life, the instinct, and the impulsive against the forces of normality — did provide them with a certain measure of heterogeneity. For Bataille, the concept of the "heterogeneous" could therefore be extended to all marginalized social groups, including revolutionaries and poets. The crucial thing was that "heterogeneous reality remain that of a force or a shock."[13] The idea that the heterogeneous could successfully incorporate marginalized political groups as well as poets extends itself, however, in problematic ways. Unlike the surrealists who could fall back on their sympathies with traditional Marxist principles, Bataille ascribed to fascist leaders a heterogeneous existence not dissimilar to that of the radical poet. Under the heading "Examples of Heterogeneous Elements" Bataille writes:

> The fascist leaders are incontestably part of heterogeneous existence. Opposed to democratic politicians, who represent in different countries the platitude inherent to *homogeneous* society, Mussolini and Hitler immediately stand out as something *other*. Whatever emotions their actual existence as political agents of evolution provokes, it is impossible to ignore the *force* that situates them above men, parties, and even laws: a *force* that disrupts the regular course of things, the peaceful but fastidious homogeneity powerless to maintain itself (the fact that laws are broken is only the most obvious sign of the transcendent, *heterogeneous* nature of fascist action). (*Visions of Excess*, 143)

Using words such as "platitude" to describe homogeneous society, and "agents of evolution" to describe fascist leaders, to Bataille homogeneity is fastidious, slow moving, and above all, weak while fascism is forceful, progressive, and capable of transcending the status quo (the italics Bataille's). If the fascist leaders are indeed forces beyond parties and laws, Bataille ignores the fact that an existing political apparatus provided these "agents of evolution" with the means to gain power. The expression "agents of evolution" reflects the use of anthropology to prove the historical necessity of abstract power to propel society forward, but it also adds to the problem of how to deal with the loss of individual identity within a system based on collective energy. Presenting the fascist leaders as agents of progression diffuses the frightening aspect of absolute power in the hands of few, and sanctifies the means without specifying what the leaders are working toward, other than something which in an abstract sense is stronger than them, namely an evolutionary idea of unhindered political process. Fascism recreates an organic and physical model of heterogeneous expenditure within a legalized and ritualized context, legitimizing the notion that society needs ritual and violence in order to break out of a homogeneous complacency. What Bataille tends to forget, and what Miller is crucially aware of, is the price paid by the individual as he/she is swallowed up by the collective.

I have said that Bataille's theories on human nature cannot be divorced from the historical context of the 1930s, and it is therefore important to keep a historicized perspective on the psychological, sociological and anthropological angle used by Bataille as well. In 1933, Bataille may have felt that he was discovering political devices, which far from vindicating fascism, presented a liberating possibility for the left from a long-term perspective. The rhetoric used is actually surprisingly close to that employed by Breton in his propositions concerning automatic writing as an absolute force in its own right. In this respect, the desired radicalization of the arts — whether it be from a surrealist or heterogeneous perspective — is very much about how it is situated. Using the heterogeneous instead of the unconscious as the site for a potential political and aesthetic revolution involves a leap; but just how big a leap is not always that easily discernible.

The use of the fascist phenomenon to prove that people in general have an excess of energy, a need for "unproductive expenditure" thus mimics the surrealists' use of the unconscious as a mental form of "excess." Similarly, one could say that Bataille took the fundamentals of psychoanalysis and incorporated it into his vision of a society governed by desires of an often irrational and disturbing character. The inherent "need" to rid oneself of excess indirectly proves the potentially revolutionary status of the heterogeneous as a concept wherein: "the poor have no other way of re-entering the circle of power than through the revolutionary destruction of the classes occupying that circle — in other words, through a bloody and in no way limited social expenditure" (*Visions of Excess*, 121). Because physical violence signals a "bloody," yet necessary expenditure, the heterogeneous attains an organic/physical aspect. This physical aspect manifests itself in waste (we cannot absorb all that we eat for example) and on a mental level, in arts that have no direct commercial value. Similarly, the erotic impulse is heterogeneous by nature because it feeds on sexual practices where the aim is nonreproductive. An example of such heterogeneous expenditure would be Miller's search for pleasure in the *Tropics*. Because Miller consistently seeks sexual gratification rather than a re-affirmation of the family structure, his "sexual" expenditure becomes a possible way to negate bourgeois society.[14]

According to Bataille, "Unproductive Expenditure" emanates from a variety of sources, but in order for it to operate effectively is must *speak* to the collective. Fascism speaks, in this sense, to the masses by providing them with an idealized leader object, creating a: "common consciousness of increasingly violent and excessive energies and powers that accumulate in the person of the leader and through him become widely available" (*Visions of Excess*, 143).[15]

In "Between Eroticism and General Economics: Bataille" (1984), the German theorist Jürgen Habermas questions precisely this reactivation of violence under the guise of the heterogeneous:

> Without such a violent transcending point of reference, Bataille runs into difficulty making plausible the distinction that remains so important for him — namely, that between the socialist revolution and the fascist take-over of power, which merely seems like the former. What Benjamin affirms of the enterprise of surrealism as a whole — that it wanted "to win the energies of intoxication for the revolution" — Bataille also has in mind; it is the dream of the aestheticized, poetic politics purified of all moral elements. Indeed this is what fascinates him about fascism: "The example of fascism, which today calls into question even the existence of the labor movement, suffices to demonstrate what we might expect from a favorable recourse to renewed effective forces." But then the question arises as to how the subversively spontaneous expression of these forces and the fascist canalizing of them really differ. The question becomes uncomfortable if, with Bataille, one proceeds from the assumption that the difference should be identified already in the forms and patterns of politics and not merely in their concrete material consequences.[16]

Bataille's undaunted embrace of violence or "unlimited social expenditure" resembles the "aestheticization of political life" for which Bataille criticized the surrealists. In his eagerness to see the return of "renewed effective forces," or of primary and pure energy, Bataille, as Habermas realizes, seems ready to accept an expulsion in fascist terms rather than the stagnation implicit in an ineffective socialism.

The radical alternative to this expulsion in fascist terms, and the one which Miller describes in much of his early work, is to embrace a sense of imminent annihilation in apocalyptic terms. In this respect, Miller's language is anarchistic rather than fascist, based on the definition of anarchy as "a state of lawlessness or political disorder due to the absence of governmental authority."[17] While fascism is largely determined by the presence of a strong leader figure, anarchy is defined by the very "absence of authority." Miller's patronizing attitude to the "masses" is part of this anti-authoritarian posture, but he never reconciles himself to the notion of a "leader-figure." In Miller's doomed world the artist, once again, stands alone:

> Walking towards the mountain top I study the rigid outlines of your buildings which tomorrow will crumble and collapse in smoke. I study your peace program which will end in a hail of bullets. I study your glittering shop-windows crammed with inventions for which tomorrow there will be no use. I study your worn faces hacked with toil, . . . I study you individually and in the swarm — and how you stink all of you![18]

The image of modernity presented here, like that of Bloomingdale's, is on the verge of collapse. More interestingly, though, are the comparisons drawn between modernity, the failed peace programs, and the increasing commodification of life in general. Miller invokes his artistic prerogative and becomes the "sociologist," a man who studies humanity both individually and collectively. The realization that both the collective and the individual are inconsequential entities in the face of impending doom is crucial. What is consequential, is the juxtaposition between the world's downfall and the artist's subsequently idealized position. In the face of violence, Miller *the writer* is paradoxically reborn: "The evidence of death is before my eyes constantly; but this death of the world, a death constantly going on, does not move from the periphery in to engulf me, this death is at my very feet, moving from me outward, my own death a step ahead always" (*Black Spring*, 27).

On the one hand, this reads as a rather fearful suppression of mortality, as Miller, like Moses, parts the dying in order to pursue his own path. On the other hand, Miller recognizes that his "own death is always a step ahead" of him, that his writing — in other words — may be death driven rather than life-affirmative. Bataille returns to this point in his later defense of Miller, but in *Black Spring* the apocalyptic imagery is so overwhelming that one might question whether it functions as a smoke-screen for something else. In the chapter entitled "Third or Fourth Day of Spring," Miller's America has become utterly symptomatic of a failed modernity: "Aye, the great sun of syphilis is setting. Low visibility: forecast for the Bronx, for America, for the whole modern world. Low visibility accompanied by gales of laughter. No new stars on the horizon. Catastrophes . . . only catastrophes!" (*Black Spring*, 24). According to Bataille, the smoke-screen — among other things — covers a "failed" modernity and Miller's inability to take the consequences of this failure as a "modern" man. Bataille cannot recognize, partly because it does not fit his concept of the heterogeneous, the satire which underpins Miller's rhetorical stance. Partly sexual — the allusion to syphilis as the penalty for promiscuity — Miller's apocalyptic visions are nevertheless "accompanied by gales of laughter." The person left laughing is undoubtedly the writer whose ability to prophesy the end of America leaves him — once again — in a position of power:

> I am thinking that in that age to come I shall not be overlooked. Then my history will become important and the scar which I leave upon the face of the world will have significance. . . . If I was unhappy in America, if I craved more room, more adventure, more freedom of expression, it was because I needed these things. I am grateful to America for having made me realize my needs. I served my sentence there. At present I have no needs . . . I am not concerned with your likes and dislikes; it doesn't matter to me whether you are convinced that what I say is so or not . . . I am not an atomizer from which you can squeeze a thin spray of hope. I see America spreading disaster. I see America as a black curse upon the world. I see a long night settling in and that mushroom which has poisoned the world withering at the roots. (*Black Spring*, 25)

Once again, America is set up as the scourge of the modern world; a prison-house from which Miller the artist has narrowly escaped. But what is more important is the link made between the impending doom, "the long night settling in," and Miller's elevated position as a sovereign figure unconcerned with humanity's "likes and dislikes," or as Bataille would say "situated above men, parties and even law." As a writer, Miller dismisses any obligation towards realism, towards having to convince his readers of the veracity of his writing and by extension he refuses to supply even the smallest measure of hope. While the nihilistic outlook fits Bataille's notion of the heterogeneous as the antithesis to civilization's dream of progression, Miller's promise to leave "a scar on the face of the world" epitomizes the inevitability of writing as a form of violent expulsion. In *Literature and Evil* (1957) Bataille defines certain writers as "heterogeneous," not because they function on the fringes of society, but because their art mimics as well as represents the sovereign desire for power and self-assertion. In pairing sovereignty with the need for heterogeneous expulsion, writing becomes a mode of creation by means of loss, or as Miller puts it: "At present I have no needs. I am a man without a past without a future. I am — that is all" (*Black Spring*, 25). To accept this "loss" creates the necessary circumstances for, and similarity between, the unfettered movement of heterogeneous forces and literary creation. Literature is therefore potentially emancipatory as well as evil; evil because, according to Bataille, truly revolutionary writing combines excess, sovereignty, and sacrifice — the three key elements of fascism.

In "Sacrificial Mutilation and the Severed Ear of Vincent Van Gogh" (1930), Bataille defines sacrifice in creative terms as: "the necessity of throwing oneself or something of oneself *out of oneself*," and as, "the rupture of personal homogeneity and the projection *outside the self* of a part of oneself."[19] Thus the artist inevitably reflects the constant pull between opposite forces: the desire to communicate, to "throw something outside of oneself," and the desire to remain intact and sovereign. In Miller's "death" imagery, such anxieties are made manifest in the uneasy alliance between the construction of the self as "immortal" and the desire to relinquish authorial control — to move away from death once and for all. The question is then whether Miller, like Bataille, is trying to write out an anti-rationalist stance within a discernibly literary format; an impossibility for a writer who doesn't want to fall into the trap he has previously accused automatism of — namely wanting to communicate what is essentially incommunicable. Bataille's attempt to delineate this paradox in Miller's work is formulated in his essay "La Morale de Miller."

"La Morale de Miller" (1946)

In Bataille's case, the search for an aesthetic based on violence as a transcending force sought to combine a scientific approach via anthropology with a notion of writing based on the heterogeneous. Bataille's problem, as Habermas pointed out, was that he had to legitimize this standpoint from an "organic" rather than rational perspective, not unlike the earlier defense by the surrealists concerning automatic writing. Just as Habermas recognized the fascist aspect of such an approach in political terms, literary criticism had to deal with the threat of an anti-rationalist stance in aesthetic and political terms. While Bataille's essay on Miller appears to support his theories on the heterogeneous within writing, Bataille — as we will see — in his eagerness to define a particular radical aesthetic forgets to acknowledge the limitations of his own anti-rationalist stance.

The essay "La Morale de Miller" grew out of two concurrent events. In 1946 Daniel Parker instigated what became known as the

"Affaire Miller"; an accusation of obscenity relating to the recent publications of the *Tropics* translated into French. In his role as *Président du Cartel d'Actions Sociales et Morales*, Daniel Parker had brought legal action against Miller, his publishers and translators. Within weeks the literary establishment rallied in Miller's defense. A *Defense Committee for Miller and Free Expression* was promptly formed, composed of such figures as André Gide, Jean-Paul Sartre, André Breton, Paul Eluard, Albert Camus, Pierre Seghers, Raymond Queneau, Maurice Nadeau, and a number of other well known literary figures. Not only did the sale of Miller's books increase, but the Daniel Parker case — due to public demand — was eventually dropped.

At the same time the opening essay to appear in the first issue of *Critique* was "La Morale de Miller." Founded in response to earlier surrealist organs, together with Pierre Prévost, Maurice Blanchot, and Pierre Josserand, *Critique* continued earlier editorial work by Bataille in *Documents* (1929–1930) and *La Critique Sociale* (1931–1934). *Critique* was different in its outlook from the earlier journals, broader in its scope, it was meant to have a more international agenda (one of the reasons why it was launched with a review of an American writer), and it was, in general, less overtly political than its predecessors. While *La Critique Sociale* and *Documents* had been closely aligned with Bataille's *College de Sociologie* (started in 1937), *Critique* was to have a less underground profile, a more global orientation, and aspire towards a more public intellectual and cultural forum. The journal was quickly propelled into the forefront of post-war intellectual debate and in 1947, only one year after its inception, the national journalists' guild awarded *Critique* first prize as journal of the year.[20]

The importance Bataille accorded *Critique* can be seen in the later preface to *Literature and Evil* (1957), a collection of essays originally published in *Critique*. In the preface, the essential ideology behind the essays is presented retrospectively in opposition to surrealism and as a continuation of Bataille's attempts to dislodge traditional boundaries between the critic and his subject. While Bataille strove to represent the totality of radical experience in writing from an aesthetic as well as political point of view, he also strove to deal with the possibility — or impossibility — of placing his writing *outside* rational and dialectical definitions of morality; and it is this crucial point which paradoxically returns in Bataille's essay on Miller.

The preface from *Literature and Evil* touches on this issue of morality and re-inserts the concept of the heterogeneous, witnessed earlier in its political guise, within the context of literary criticism. The structure of the preface, with its breakdown of principal terms and definitions, starting with a personal perspective and ending with a "grand" statement, is also typical of Bataille's style in general. Although Bataille states the book's progression from his earlier surrealist inspired work, it is nevertheless derivative in form, if not content. The preface to *Literature and Evil* criticizes the ineffectiveness of surrealism's attempts to transcend traditional notions of poetics and instead, offers up morality and evil as alternative and crucial elements in "intense communication":

> I belong to a turbulent generation, born to literary life in the tumult of surrealism. In the years after the Great War there was a feeling which was about to overflow. Literature was stifling within its limitations and seemed pregnant with revolution.
>
> These studies, which are so strikingly coherent, were written by a mature man. Yet they were generated in the turbulence of his youth, and they faintly echo this.
>
> I find it significant that a part of the first version of these essays should have appeared in *Critique*, a review which owed its success to its serious character. But I must add that, if I occasionally had to rewrite them, it is because, at first, I could provide no more than an obscure expression of my ideas owing to the turmoil in my mind. Turmoil is fundamental to my entire study; it is the very essence of my book. But the time has come to strive towards a clarity of consciousness . . .
>
> These studies are the results of my attempts to extract the essence of literature. Literature is either the essential or nothing. I believe that the Evil — an acute form of Evil — which it expresses, has a sovereign value for us. But this concept does not exclude morality: on the contrary, it demands a "hypermorality."
>
> Literature is *communication*. Communication requires loyalty. A rigorous morality results from complicity in the knowledge of Evil, which is the basis of intense communication.
>
> Literature is not innocent. It is guilty and should admit itself so. . . . I wanted to prove that literature is a return to childhood. But has the childhood that governs it a truth of its own?[21]

The initial tone of the preface reads as an apology about the "obscure" writing of his youth; writing which now has been made more precise by revision, in fact, "strikingly coherent." The implication is that Bataille has aged and as his work has matured, accentuated by the switch from first person to third, a distance has developed between what he is now and was before. This "distance" partly emphasizes the progressive state of Bataille's theorizing, but more importantly, it attests to a new-found intensity of communication, a recognition of the representation of evil as an intrinsic part of the literary process. Bataille's use of evil as a distinct literary mode does not diminish the complexity of his notion of a "turbulent youth," instead, it connects it to the idea of childhood as indicative of the heterogeneous.

Underlying the question of how a "mature" writer uses and develops a dialogue with his past is the notion of childhood and what it represents. In the early attacks on surrealism Bataille accused Breton of "servile idealism": "Servile idealism rests precisely in this will to poetic agitation rather than in a strictly juvenile dialectic" (*Literature and Evil*, 41). In the preface, the word juvenile turns into puerility, a puerility born out of and contained in the use of childhood as an imagined area of freedom. This progressive narrative of childhood to adulthood reconstitutes the re-imagined childhood as an alternative commentary on the nature of rationality. It also constitutes a separate sphere, a place one can re-enter through literature. The sphere of childhood becomes the antithesis to a society based on rationalization and utility; a location which in literary terms restates the anti-utilitarian values of the heterogeneous:

> The forbidden domain is the tragic domain, or better still, the sacred domain. Humanity admittedly, banishes it, but only in order to magnify it, and the ban beautifies that to which it prevents access. . . . The lesson of all religions, is that there is an instinctive tendency towards divine intoxication which the rational world of calculation cannot bear. This tendency is the opposite of Good. Good is based on common interest which entails consideration of the future. Divine intoxication, to which the instincts of childhood are so closely related, is entirely in the present. In the education of children preference for the present moment is the common definition of Evil.
>
> (*Literature and Evil*, 22)

Revolt is represented by violence and puerility, a combination which exemplifies the individual search for freedom, another form of expulsion in heterogeneous terms. It is anti-social because it does not take the collective good into consideration and instead strives to express itself in the present rather than according to future goals. The sphere of childhood, as seen in Miller's work, can also be a collective force: represented through the friendships and gangs of childhood. Childhood is, in other words, a heterogeneous force because it functions in opposition to "the rational world of calculation" and communicates an attack on the "common interest." In addition, childhood represents "the power to rise, indifferent to death, above the laws which require maintenance to life"; once the child chooses to live in the present, to go against Good, the heterogeneous occurs. Thus, Miller's promise to live for the present — a present in which he has "no needs" — can be seen as an attempted return to the actual state of childhood:

> The fragmentation of maturity. The great change. In youth we were whole and the terror and pain of the world penetrated us through and through. There was no sharp separation between joy and sorrow: they fused into one, as our waking life fuses with dream and sleep. . . . And then comes a time when suddenly all seems to be reversed. We live in the mind, in ideas, in fragments. We no longer drink in the wild outer music of the streets — we remember only. Like a monomaniac that picks up the thread over and over and spews it out according to some obsessive, logarithmic pattern. *(Black Spring,* 14–15)

For Miller, the idea of childhood — rather than an actual return to his past — is what is crucial in literary terms. As childhood, or youth, becomes an idealized time of purely sensual experience, adulthood can only be second rate, a poor imitation based on the act of remembrance rather than on actual lived experience. Miller connects the unfettered movement of life in childhood to the streets as well as to the unconscious, the place where "our waking life fuses with dream and sleep" and like a sleepwalker, the writer is left with no option but to obsessively return to the same place. Compared to the surrealist eroticization of the city, Miller's "streets" — in this instance — function predominantly as backdrops for the artist's awakening, and as such, the apocalyptic tone becomes a set-up for another rebirth of the artist rather than a sincere vision of things to come. Partly an issue of the literary zeitgeist, as mentioned before, Miller's representations of the "streets" of childhood are also searches for that in-between state of adolescence where rules and sexuality are tested, where the entry into bourgeois society is delayed as well as questioned. The state of adolescence, in other words, is not one of ignorance, but one which operates within a heightened state of awareness: a place where the child is privileged because it has not yet been forced to chose an occupation of a utilitarian nature. Once the child enters the adult sphere, where work determines one's value within society, he or she is "separated from the privileged moments of powerful communication . . . based on the emotions of sensuality, festivity, drama, love, separation and death" (*Literature and Evil,* 204).

As the idea of childhood becomes a crucial part of literary creation, it too must be open to "the terror and pain of the world." Childhood, as Miller puts it, is the one time when the "terror and pain of the world penetrated us through and through." The fact that this "terror and pain" operates on a larger and more abstract scale does not mean that it is necessarily "negative." According to Bataille, "Evil is not opposed to the natural order, since death is the condition of life, Evil which is essentially cognate with death, is also in a somewhat ambiguous manner, a basis for existence" (*Literature and Evil*, 27). Similarly, vice can only work if the "sinner" is acutely aware of the moral framework, without which, vice would no longer exist. In literary terms "the deliberate creation of Evil — that is to say, wrong — is acceptance and recognition of Good. It pays homage to it and, by calling itself wicked, it admits that it is relative and derivative — that it could not exist without Good" (*Literature and Evil*, 36).

The fact that Evil is felt more intensely by those in whom ethical values are most deeply rooted, means that the writer who deals with evil embarks on a dangerous process. In *Literature and Evil*, Bataille uses Baudelaire as an example of a writer whose life may have been "a long rejection of productive activity," but who nevertheless fell prey to a "capitalist society in full swing." Baudelaire's curse was his bourgeois position in society, a position in which the future was threatening because it would "put an end to the splendor of the ancien régime and replace glory by utility." Bataille focuses on the external political and social contexts for Baudelaire's rebellion against utility in order to show that he was caught up in an "unparalleled tension which not only expressed individual necessity . . . but was also the result of a material tension imposed, historically, from without" (*Literature and Evil*, 54–55). Because Baudelaire's attraction to Evil, rather than linked to the freedom of childhood, is a desperate attempt to counter historical progress, the heterogeneity which follows in its wake is an illusion rather than an conscious stance.

This critique of Baudelaire's false posture as a heterogeneous artist (also originally published in *Critique*) echoes Bataille's perspective on Miller. Paradoxically, it also represents a reversal of Benjamin's critique of the surrealists, a critique based on the surrealists' inability to take historical circumstances into consideration in their definition of the marvellous. On the contrary, the heterogeneous, for Bataille, necessitates a disregard for historical process, otherwise, it becomes a weak form of protest unable to claim the required indifference necessary for the puerile attitude. In this sense, very few writers fall into Bataille's desired category of wanting "to remain within the puerility of a dream." Ultimately, the heterogeneous can only be achieved once the writer eliminates his or her desire for acceptance and life affirmation, characteristics which for Bataille are an inherent part of the rational society he wishes to circumvent. In the end, death stands alone as the ultimate form of heterogeneous expulsion and the sphere of childhood as the only state which approximates it (*Literature and Evil*, 154–58).

In "La Morale de Miller," Bataille acknowledges Miller's desire to transgress, but sees the writing in *Tropic of Cancer* and *Tropic of Capricorn* as marred by an individual subjectivity which overshadows the violence and obscenity necessary for an entry into evil. In other words, Miller thrives too much on being the creation of those who condemn him to really care about the subversive qualities of his writing. Bataille's analysis of Miller proposes, among other things, that Miller is communicating with himself, rather than the reader, and this in turn is linked to the idea of literature as confessional by nature. For Bataille, it is precisely the confessional stance which indicates a portrayal of the writer as he truly is, even when he is immoral:

> Miller's books may not be first class but they are however explosive and what they occasionally say with sublime eloquence responds to an extreme anguish and pain and not only to the desires of a difficult exaltation. In this case if one tries to meddle with Miller, what will be interrupted is not, as those who have taken the initiative to prosecute him seem to think, the commerce of dirty books, but the activity of a human spirit who must express clearly and entirely "what he is."[22]

According to Bataille, the search for personal liberation elevates the writing and carries it into the sphere of the sublime in spite of the fact that it is painful and anguished. Because Miller presents himself for "what he is" ("seul et nu"), he confronts the reader with an image of truth rather than a glorified hero. Nevertheless, Miller also masks his true identity even as he claims to present himself as truthfully as possible. According to Bataille, it is easy to be distracted by Miller's "lyrical, dreamlike, rather fantastical" style, and yet, his "works are grounded" and possess "a feeling of preciseness." The presentation of different Miller personas; the obscene voice of the erotic interludes, the sentimental descriptive voice of reminiscence, are all part of an overall plan, a design by Miller to portray an enigmatic character, namely himself. Miller's obscenity may appear "seemingly easy" but it is "in reality complex and deserves to be re-read" (*Oeuvres Complétes*, 40–41).

Striving to avoid conventional notions of the artist as an alienated and heroic figure, Bataille nevertheless defines Miller as a saint of modern illumination — partly as a way to elevate the position of the heterogeneous artist. This paradox, although arguably useful for Bataille's notion of the heterogeneous as both a deliberate stance and a marginalized position enforced by society, prompts him to see Miller as caught between his own "knowingness" and the attempt to render as multifaceted a representation of himself as possible. "The result of this untenable challenge is a being who is difficult to define. . . . And thus the rebel condemns himself to a certain ambiguity, to the point of becoming inaccessible to even himself." This idea, that Miller's writing can somehow move beyond his own control, is not unlike the surrealist belief in the forcefulness of the unconscious. But more importantly, it is an idea which Bataille needs in order to slot Miller into a romanticized vision of ecstatic and sublime writing. In writing on Miller, Bataille inadvertently displays the same romantic leanings as the surrealists. Additionally, in order to escape a strictly psychoanalytical terminology of the unconscious, Bataille turns to a religious rhetoric in order to describe what he calls Miller's "transcendent terminology."

Vehemently against institutionalized religion, Bataille nevertheless uses (or abuses) religious terms in ways similar to the surrealists: to indicate a sacred, holy aspect of the writer "who illuminated, ecstatic, speaks like a prophet." Miller's prophetic capabilities are thus defined as his ability to "change the perspectives from which we are made "in order to substitute them with "an ecstatic vision of a reality which eludes us." "Only when meaning is lost can there be new meaning."[23]

The vision of "a reality which eludes us" — in Miller's case — is once again that of childhood. According to Bataille, Miller "does not want to simply accept the established system, what he really does is maintain the shifty attitude of the child." Ironically, such a statement is similar to Breton's critique of Bataille's violent and yet ineffective politics, while at the same time, supporting Bataille's theories on the importance of maintaining "the puerile voice" (*Oeuvres Complétes*, 42–43). In "La Morale de Miller" Bataille uses as examples Miller's childhood descriptions of New York around the turn of the century in the *Tropics* and *Black Spring*. On the streets, Miller and his friends live in gangs which "form a microcosm of a world turned upside down in which laws are governed diametrically opposite to adult society." The "games" these youths enact turn the established rules of civilized conduct around, and during one incident, a rival "gang" member is killed during a rock-throwing fight. Twenty years later, Miller meets the cousin who was with him on that fatal day:

> When we did meet what deeply impressed me was the look of innocence he wore — the same expression as the day of the rock fight. When I spoke to him about the fight I was still more amazed to discover that he had forgotten that it was we who had killed the boy; he remembered the boy's death but he spoke of it as though neither he

nor I had any part in it. . . . He considered it extraordinary that I should remember such things. (*Tropic of Capricorn*, 125)

In keeping with the descriptions of childhood in terms of violence and freedom, the fight sequence in *Tropic of Capricorn* carries far weightier moral implications than Miller ever imagines in the life of his contemporary adults. While his cousin shows a remnant of the laissez faire attitude which enabled the boys to get away with their crime in the first place, Miller, upon returning to his old neighborhood has now entered a different world, one in which moral implications have changed retrospectively. Bataille applauds the representation of childhood in terms of transgression, in opposition to the adult sphere of productivity, but also recognizes that Miller is now living "in a sort of exile and in this exile the children . . . bring him news from a lost land" (*Oeuvres Complètes*, 42). In this respect, the image of the writer recreating in his fiction what he can never relive is somewhat sentimental. But Bataille does not take into account that Miller's descriptions function as *constructed* images of the past, chosen for a specific purpose. Miller passes on his phobias and sense of childhood repression, but he also constructs an idyllic image of a life made sacred by the absence of conventional morality:

> In our ungratefulness was our strength and our beauty. Not being devoted we were innocent of all crime. The boy whom I saw drop dead, who lay there motionless, without making the slightest sound or whimper, the killing of that boy seems almost like a clean, healthy performance. The struggle for food, on the other hand, seems foul and degrading, and when we stood in the presence of our parents we sensed that they had come to us unclean and for that we could never forgive them. The thick slice of bread in the afternoons, precisely because it was unearned, tasted delicious to us. Never again will bread taste like this. It had a slight taste of terror in it which has been lacking ever since. And it was received with tacit but complete absolution.
> (*Tropic of Capricorn*, 127–28)

Bataille's reading of this specific instance focuses on the use of childhood as a social critique rather than a purely biographical moment. The "unearned" slice of bread, the unclean parents who have turned into a commodity, all conveniently slot into a belief in heterogeneous expenditure as possible only within the immoral sphere of childhood. As Bataille puts it: "It is rare that anything but the childhood stage of one's life is lived more intensely. Rare also that it should have such consequences for one's later life." Bataille shrewdly connects Miller's use of his past with the psychological sense of being at home, in one's own country. Growing up, in other words, constitutes a form of involuntary exile (Miller did write *Tropic of Capricorn* while in exile — although voluntarily as an expatriate). What the *Tropics* are also about, then, is how Miller recreates America while in Paris.

Bataille, however, is not interested in geographical reality, time and its ability to provide the artist with a sense of absolution is really the issue. Becoming an adult effectively means that the writer is exiled by the progression of time itself — a tragedy which by nature is inevitable — whereas a voyage away from a specific culture can be reversed. In this respect, one of the weaknesses in Bataille's analysis is his refusal to contextualize Miller within a wider tradition of American expatriate writers. By reading Miller's narrative move in terms of childhood and maturity, Bataille focuses on deeper societal schisms, but neglects the political, sexual, and cultural freedom, European exile entailed for an American at the time. Above all, Bataille insists on the past as linked to the author's sense of belonging (in America) as well as to his freedom (although he found this by leaving New York): "His early youth seemed to be a universe without limits, so much so, that the life which followed, the life of an adult, is a diminished domain" (*Oeuvres Complétes*, 42).

Miller's descriptions of childhood are symptomatic of his need "to aggressively oppose the moral values of the adults," thus re-introducing the link between literature and evil. In the realm of the child the "Evil which the parents forbid, becomes . . . that which is most sacred for the children," and the fighting which these gangs engage in, acquires a deeper meaning only if opposed to the rules and regulations of the adult world. Being disobedient is not simply childish behavior but a conscious attempt to fight back the inevitable entry into the world of the adult, just as being disobedient for the writer is a way to re-enter the world of the child. The parents on the other hand, "have the responsibility and obligation to introduce the child into 'La sphére de l'activité'" — the sphere of activity or production. As the sphere of production stresses "l'utile à la saveur," what is profitable and utilitarian rather than sensual, the child will feel an immediate hostility towards the adult sphere and "unless he is completely obedient, the child will confuse life with evil — capriciousness, violence and sensuality — for him the real taste of life lies within the confines of evil" (*Oeuvres Complétes*, 43). Bataille actually reverses the Freudian notion of childhood as a time of repression, a time where the child undergoes as series of events which lead to the formation of his later psyche. Instead, repression is shifted to the specific point in time when childhood turns into adulthood (what Miller called the "great change"), when the child is forced to solidify his position as a valuable member of society.

By grouping capriciousness, violence, and sensuality with the notion of evil, Bataille defines an alternative sphere where the child tries to remain free at the expense of conventional notions of morality. The domain of childhood, in this manner, becomes indirect proof of Miller's attraction to evil. The attraction to evil does not mean that the child is "immoral, on the contrary." Instead, the child's morality places itself within the sphere of the gangs and as such "the authentic test of morals is what he sees in the gang he is a member of; generosity, loyalty and a feeling of equality and justice." The implication is, then, that the child operates in opposition to adult notions of law and justice but not outside actual notions of good and evil. An alternative and less binary reading, would be to see Miller's childhood representations as a stopover on a voyage of self-discovery rather than a lost paradise of sorts. In *Tropic of Cancer*, the sphere of childhood contains *and* instigates Miller's search for freedom and a voice he can call his own. Bataille neglects the possibility that Miller's descriptions are representations of himself *in the process* of realizing an inner necessity to write, and as such, are not necessarily idyllic visions of a freedom no longer attainable. This is how Miller describes the realization that only in the self can freedom be found:

> I was truly alone and whenever that happened the book commenced to write itself, screaming the things which I never breathed, the thoughts I never uttered, the conversations I never held, the hopes, the dreams, the delusions I never admitted. If this then was the true self it was marvellous and what's more it seemed never to change but always to pick up from the last stop, to continue in the same vein, a vein I had struck when I was a child and went down in the street for the first time alone and there frozen into the dirty ice of the gutter lay a dead cat, the first time I had looked at death and grasped it. From that moment I knew what it was to be isolated . . .
>
> (*Tropic of Cancer*, 51)

This passage illustrates some of the differences and similarities in Miller and Bataille's visions of creativity. While they both acknowledge death as a literary trope which illuminates vulnerability as well as strength, Miller sees his own strength as based on the realization that ultimately there is only an individualist ethos to fall back on. In other words, the material for a book representing the "true self" can only come from within (as in the Bergsonian premise). Nevertheless, Bataille focuses on Miller's communal and ritualized childhood activities, and not, as this part of *Tropic of Cancer* indicates, the Miller who defines creativity as a continuous never-ending process born in solitary contemplation.

The premise, that the child's morality must be seen primarily vis-à-vis the adult structure which constitutes society, thus fails to take into consideration the complexity of Miller's "hopes" and "dreams." "Living on the edge of the infantile revolution" becomes Miller's prerogative, but not necessarily one that circumvents the society he seeks to escape and yet needs as an artist. Bataille wants Miller to escape the responsibilities of adulthood: "The child's opposition can only fail: it is possible marginally and through trickery" but Miller's trickery operates on several levels. In one sense, it represents the trickery against the world as a rebellious child and writer, but it also represents an ambiguity deliberately designed to oppose Bataille's or any other critic's attempts to push Miller into a clear political stance. If Bataille aims to show that Miller's return to the past cannot be anything but an unsuccessful attempt to hold on to the puerile voice, he fails to take into account that Miller, through his capacity to recollect, does not feel that he has lost anything:

> It was like a state of grace, a state of complete ignorance, of self-abnegation. Whatever was imparted to me in these moments I seem to have retained intact and there is no fear that I shall ever lose the knowledge that was gained. It was just the fact perhaps that it was not knowledge as we ordinarily think of it. (*Tropic of Capricorn*, 128)

The challenge which Miller thus sets himself, to live on the edge of the infantile revolution as an adult, accentuates the "radically insubmissive" attitude but is also non-threatening. In remaining "faithful to his childhood," Miller chooses to continue the fight marginally, albeit on his own terms. But this is a dubious practice, according to Bataille, since the child often seems non-serious, humorously inefficient: "the revolt condemns itself to a certain ambiguity, to the point of becoming almost inaccessible to Miller himself." Miller is therefore "a being who is difficult to define," not simply because of his constant jolts from childlike naiveté to adult anger, but because his writing is caught in a gray area between the past and the inevitable future. Thus, while Bataille sees Miller as trapped in an area where the past cannot be recaptured and the future is of no importance, he fails to see that this dichotomy *in itself* may be Miller's definition of freedom. *Tropic of Capricorn* illustrates that Miller's prime concern is how the artist absorbs and uses his past, rather than how he may return to it. In this case, Miller knows that it is impossible. Confronted with this possibility, Bataille accuses Miller of doing exactly what Breton accused him of: "Miller exasperated, sensibly asks himself whether one of the ways to address these problems is not to hide himself, to refuse to submit," and in fact this is what Miller does; refuses to submit to the reader, to his surroundings, and above all, to the moral expectations of his contemporaries. "Under these conditions, one can only be the way Miller is, the monster who acknowledges that his books are unbearable in every sense" (*Oeuvres Complétes*, 45–46).

Bataille therefore concludes that Miller's books are ultimately a sort of playground, in which he can, for a short time delay the inevitable entry into "the reality of the social order." According to Bataille: "this method is dangerously inconvenient," but the question is whether it inconveniences Miller or Bataille. By focusing on the fact that Miller is no longer a child, the constant and insistent representation of himself as "down and out," as living only for the moment without consideration for those who surround him, becomes in Bataille's eyes an effort in itself. "The effect that this obtains does not constitute a new world order" and while it is clear that "as a child Miller could have confirmed himself in this manner," now — in looking back — he cannot.

In *Black Spring* Miller confirms his identity by positioning himself as a patriot of the 14th Ward, Brooklyn, a citizen whose sense of exile is crucial for his sense of belonging as well:

> One passes imperceptibly from one scene, one age, one life to another. Suddenly, walking down a street, be it real or be it a dream, one realizes for the first time that the years have flown, that all this has passed forever and will live on only in memory; and then the memory turns inward with a strange clutching brilliance and one goes over these scenes and incidents perpetually, in dream and reverie . . . suddenly but always with terrific insistence and always with terrific accuracy, these memories intrude, rise up like ghosts and permeate every fibre of one's being. Henceforward everything moves on shifting levels — our thoughts, our dreams, our actions, our whole life. A parallelogram in which we drop from one platform of our scaffold to another. Henceforward we walk split into myriad fragments . . . we walk with sensitive filaments that drink avidly of past and future, and all things melt into music and sorrow; we walk against a united world asserting our dividedness. (*Black Spring*, 10)

Signaling the influence of Proust (whose *Albertine Disparue* he read while writing *Black Spring*), this passage shows some of the narrative psychology at work in Miller's descriptions of his childhood in Brooklyn. In it, Miller explores the relationship between the remembered self and the remembering self; a relationship wherein the recreation of the past as present provides an image of reciprocity: like parallelograms, we drop from one level to another but without necessarily loosing sight of what we left behind. The ability not to be overwhelmed by memory, while at its mercy, is at the heart of this representation of the self, and in this belief alone, lies an optimism which contradicts Bataille's claim that only the puerile voice can regain the dream of childhood. If man is divided once he enters the adult sphere, the trauma of growing up is diffused by Miller in an alternative world of dream and reverie. Miller recollects a time when human values were an integral part of an operable cultural system, but the primary reference is to a state of mind rather than the actual non-productive life of the child in utilitarian terms. As such, Miller's reminiscence is of a mythic, rather than lost America in the 14th. Ward, a place where "the foam was on the lager and people stopped to chat with one another." This is largely an image of a paradisiacal sphere where the young Henry Miller played the "orange blossom waltz" in the local saloon and "wore a velvet suit because velvet was the order of the day" (*Black Spring*, 13).

Miller's recognition that adult life is spent trying to compensate for this sense of loss, provides the necessary conditions for a re-birth of the artist. In this respect, nostalgia has a use-value which matches if not supersedes that of childhood as a form of heterogeneous expenditure, something which Bataille conveniently ignores. If Bataille ideally would like to avoid language as a way to communicate the heterogeneous, then Miller, in an opposite sense, sees literature as a crucial way to portray the self. Thus by writing about his childhood, Miller has not lost anything which he has not regained again — in looking back. In addition, the concept of exile in *Black Spring* allows him to invent, through metaphors of death and rebirth, not a single identity but a succession of identities, all of which are valuable because they examine the remains of previous selves.

Bataille is left with a conundrum: he accepts Miller's anarchical visions in the *Tropics* and yet finds it unacceptable that Miller's social critiques accentuate the artist's struggle to find his own voice. Bataille cannot accept the fact that Miller's freedom proceeds from the assumption that he is destined to become an artist. As an artist Miller's "access to the present is voluntary and active," which implies that Miller has given himself sovereign rights without taking the necessary step towards evil and death. Miller's confessional style is therefore centered in a joyful sense of expenditure rather than in pain and violence. Bataille tries to come to grips with this by linking Miller's transgressive quality to the issue of obscenity. On one hand, for Bataille, Miller's use of obscenity is that of someone who considers it a natural and legitimate way to manifest the physicality of life: "If Miller is obscene, his obscenity is like his breathing and he does so avidly, fully, totally." On the other hand, in order to illustrate Miller's ignorance towards the ways in which he negates the potential of his own obscenity, Bataille connects the use of obscenity with an ambiguous attraction to excess or limitless expenditure. According to Bataille, as long as Miller's obscenity constantly struggles between aversion and desire it will never be truly heterogeneous.

In spite of this, Miller "is honest about the fact that the games of the flesh please him." The problem is that Miller's obscenity is made sordid by his disregard for the desired object. For Bataille "seduction without respect is no longer 'real' seduction" and the *Tropics*, in accentuating the "vulgar and stupid element," become the equivalent of "a sordid obscenity." In addition, Bataille finds the actual descriptions of sex in Miller's fiction, vis-à-vis his expositions in such essays as "Obscenity and the Law of Reflection," oddly inconsistent. The Miller who speaks of achieving "understanding of an order and harmony which is beyond man's conception and approachable only through faith" seems out of synch with the man, according to Bataille, who "despises women" and "even steals from them" in the *Tropics*.

Bataille comes to terms with this incongruity by connecting Miller's use of obscenity with religion, in the hope that the religious aspect will validate Miller's sexual excess and accentuate the search for a sacred sphere beyond the enjoyment of physical sex.[24] As a way to defend Miller, Bataille is thus willing to place his obscenity somewhere between good and evil, between perfection and its opposite. The *Tropics* are elevated by the fact that the sordid operates in more than just sexual terms. In this version, "l'ordure," that which people throw away, the unusable within the sphere of production also constitutes Miller's obscenity: "which he displays, without any excuses. Miller's attraction to religion is compensated by just as significant an aversion towards perfection" (*Oeuvres Complétes*, 50). As Miller puts it in "Obscenity and the Law of Reflection": "discussing the nature of obscenity is as difficult as discussing the nature of God." "When obscenity crops out in art, in literature more particularly, it usually functions as a technical device; the element of the deliberate which is there has nothing to do with sexual excitation, as in pornography. If there is an ulterior motive at work it is one which goes far beyond sex. Its purpose is to awaken." The awakening is ultimately for Miller's own sake, and not in the service of a wider radicalization of society. Miller's obscenity, rather than designed to shock the reader, presents the emotional turmoil of the author through sex, or as Bataille puts it: "the level of illumination which the author himself reckons to have achieved." It is only once the author has passed into "another dimension of reality" that "he no longer feels the need of forcing an awakening" (*Remember to Remember*, 287–89). Bataille concludes that: "in speaking on the topic of obscenity Miller sounds like a religious preacher" (*Oeuvres Complétes*, 50).

On the one hand, "La Morale de Miller" constantly swerves from positing Miller as a religious mystic, and on the other hand, reserves the right to condemn his use of obscenity as "sordid." On one level, Bataille needs the link between eroticism and religion in order to provide his chosen literary examples "with the intention of fathoming a mystery which is no less profound, nor perhaps less 'divine,' than that of theology" (*Literature and Evil*, 116). On another level, there is also a certain amount of moralizing on Miller's account when the coexistence of the "philosophical" and the sexually active Miller becomes proof of a sordid notion of obscenity. In these terms, Bataille can conveniently define the essays on obscenity as Miller's religious side, whereas the fiction indicates an aversion to perfection which manifests itself in an attraction to "the repulsive aspects of carnal life." Such obscenity can only lead to a false sovereignty, and, "like the conqueror amidst the ruins of a devastated city" Miller barely survives the aftermath of the sexual conquests which he has in the course of his "puerile" existence (*Oeuvres Complétes*, 53).

Compared to Bataille's definition of the heterogeneous in terms of fascism, "La Morale de Miller" is ultimately a considerably more conservative reading of sexual ethics. The heterogeneous in this respect, and what it really entails, comes to an impasse as far as obscenity is concerned. Bataille's "sordid obscenity" implies that there is a form of "pure" obscenity, that obscenity *can* entail an element of seduction as well as respect, which makes the puerile voice, although capable of transgressing adult utilitarianism and production, ill-suited for obscenity. Nevertheless, Bataille finds it hard to illustrate precisely what he means by Miller's "sordid obscenity," merely that his erotic scenes have an "aura of fatality," "an element of depression." In order to engage in this sordid obscenity Miller must also despise the women he sleeps with enough to leave them at a moment's notice. This choice extends itself to friends as well, insists Bataille, for they live "childishly in the present," and represent mini-versions of a womanizing, egotistic Miller.

The problem is that these mini-versions of Miller accentuate Miller's personal story of redemption. They represent the waste, the "ordure" which forms an integral part of the sphere of the obscene, and as such their actions are valuable in the same way that Miller valued his fellow gang-members in his youth. As Bataille puts it: "Thus the glory of the imperfect man, where filth is his characteristic, is ultimately more seductive than the glory of God," giving "the price of Miller's vulgarity a decisive value." Bataille then goes on to paraphrase "Obscenity and the Law of Reflection," "Those who want to conquer . . . the world must ruin themselves and suffer under their own devastation." The religious act of throwing oneself into the "ordures" of civilization, "before any resurrection is possible," becomes Miller's greatest accomplishment. In other words, the only way to achieve power is through a systematic debasement of the self; a rather Catholic view of the martyr as someone who inflicts pain upon himself in order to reach a higher spiritual sphere. As far as "Obscenity and the Law of Reflection" is concerned, the rhetoric does seem to point towards a divine sphere of "order and harmony." The "lust to convert" may start out as a desire to rebel but it ends, in Miller's case, with an acknowledgment that only the self can be saved.

Written around 1941, Miller's essay on obscenity pre-empts "La Morale de Miller," and accounts in a large measure for Bataille's view of Miller as a mystic. The essay contains many of the key factors in Bataille's own theories on obscenity, on the link between sexuality and the sublime and how the religious and the sexual exists in close conjunction with one another. As Bataille puts it in "La Morale de Miller," "It is not in the stars but in the gutter that the empire of seduction hides itself. . . . Only by going through denigration and wallowing in it, can one once again grasp the past." In spite of this, what Miller's fiction lacks, from Bataille's point of view, is the crucial move from transgression into a state of indifference and death. In *Black Spring* the return to childhood was a process wherein the artist may find his true identity. Bataille, however, while not adverse to the notion of rebirth, is in a radically different position. For Miller to acknowledge "the pain inherent in being human," he must see beyond his own art, according to Bataille. The problem is that he "wants above all to provoke adults" and by "pushing this desire to the point of absurdity, he reaches the point where he no longer worries about anything." If art is "only a sort of play," then the artist who refuses to compromise his art "will never admit that art is a luxury, and that the seriousness of existence lies elsewhere" (*Oeuvres Complétes*, 45).

Paradoxically, Bataille's sense of Miller is astutely correct, for Miller "the seriousness of existence" *is* art. Going back to Benjamin's call for a politicized way to describe the experience of modernity, both Bataille and Miller fail, in so far as they seek answers outside the traditional sphere of party-politics. The great investment by Miller in his literary production, lies then, not so much in the creation of an obscene voice, as it does in his attempts to get to the heart of what constitutes creativity. This provides Bataille with a basic conundrum: if literature is the experience of limits and the author is responsible for maintaining his text at the edge of meaning, then death — the absolute negation of meaning, reasoning, and utilitarianism, is also the death of literature. Bataille says it himself in "La Morale de Miller," "if one refuses the 'possible,' one accepts on the other hand to be torn apart, to remain in the grasp of the 'impossible'" (*Oeuvres Complétes*, 46–50).

Such a critique is almost identical to Habermas's observation on Bataille's use of fascist aesthetics. The question remains of how to synthesize a vision of an ecstatic and violent breakthrough in aesthetic terms without dismissing the rational and speculative philosophy which enables such a thing in the first place. In a similar manner, Bataille dismisses Miller for not providing a dialectical resolution to the issue of childhood, and thus, indirectly retracts one of the major premises for his own definition of the heterogeneous. Ultimately, Bataille feels capable of critiquing Miller on the grounds of a "sordid obscenity" but Bataille needs the idea of a "sordid obscenity" in order to posit the existence of the heterogeneous in the first place. The fact of the matter is that Bataille's own writing does not tolerate the type of scrutiny which he himself applies to Miller. According to Bataille, Miller "changes the perspectives from which we see things" by subverting our conventional notions of what constitutes morality, but he fails in "substituting them with an ecstatic vision of a reality which eludes us."

The accentuation of childhood as a sphere which escapes rational progress in economic, moral, life-affirmative, and indeed literary terms, is a problematic one to say the least. It implies, as does fascism, that society can successfully negotiate its way around violence by allowing sporadic outlets of heterogeneous expenditure. In terms of a "puerile" language, Bataille has to believe in the possibility of a fictional as well as theoretical voice capable of stressing the limitations of discourse in general. This schism also repeats the problem at the root of automatism; can sovereignty in literary terms be attained without recourse to a rational and dialectical discourse?

In this respect, Miller's use value for Bataille could be seen as rather limited. However, Miller's refusal to abide by conventional standards of morality — especially in his representations of a sexually promiscuous narrator — provide him with the necessary measure of heterogeneity for Bataille to establish him as an example of heterogeneous expulsion;

certainly in creative if not outright political terms. That said, Miller's distrust in absolutist notions of creativity cannot be ignored as a factor in how *he* was read by his contemporaries and in turn, how Miller read other writers. After the Second World War, Miller's apocalyptic scenarios in *Black Spring* undoubtedly seemed a little too close to the bone. Miller now decided himself to analyze some of the perils encountered by the writer in search of an aestheticized politics of writing. In order to do so he chose a self-confessed fascist and a writer whom he admired immensely.

"Reflections on the Death of Yukio Mishima"

The question of how literary criticism deals with the literary aesthetics of an anti-rationalist remains, as it did in Bataille's *Literature and Evil*, at the forefront of Miller's examination of Mishima's fiction. For Yukio Mishima, the regeneration of a dying culture — Japanese Imperialism — provided the background for a literary, as well as personal quest for a sexual and political identity. Best known for his spectacular death by ritual seppuku (suicide) in 1970, Mishima's untimely death represents one of the strangest collusions between the role of militant patriot, modernist writer, and the attempt to regenerate Japanese myths of masculinity. In this respect, his suicide was not only a protest against modernization and Westernization, which he saw as the main reasons for the moral and spiritual decay of Japan, but a gesture indicative of a last escape; an escape from the "impossibility" of literature as an agent of radical transformation — hence the anti-rationalist ethos behind his death.

   To a large extent, Mishima exemplifies Bataille's definition of the heterogeneous artist par excellence. Ready to make the move from purely literary transgression into a state of death, Mishima, in a sense, does exactly that from which Miller ultimately backs off — namely renounces the life of the artist in favour of direct action. Although Miller does not directly examine the literary seeds of this ethos in Mishima's fiction, the act of suicide itself begs the question of how one aligns life with art. As Miller puts it: "To open most any one of his books one senses immediately the pattern of his life and his inevitable doom" (*Sextet*, 43). Beyond their shared status as underground writers lies the issue, then, of what it actually means to be anti-establishment, the selfsame issue which Bataille hoped to resolve through the heterogeneous.[25] As we will see, for Miller, the idea that fascism may be a liberating act is actually secondary to this; what Miller really wants, is for Mishima's death to illuminate *Henry Miller's* creative survival:

> I know that in speaking thus I appear to be white-washing Mishima (I am aware of all the things he has been accused of). But it is not my intention to white-wash Mishima nor to condemn him either. I am not his judge. I speak thus because his death, the manner and purpose of it, caused me to question some of the things I valued . . . caused me in brief to re-examine my own conscience. When I question Mishima's ideas, his motives, his way of life or whatever, I question my own at the same time. (*Sextet*, 29)

Miller is deliberately vague when it comes to any literary affinities, rather, it appears to be the act of suicide, the very violence of it, which Miller feels impinges upon his own conscience. Although never overtly stated, it is almost as though Miller sees himself as potentially in Mishima's place. Culturally and sexually, the connections between the two writers appears rather tenuous but in psychological and personal terms, Miller has found another literary exile: "He gives us the feeling of being an exile here below. Obsessed by the love of things of the spirit, everlasting things, how could be help but be an exile among us?" (*Sextet*, 43). The image of the samurai writer as a transcendent angelic figure is a rather droll one, but it supports Miller's vision of the writer as prophet and truth-sayer. Miller realized that Mishima, like himself, had constructed an elaborate persona in his fiction. For both of them the crux of literary creation lay in the narrator's search for identity.

It is no coincidence, then, that Mishima's first literary success was called *Confessions of a Mask* (Kamen no Kokuhaku, 1949). Although the main character's overt homosexual tendencies shocked as a literary subject in itself, it was the attitude toward the war, diametrically opposed to the humanistic criticism of the times, which expressed an unprecedented and shocking new temperament. Written in the first person, *Confessions of a Mask* is largely autobiographical although Mishima stressed that it should not be taken as an authentic account of his private life. According to him, the main goal was not authenticity but the use of his own experiences as a setting for an exposé of the "real" face of the protagonist. As such, the narrated events are chiefly props, placed to facilitate the removal of the social masks and gestures which hinder the protagonist from realizing and analyzing his inner self. The symbol of the mask is then both a self-revelation and a means of fictionalizing an inner drama.[26]

Upon a closer reading, Mishima's desire for self-revelation stems from reasons other than merely ethical or artistic. Although the first person confessional mode provides the structure and the materials (for both Miller and Mishima) it is foremost an attempt to construct a fictional world different from that of everyday life. The result is unorthodox in the sense that it deals with the revelation and representation of an unusual psyche, rather than an attempt to show, as a more typical narrative of psychoanalytic explanation might, how this psyche arrived in the first place.

In common with Miller, Mishima rarely questions the mind-set of his narrator, but instead, challenges the reader to accept him as a being who cannot and will not change. Psychological clues are set in order to draw the reader into the synchronic depths of the protagonist's world, while the stylistic structure of the novel simultaneously attempts to draw the reader's attention to the novel as another "mask," a picture presented to the outside world. In essence the mask enables the writer to survive intact. Within the constructed narrative of self-revelation we are given enough information to identify him as a social being, but crucially, a being who also withholds enough information to survive as a writer. The use of this balancing act in fiction-writing is an essential ingredient for the success of both Mishima's and Miller's novels. What connects the two to Bataille's notion of the heterogeneous is the overriding theme of beauty and sexuality as dependent on its impending annihilation. For Mishima, in particular, the sensational surge felt within the proximity of heterogeneous forces, whether it be violence or madness, is erotic. In addition, Mishima's homosexuality — with its accentuation on sado-masochistic practices — becomes an example of his "otherness," his heterogeneity and marginalization complicated by the fact that he admires the masculine ethic of the samurai.

It would be a mistake, however, to see Mishima's violent form of eroticism as yet another binary opposition to established ideas of what constitutes normality. In line with Bataille's definitions of the heterogeneous as existing on the margin of society, rather than directly in opposition, the erotic sphere, like that of war, becomes the setting for a complex series of games. The object of the game is not to win, but to determine the precise moment of transgression in psychological terms. Iris Gillespie, in "Mishima and the Archaic Mind" (1988) makes a distinction between a sacrifice of a violent nature for "hearth and home" and the type of sacrifice made by Mishima. She sees Mishima's "mystique of death" as a gift of "excess" which ensures the survival of the community:

> The mystique of death for a sacred monarch belongs to a different category from that of simple but honorable death for hearth and home. Above all, it guarantees the immortality of the ruler in a super-natural sense and implies some degree of participation for his loyal dedicatee. This archaic belief is a displacement of a former system whereby the ruler himself secured sanctity and immortality by ritual self sacrifice, . . . In its military/heroic context, this principle evolved from the ritual deemed essential for the fertility of the tribal unit.[27]

Gillespie focuses on Mishima's belief in the possibility of re-enacting a truth lost to a new generation of Japanese artists. Gillespie proposes Mishima's death as a response to a sense of cultural rape; a cultural rape promulgated by the acceptance of European supremacy in military, po-litical, and cultural terms. This sense of cultural rape, which activates the desire for a return to a "mythic golden age," is represented in a system where "sanctity and immortality" are ideas actively upheld and not privileges given by benevolent conquerors. For Gillespie, Mishima is a heroic rather than tragic figure, fortunate enough to believe, like the "sacred monarch," in a sense of cultural continuity as achievable through his own actions:

> The children of cultural rape, which may be long past, digested, sub-limated, occasionally respond by a determined striving for an earlier unalienable identity . . . by the invention of a mythic golden age. . . . For a fortunate few, a revival of archaic ritual may establish the illusion of cultural continuity. But for most, the deprivation of the past is transmuted to contempt. ("Mishima and the Archaic Mind," 12)

Gillespie's analysis of Mishima is not dissimilar to Bataille's definition of the heterogeneous as a form of sacrifice which ensures cultural identity. The difference is in Gillespie's realization that the re-enactment of ritual only provides the illusion of cultural continuity, not a real sense of indi-vidual identity. In Mishima's case, the trauma of "cultural rape" can be pinpointed more precisely in the effect of the Second World War. Like many young Japanese writers, Mishima felt lost in the post-war era of peace, simply because the threat of immediate death, having been drasti-cally diffused, also deprived his writing of its underlying metaphysics.

In *Confessions of a Mask*, the aristocratic setting and the background of the newly finished war provides a fascist as well as militaristic context for the narrator's disillusionment. As mentioned before, the initial out-rage over the book was not because of its homosexual element, but be-cause of the provocative way with which the war was dealt. In one scene the narrator returns to Tokyo on March 10, 1945, following the destruction of an area mainly populated by working-class families:

I was emboldened and strengthened by the parade of misery passing before my eyes. I was experiencing the same excitement that a revolution causes. In the fire these miserable ones had witnessed the total destruction of every evidence that they existed as human beings. Before their eyes they had seen human relationships, loves and hatreds, reason, property, all go up in flames. And at the time it had not been against the flames they fought, but against human relationships, against loves and hatreds, against reason, against property. At the time, like the crew of a wrecked ship, they had found themselves in a situation where it was permissible to kill one person in order that another might live. A man who died trying to rescue his sweet-heart was killed, not by the flames, but by his sweet-heart; and it was none other than the child who murdered its own mother when she was trying to save it. The condition they had faced and fought against there — that of a life for a life — had probably been the most universal and elemental that mankind ever encounters. (*Confessions of a Mask*, 111)

The returning narrator almost laments the death denied him. In one of Mishima's many glorifications of the moment which precedes death, the inability of people to survive as a unit only exemplifies man's essentially solitary condition. As war always operates on various levels, survival often necessitates "a life for a life," a rather bleak view of human nature under distress, especially if the premise is that in the extreme, murder becomes "permissible," "the most universal and elemental condition that mankind ever encounters." The narrator finds himself "emboldened and strengthened" by the misery (bringing to mind Miller's hyperactive visions of impending doom), relieved over having been spared, but also annoyed at not being part of "the total destruction."

Adding to the horror is the fact that the relationships which disintegrate in the face of death are the sacred ones, mother and child are opposed, two lovers part, and so forth. There is no respect or reverence towards "the family," nor in the descriptions of traditional love affairs. Instead, the descriptions show how the public sphere, in this case the army, and the private collide destructively in wartime; rather than dramatize the events, the destruction is described from a distance, from a solitary rather than collective viewpoint.

Mishima's fascination with the aesthetics of violence and death, as witnessed in this extract from *Confessions of a Mask*, is elaborated on in his later work on Bataille. In "Georges Bataille and Divinus Deus" (1968) Mishima praises Bataille's writing for its "vivid, harsh, shocking and immediate connection between metaphysics and the human flesh."[28] The protagonist in *Confessions of a Mask* is similarly obsessed with his own flesh and defines his self-consciousness as "a matter of sex, of the role by means of which one attempts to conceal, often from himself, the true nature of his sexual desires" (*Confessions of a Mask*, 72). In an essay published only a few months before his suicide — "Sun and Steel" — Mishima states: "If the body could achieve perfect non-individual harmony, then it would be possible to shut individuality up forever in close confinement."[29] Such a comment illustrates Mishima's attempts to bypass Western notions of mutuality and reciprocity, and to incorporate what Bataille would designate distinctly heterogeneous features. Mishima's constant simultaneous distancing from and provocation of the reader's expectations is a "game" akin to Miller's proclamations of sexual and emotional independence. The difference is that while Miller glorifies his "free" bachelor life, he is inevitably drawn to that which will complicate his "freedom," namely women. By actively seeking, and indeed humiliating the narrator during the search, Miller allows something "other" to break the cycle of narcissism which Mishima adamantly takes upon himself, to "shut individuality up forever in close confinement."[30]

The urge to be identified as a rebel and tragic hero at the same time can be viewed, according to Bataille, as another way to penetrate the boundary between the heterogeneous and homogeneous. The hero/rebel wants to go "beyond the reach of human infirmities," to attain complete sovereignty. Mishima's tragedy — the fact that death was the only way to "participate" in the heterogeneous — ironically becomes Miller's salvation, as Miller, rather than attempt to break through his own narcissism embraces *it* and death simultaneously. For Mishima, however, "there were two contradictory tendencies within myself. One was the determination to press ahead loyally with the corrosive function of words, to make that my life's work. The other was the desire to encounter reality in some field where words should play no part."[31]

Mishima recognizes this self-same dichotomy in Bataille; the sacred, indicative of an erotic and heterogeneous mode of writing, is also impossible to attain:

> What is certain, nevertheless, is that, being aware that the sacred quality hidden in the experience of eroticism is something impossible for language to reach (this is also due to the impossibility of re-experiencing anything through language), Bataille still expresses it in words. It is the verbalization of the silence called God, and it is also certain that a novelist's greatest ambition could not lie anywhere else but here. (*My Mother*, 12)

The complete exclusion of all discourse is of course impossible, but, as Mishima realizes, the elevation of the attempt into a "sacred" act is perhaps not. According to Bataille: "the door must remain open and shut at the same time. What I wanted: a profound communication between beings to exclusion of the links necessary to projects, which discourse forms."[32] Bataille invokes a "profound communication," and although Bataille's communication stems from a Catholic and Western tradition, Mishima is engaged in a similar act of sanctifying writing by invoking God. The transgressive, heterogeneous quality which politicizes the act of writing is now also mystified in semi-religious terms.

Considering Habermas's critique of violence as a transcending point of reference, Mishima appears as an example of someone whose search for the ultimate mode of literary transcendence lead him to fascism in a political sense. In looking for direct action which could supersede literary activity, Mishima discovered *Bunbu Ryodo*: the ethical principle of the traditional samurai. Bunbu Ryodo demands samurai discipline in both the military and literary arts; In other words, a perfect soldier and a perfect poet is one who is perfectly prepared for death.[33] In his last years, Mishima formed the Shield Society — Tatenokai, a small private army dedicated to the defense of the emperor. The western emblem of the society remained "SS" in spite of the obvious connotations.[34] The purpose of the Tatenokai, to restore the emperor to his previous rank as both mystical and effective ruler, was from the onset politically suspicious. By the late 1960s, the emperor Hirohito had renounced his godhead for over thirty years and was considered a figure head rather than a divine and active political figure in need of a private army.[35] In spite of this, the Tatenokai adopted the sword as a promise of strength; symptomatic of the desire to change the post-war trend in Japan towards democracy and plurality. By 1970, firmly convinced that his literary endeavors were feeble political devices, Mishima attempted a coup at the headquarters of Japan's Self-Defense Force. When the soldiers refused to follow him, Mishima killed himself by Seppuku after crying out: Long Live the Emperor (Tenno Heika Banzai!).[36]

Whether Mishima's suicide was a well calculated public gesture or the desperate act of a man who knew he had gone too far is impossible to know. Ultimately, Mishima seems to have been disillusioned with his literary effort, or in any case impatient with its results. Yet, it is clearly too simplistic to dismiss his suicide as the natural outcome of a man disillusioned by the ineffectiveness of his own literary career in political terms. In Gillespie's words: "Although in its public manifestation, the death of Mishima was dramatically speaking, a 'flop': and although

open to morally reductionist interpretations from Western or Western-
ized contemporaries, it was totally consistent with his vision of religious
orthodoxy, and therefore, a perfected deed." ("Mishima and the Archaic Mind," 32). As Miller pragmatically puts it: "Fortunately for
Mishima, he was able to blend all his notions about taking his own life
with the higher one of thereby serving his country. It was the artist in
him, no doubt, that decided how to make the best use of his death. . . .
One cannot say that it was the work of a madman or even of one tem-
porarily deranged (*Sextet*, 28).

The notion of literature as operating within the realm of action, the
ancient Japanese notion of the sword and the pen as one, partly explains
why Mishima's move to the extreme right was not a sudden act of
"madness." In "Patriotism" (Togoku, 1966), the young Lieutenant Takeyama returns to his home following an aborted revolt by the right-
wing officers under his command. The story follows his and his wife's
last moments before committing ritual suicide, their stoic and heroic
methodical preparations for the act. Takeyama never falters in his decision, but instead, infuses his last moments with a mystical grandeur and
beauty. "Patriotism" was later made into a film, directed by and starring
Mishima in the role as Takeyama. "Patriotism" deals with the aftermath
and the psychology of disillusionment, and shows how Mishima's revival
of samurai traditions in the service of emperor Hirohito provided him
with a ruling metaphor, namely that only through acts of courage could
true beauty, loyalty, and wisdom be found. With its emphasis on male-
ness and bonding through rigorous physical training, the samurai code
provided an ideal touchstone for Mishima's ideals.[37]

It is no coincidence, then, that *Confessions of a Mask* posits death as
the ultimate proof that man's most singular gesture of sovereignty is his
capability to take life into his own hands. Mishima's fiction exemplifies
Bataille's theory that absolute power "manifests, at the top, the fundamental tendency and principle of all authority: the reduction to a personal entity, the individualization of power" (*Visions of Excess*, 148).
Mishima achieved an absolute "reduction to a personal entity" the
moment he ended his totalitarian political career in an act of defiance
which simultaneously cut him off from any future political activity. The
question of whether Mishima died to gratify his own tendency towards
annihilation, or for a larger cause, is precisely what Miller questions in
"Reflections on the Death of Mishima."[38]

As mentioned before, Mishima and Miller both broke into the literary scene via semi-autobiographical fictions which set out to present a
truthful picture of physical life. In the process, however, they both end

up presenting complex narrative personas, male characters who learn by default and who try to remain intact in a world of increasing strife and confusion. Although Mishima imposes an extremely calculated tone of voice for his first person narrator, and Miller's is forever digressing, analytic comments connect the episodes in the narratives, and in both cases lead to a concentration on the main characters' sexual impulses. The calculated aura of sexual exposure, in both cases, is meant to deflate any suspicion of dishonesty, a relatively easy way to dismiss possible charges of deception and hypocrisy. While Mishima's first person narrator struggles to keep his homosexual responses free of ambiguities, the combination of paranoia and affection which he feels towards the men he desires is not unlike Miller's muddled behavior towards June/Mona/Mara. While Miller realized that *Confessions of a Mask* was not simply a record of a closet homosexual, just as the *Tropics* were not simply the memoirs of a womanizer, he avoids any closer analysis of their respective sexual behaviour.

This explains Miller's affinity with Mishima, but only in a limited sense. The "official" agenda of "Reflections on the Death of Mishima" is to lament the fact that Mishima did not realize the futility inherent in pursuing military rather than literary power. While this is the more obvious motivation behind Miller's critique, what is more interesting is the accusation that Mishima, not unlike Miller, aestheticized politics for the sake of exemplifying his own personal obsessions. Rather than make the connection outright, Miller anecdotally connects himself with his subject:

> The shock I experienced on learning of Mishima's dramatic and gruesome death was reinforced by the recollection of a strange incident which happened to me in Paris about thirty five years ago. One day, I happened to pick up a magazine, in which there were photos of the decapitated heads of Mishima and his comrade on the floor. Two things struck me at once: one, the heads were not lying on their sides but standing upright; two, one of the heads bore a striking resemblance to my own which I had once seen lying on the floor, but in pieces. Whether real or imaginary the resemblance between Mishima's head and my own was frightening. (*Sextet*, 41)

In 1936, a young artist friend had sculpted a head of Miller, "a very true likeness, which has always haunted me," and which Miller then accidentally knocked over. If we compare this seemingly inconsequential anecdote with Bataille's ideal state of the body politic, namely freed from intellectual and reasoned rule — i.e. in its most heterogeneous form — then Miller's "headless" body could be seen to symbolize this state. Although Miller is not comparing himself to the "headless" body politic, the analogy is useful in that it portrays the body as a place where everything is symbolic, and where the principal part of Miller — his head — has been made unrecognizable by himself.

If "the body" is symbolic, then Miller's decapitation scene is a way for him to project his own presence into a situation where he has no place to be, or one could say, into a story which is not his own. He is, after all, meant to be writing about Mishima. The fact that the decapitated heads of Mishima and his comrade were standing upright has no bearing on the actual point of the anecdote, it is the resemblance that Miller finds uncanny. The resemblance may be a projection, but it is a particularly disturbing one as it implies that Miller wants to resemble Mishima in death. Miller narrowly escapes any actual resemblance; his 1936 "self" shattered in an accident which he himself caused.

If one compares the symbol of the mask with the shattered head, a dichotomy appears. While the mask can be worn or taken off alternatively, the head is forever gone, irreplaceable as an object and indicative of Miller's past nihilistic ideals which have now been superseded by a more pacifistic attitude. If Miller indirectly tells the reader that the Mishima side of him is in the past, then he also indicates that the desire for death towards which Mishima was obsessively driven, can be defeated. For Miller, the heterogeneous elements in Mishima are those of tragedy first and foremost, and thus Mishima's tale, as far as Miller is concerned, is that of a man obsessed beyond redemption:

> Youth, beauty, death — these are the themes which inform Mishima's writing. His obsessions we might call them. Typical, one might say, of Western poets, or the romantic ones at least. For this Trinity he crucifies himself. . . . Mishima's love of youth, beauty, death seems to fall into a special category. And it is tainted with Narcissism. To open most any one of his books one senses immediately the pattern of his life and inevitable doom. He repeats the three motifs, youth, beauty, death, over and over again, like a musician. He gives us the feeling of being an exile here below. (*Sextet*, 43)

The analogy between Christ and Mishima provides a religious and redemptive value to Mishima's death. "He who was endowed with high intelligence, did he not perceive the hopelessness of trying to alter the mind of the masses? So far no one has ever yet been able to accomplish this. Not Alexander The Great, not Napoleon, nor The Buddha, nor *Jesus*." "I ask myself again and again — did Mishima really hope to change the behavior of his countrymen? I mean, did he ever seriously contemplate a fundamental change, a genuine emancipation?" (*Sextet*, 34).

Incapable of abstracting from Mishima's blatant militarism, Miller writes: "Judging from what I have read of you, my dear Mishima, this subject of peace does not seem to occupy a great place in your work. Today the whole 'civilized' world is nothing more than an armed camp in which the victims are silently screaming 'Peace, Peace, give us Peace!' And you, my dear Mishima, seem to have been strangely unconcerned" (*Sextet*, 53). In questioning the purpose of the attempted coup, Miller realizes that Mishima's actions are prompted by a firm belief in force, and in this respect, the concept of physical violence as an unavoidable part of the heterogeneous becomes one of the major differences between Miller and Mishima. Miller may believe in the importance and effectiveness of a radicalized mode of writing, but his distrust in the established and militarized political sphere leads him to exclude all marginalized political groups — whether they be leftist or right wing — from his concept of the heterogeneous.

Instead, Miller's focus is almost uniquely on the subversiveness of the poetic act in itself, the act of *writing out* one's violence, rather than enacting it in the "real" world. At stake is the role of the artist in times of social and political upheaval:

> The reason why the truly great artists are immune to wars and revolutions is because they realize the futility of these events or conditions. They see in them a mere periodicity, a rotation around ideals, a change of tyrannies. The fact that the religious teacher and the artist also incite wars is no contradiction of the forgoing. They stand for a state of perpetual war, an anarchy that is god-like, a constant and persistent iteration of personal values, emphasis on being and not doing. These great types have always been against, always been intransigent to a degree of fanaticism. The simple reason is that the great mass is peaceful, lethargic, stagnant, resigning itself constantly to a biological life, to collective immortality, either through sexual perpetuation of the species or through religious ideology.
>
> (ms. notebooks, 1930–35, UCLA)

This extract from Miller's 1930s notebooks presents the artist, once again, as a visionary, able to see through political hypocrisy and thus valuable within the social sphere on an equal footing with religion and politics. Within Miller's particular framework, the artist is both powerful, capable of inciting wars, and yet curiously indifferent to the collective good, which is why he laments the fact that the mob is governed by religious restrictions, restrictions which condemn sex for anything but procreation, or as Miller phrases it: "the biological life." In this context, the mass is always secondary to the primary aim of the artist:

"a constant and persistent iteration of personal values." The "anarchy that is god-like" is not so much a warning, as it is a recognition of the turmoil necessary for the creative mind: "the perpetual state of war" which the individual must channel into an "iteration of personal values" first and foremost. This "perpetual state of war" as a description of the writing process itself, is not dissimilar to Bataille's premise that the artist is someone who has recognized "excess," the ability to "give," as a prerequisite for an enactment of the heterogeneous.

The lineage between Miller, Mishima, and Bataille is thus both a stylistic and thematic one. In spite of the fact that Miller, unlike Bataille, did not believe in the search for an aesthetic purified of all moral elements (to use Habermas's expression), he was sympathetic to Mishima's attempts at pursuing an autobiographical voice wherein representations of sexuality also became a way to signal the body-politic. Like the surrealists, Miller wanted to shock, to use the energies of intoxication in his writing, but the means to do this was often via sexuality as a provocation against the establishment which is not equal to a desire to abolish the establishment itself. Above all, Miller seems to have been disillusioned by the death-driven aspects of Mishima's nihilism and in order to provide the creative process with a future, Miller adds a crucial element, namely the concept of love:

> In the realm of love all things are possible. To the devout lover nothing is impossible. For him or her the important thing is — to love. Such individuals do not fall in love, they simply love. They do not ask to possess, but to be possessed, possessed by love. When, as is sometimes the case, this love becomes universal, including man, beast, stone, even vermin, one begins to wonder if love may not be something which we ordinary mortals know but faintly. (*Sextet*, 43)

Miller reactivates sovereignty, not via a violent expulsion, but via love. This possible expenditure of energy, which in its universal and generous nature does not engage in the necessity of games or masks, is an awareness of an expanded ability to love, and a breakthrough into something immortal and universal. The concept of love is not presented as a solution to an increasingly hostile and militarized world, but as an alternative to the deadly trilogy of Mishima, where youth, beauty, and death are concepts which fade with time. For Miller "love" is everlasting, described in cosmic terms and ultimately beyond our control.

One could easily claim that Miller's abstraction of love is as "impossible" to attain as Bataille's so-called sacred sphere of the heterogeneous. This could be true, in so far as Miller defines love as somehow exceeding *both* the heterogeneous and the homogeneous. If love connects "man, beast, stone," then a sort of cosmic sovereignty can be found once the individual learns to love rather than hate. Revolution, in this respect, is first and foremost a personal realization and ultimately fascism, the need in Bataille's terms to "accumulate excessive violent energies in the person of the leader" is not a necessity for revolution. Miller recognizes Mishima's suicide as a heterogeneous gesture but within Miller's own creative framework it is also a failure.

Miller wrote until he was eighty-nine, surviving both Mishima and Bataille by several decades. Partly influenced by the sixties counterculture, he also changed his thirties inspired anarchistic viewpoints to a much more popular version of Pacifism and Buddhist aesthetics in his later life. For Mishima, on the other hand, only death could bridge the complex separations between self and activity and ultimately provide him with a raison-d'être. In opposition, Miller makes his position clear: if there is nothing else of which we can be sure, we must acknowledge that love is a necessity for survival. Narcissism must not be at the core of literary creation, even if this means a return to more traditional concepts of romantic love as fueling the creative process. Bataille's model of revolution via violence and transgression is useful in looking at literary impulse from different perspectives, as witnessed in Bataille's reading of Miller's writing. But, however obsessed or obscene he appears at times, Miller is essentially too "possessed by love" to not believe that text is always fertile and life-affirming rather than pointed towards death.

The concept of the heterogeneous goes a long way in illuminating the attraction to fascism felt by such writers as Bataille and Mishima. While Bataille's writings on fascism indicate a political leaning, as opposed to the dogmatic and ultimately lethal consequences of Mishima's embrace of imperial culture, Miller's response is equally indicative of the anxieties felt by writers operating within a self-acknowledged "radical aesthetic." Such an aesthetic, as we have seen, is not necessarily determined by its sexual content so much as by its representations of mass-psychology and violence. What Miller's essay on Mishima illustrates is partly how he moved from a tendency to embrace apocalyptic visions of modernity in the 1930s, to a more life-affirmative — if not necessarily more interesting — stance in the post-war years.

Miller's tendency in the *Tropics* to incorporate aspects of the heterogeneous into accounts of urban life and sexuality for purposes other than sensationalism was acknowledged by few of his contemporaries. While Bataille's own theories on the links between literature and violence may seem dangerously inept, at least when it comes to the realpolitik of the post-war period, his readings of "difficult" writers in the journal *Critique* are impressively astute. For decades, Miller's use of childhood, his philosophizing on obscenity as a representative force in political, not simply titillating, terms remained an unexplored avenue. While Bataille lately has been re-discovered through his links to French deconstructionist theory, no one has made an effort to examine his essays on literature or — more importantly — queried why he would chose such an idiosyncratic writer as Miller to start off the brief but noticeable career of *Critique*. In this respect, Miller's anarchical tendencies in the 1930s could be seen in psychoanalytical terms (as Nin did) as a way to explore the full ramifications of the uncensored male voice. Nevertheless, as Bataille realized, this would detract from the unavoidable connections between fascism and the body-politic in that particular period. With hindsight we can now praise Miller's move towards a pacifist ethic in such essays as "Reflections on the Death of Yukio Mishima," but while this might have been in tune with the zeitgeist of the early 1970s, his pre-war fiction cannot be divorced from the volatile — if creatively fruitful — period when fascism and literature were inter-connected.

Notes

[1] Michael Richardson provides an in-depth account of the changing relationship between Bataille and Breton in his introduction to *The Absence of Myth: Collected Writings by Bataille on Surrealism* (London: Verso, 1994).

[2] André Breton, "Manifesto for an Independent Revolutionary Art," in *Manifestos of Surrealism* (U of Michigan P: Michigan, 1969), 184.

[3] From Georges Bataille, "The Castrated Lion" which was originally a response to "The Second Surrealist Manifesto" in *Georges Bataille — The Absence of Myth — Writings on Surrealism*, trans. by Michael Richardson, (London: Verso Books, 1994), 28–30.

Later on it appears that Bataille viewed surrealism much more leniently and indeed paid homage to automatic writing and to Breton's ability to "imbue even the smallest action with a meaning that involves the fate of mankind." Georges Bataille, "Surrealism and how it differs from Existentialism" — a review of Breton's *Arcane 17* (1945), (*Absence of Myth*, 57–68).

[4] After the Second World War, Bataille's ideas on the importance of the death drive were analyzed through a series of anthropological studies in which the notion of sacrifice became central to his theory on a general economics governed chiefly by sexuality. It is likely that Bataille had read Freud's "Civilization and its Discontents" (1929) on the irremediable antagonism between the demands of the instinct and the restrictions of civilization.

[5] Georges Bataille, "The Psychological Structure of Fascism" in *Visions of Excess — Selected Writings, 1927–1939*, ed. by Allan Stoekl (Minneapolis: U of Minnesota P, 1985). All subsequent quotes from this edition. Originally published in *La Critique Sociale* 10 (November, 1933).

[6] In "The Struggle against Liberalism in the Totalitarian View of the State," *Negations* (London: Penguin Press, 1968), 7. Marcuse concludes that in a totalitarian state authority no longer depends upon validation; neither from the electorate nor from the laws set up by those in authority. Totalitarianism must be seen as based on an ethic of transcendence, metaphysics, and the irrational: "When the totality is no longer the conclusion but the axiom, the path of theoretical and practical social criticism is blocked off. Totality is programmatically mystified." Originally published in *Zeitschrift für Sozialforschung*, vol. 3 (1933).

[7] Walter Benjamin, "Theories of German Fascism," *New German Critique* 17 (Spring 1979), 126.

[8] Jung makes this point in "The Concept of the Collective Unconscious":
"There is no lunacy people under the domination of an archetype will not fall a prey to. If thirty years ago anyone had dared predict that our psychological development was tending towards a revival of the medieval persecutions of the Jews, that Europe would again tremble before the Roman fasces and the tramp of legions, that people would once more fire the Roman salute, as two thousand years ago, and that instead of the Christian cross an archaic swastika would lure onward millions of warriors ready for death — why, that man would have been hooted at as a mystical fool. And today? Surprising as it may seem, all this absurdity is a horrible reality. Private life, private aetiologies, and private neuroses have become almost a fiction in the world of today. The man of the past . . . has risen again into this very visible and painfully real life, and this not only in a few unbalanced individuals but in may millions of people!" *The Archetypes of the Collective Unconscious*, 2nd ed. (London: Routledge, 1990), 48. All subsequent quotes from this edition.

[9] Georges Bataille, *The Accursed Share*, trans. by Robert Hurley (New York: Zone Books, 1988). All subsequent quotes from this edition.

[10] Bataille's ideas on the social as the only measurement for the classification of phenomena, as well as his acknowledgment of the overriding importance of the social sphere on individual action, were influenced by Emil Dürkheim's theories on the same. For a wider discussion of Dürkheim's influence on Bataille, Michael Richardson's *Georges Bataille* (London: Routledge, 1994) provides an anthropological reading.

[11] Roland Barthes, "The Metaphor of the Eye," in Georges Bataille, Story of the Eye (London: Penguin, 1982), 119–27. Originally published as "En Hommage á Georges Bataille," in *Critique*, nos. 195–96, August-September 1963. Barthes partly based his reading on Bataille's "The Use Value of D. A.

F. de Sade" (1929), in which Sadism is seen as the result of the expulsion of heterogeneous elements. For a wider look at Bataille's role as a "radical" writer in the 1930s see: Jean-Michel Besnier, "Georges Bataille in the 1930s: A Politics of the Impossible," in *On Bataille* (New Haven: Yale French Studies, 1990), 171.

[12] Bataille's attack on surrealism reached its height in another essay from 1929 or 1930 "The 'Old Mole' and the Prefix *Sur* in the Words *Surhomme* and *Surrealist.*" Written for the avant-garde review *Bifur*, it was left unpublished in Bataille's lifetime. Perhaps Bataille, in the light of his later more favorable approach to surrealism, regretted the essay's harshness: "It is regrettable, . . . that nothing can enter into M. Breton's confused head except in poetic form. All of existence, conceived as purely literary by M. Breton, diverts him from the shabby, sinister, or inspired events occurring all around him, from what constitutes the real decomposition of an immense world." Bataille, *Visions of Excess* (Minneapolis: U of Minnesota P, 1985), 41.

In 1935 Breton and Bataille made a brief attempt at reconciliation via the formation of a new movement, "Contra Attaque," but this quickly dissolved.

[13] Georges Bataille, "Interview with Halo-Noviny," (*Visions of Excess*, 143).

[14] Further references to the anarchic tendencies behind "pleasure-driven" sexuality can be found in Bataille's chapter on De Sade in *Literature and Evil*, (London: Marion Boyars, 1985), 103–30.

[15] Wilhelm Reich's *The Mass Psychology of Fascism* appeared in 1933, coinciding with "The Psychological Structure of Fascism." Printed in Denmark due to German censorship laws, it is unlikely that Bataille read it at the time. Nevertheless, the similarities in their analysis of a "sex-economy" (the regulation of libido) and the universal aspect of fascism as an intrinsic part of suppression in both biological and sociological terms are striking.

[16] Jürgen Habermas, "Between Eroticism and General Economics: Georges Bataille," in *The Philosophical Discourse of Modernity* (Cambridge: Polity Press, 1987), 220–21. All subsequent quotes from this edition. "Between Eroticism and General Economics: Georges Bataille" was first published in English as "The French Path to Postmodernity" in *New German Critique*, 33 (Fall 1984).

[17] According to Webster's Ninth New Collegiate Dictionary, Ninth Edition.

[18] Henry Miller, *Black Spring* (London: Grafton Books, 1988), 205. All subsequent quotes from this edition. Originally published as *Black Spring* (Paris: Obelisk P, 1936).

[19] Georges Bataille, "Sacrificial Mutilation and the Severed Ear of Vincent Van Gogh," in *Visions of Excess* (Minneapolis: U of Minnesota P, 1985), 67–68.

[20] Sources used: Georges Bataille, *The Absence of Myth — Writings on Surrealism*, trans. and intro. by Michael Richardson (London: Verso, 1994), 1–25. Jean-Michel Besnier's, "Georges Bataille in the 1930s — A Politics of the Impossible," in *On Bataille*, Yale French Studies (New Haven: Yale UP, 1990).

[21] Georges Bataille, Preface, in *Literature and Evil*, (London: Marion Boyars, 1990). All subsequent quotes from this edition. Originally published as *La Littérature et le Mal* (Paris: Gallimard, 1957).

[22] Georges Bataille, "L'inculpation d'Henry Miller" (1946), in *Oeuvres Complétes de G. Bataille* (Paris: Gallimard, 1971), vol. 7, 110. All subsequent quotes from this edition.

[23] Georges Bataille, "La Morale de Miller," in *Oeuvres Complétes*, vol. 7 (Paris: Gallimard, 1971), 53. All subsequent quotes from this edition.

[24] Miller's later trilogy *Plexus* (1952), *Sexus* (1957), *Nexus* (1959), is subtitled *The Rosy Crucifixion*, an indication that his "martyrdom" in literary as well as sexual terms is a joyful as well as painful experience.

[25] Yukio Mishima's real name was Kimitake Hiraoka. He established his pseudonym at the age of sixteen with his first book *The Forest in Full Bloom* (1941). Biographical information taken from: Marguerite Yourcenar, *Mishima: A Vision of the Void* (Paris: Gallimard, 1980).

[26] Yukio Mishima, *Confessions of a Mask* (London: Grafton Books, 1986). All subsequent quotes from this edition.

[27] According to Susan Gillespie: "The semantic overlapping of the archaic 'purity versus impurity' with the modern usage of 'good versus evil' produces innumerable confusions, historically and geographically. Mishima's 'bilingual' art juxtaposes value-systems surrealistically." "Mishima and the Archaic Mind," *Adam International Review*, 487–92 (1988), 27. All subsequent quotes from this journal.

[28] Yukio Mishima, "Georges Bataille and Divinus Deus" in Georges Bataille, *My Mother* (London: Marion Boyars, 1989), 9–20. All subsequent quotes from this edition.

[29] The sun represents Japan and the steel refers to bodybuilding as well as swords.

[30] Mishima's mania for order and classification can be detected in the ways in which he defines his own homosexuality. Introversion becomes a catch phrase for what Mishima also calls his "bad habit." But whereas "bad habit" appears to define any masturbatory activity, introversion links "the inverted and the sadistic impulses with each other." (*Confessions of a Mask*, 33).

[31] Yukio Mishima, *Sun and Steel*, trans. by John Bester (London: Secker and Warburg, 1971), 8.

[32] Georges Bataille, *Inner Experience*, trans. by Leslie Anne Boldt (Albany: Albany State UP, 1988), 92.

[33] In Japanese thinking, the entrails signify, and are the locale of human sincerity. Thus the gesture of hara-kiri is the most sincere gesture of all. Suicide is one act which cannot be reversed.

[34] *My Friend Hitler*, a play by Mishima (1968) which deals with the youthfulness and beauty of the SS, was extremely controversial when it appeared. Mishima did not hesitate in manifesting an overt interest in German fascism around the time of the Tatenokai.

[35] Mishima's short story; "The Voice of the Hero Spirits" (1966) deals with the ramifications of Hirohito's decision; a group of disillusioned kamikaze flyers of the Pacific War find their raison d'être abolished once they no longer have a divine emperor to die for.

[36] The film, *Mishima: A Life in Four Chapters* (Paul Schrader, 1985) traces the events of the last day of Mishima's life interspersed with narrative from his short stories. The original production of the film was delayed, as the Japanese authorities and Mishima's widow refused to help Schrader.

[37] Yukio Mishima, "Patriotism," in *Death in Midsummer and Other Stories* (New York: New Directions, 1966).

[38] Henry Miller, "Reflections on the Death of Yukio Mishima," in *Sextet* (London: John Calder, 1972). All subsequent quotes from this edition.

4: *Time of the Assassins*

The Writer in Exile —
Arthur Rimbaud and Henry Miller.

B ATAILLE'S ESSAY ON MILLER illustrated the difficulties of re-working literary traditions of an essentially transcendental nature into viable and operative modes of politicized writing. It also showed how Bataille's work on Miller was influenced by the belief in literature's ability to convey a transgressive voice, not unlike that of the surrealists. Symptomatic of surrealism's desire to create a "scientific" legitimization for a truly modern and radical form of writing scientism, as we have seen, could also be a dangerously convenient way to ignore literature's political and moral implications.

In contra-distinction to such "scientific" legitimizations, Henry Miller's defense of his own writing could be seen as "confessional" and subjective. Chiefly concerned with the nature of individualism, as opposed to behaviorism on a collective level (Bataille's theories on fascism e.g.), Miller paid homage to those writers whom he credited as the forerunners of the first person confessional voice. Among them, writers as diverse as Yukio Mishima and Anais Nin became, in Miller's eyes, key players in literature's concern with individualism and the erotic.

This lineage of writers, although culturally disperse, created a poetics of individualism in which "the derangement of the senses" is a crucial part of the writerly project. The term stems from the French symbolist poet Arthur Rimbaud, and is invoked by Breton, amongst others, as a necessary aspect of automatism. It is no coincidence, then, that Miller heralded Arthur Rimbaud as the one writer whose writing "touches me as the work of no other man does. . . . In Rimbaud I see myself as in a mirror."[1] What this "mirror" image is, and how it reflects back on Miller's own work is the discursive topic of *Time of the Assassins* (1946).

Time of the Assassins is also the end of the "European" chapter of Miller's life. The idea of writing a book on Rimbaud germinated during Miller's stay in Europe, but he did not finish it until he had been back in the United States for almost seven years. The book thus appropriately coincides with Miller's return from expatriatism, both in a psychological and geographical sense. After *Time of the Assassins*, Miller dedicated himself to writing on and working with American artists and topics, trying to survive financially by selling reviews, excerpts from previous work, and shorter pieces to journals throughout the United States.

By 1944 Miller had remarried for the third time, and by 1946 was living under poor circumstances in a log cabin with a new daughter and the knowledge that most of his books were unpublishable in the United States. Miller's American publishers, banking on his notoriety from abroad, had commissioned a travel-book to circumvent American censorship laws a couple of years earlier. Unfortunately, in financial terms *The Air-Conditioned Nightmare* (1945) was a disaster.[2] Nevertheless, Miller pressed ahead with the Rimbaud book. With his life as an expatriate and bachelor effectively over, *Time of the Assassins* was to be something different; a study in growing up as opposed to "the infantile revolution" of the *Tropics*.

Just as Miller's 1930s writing bears the imprint of the imminent political chaos of the war years, *Time of the Assassins* is similarly representative of post-war anxieties. The title puns on Miller's belief in an imminent nuclear holocaust and becomes a way to combine his personal fears concerning "the catastrophic end which we face" with a view of Rimbaud's "gesture of renunciation" as an act which "leavened literature." "I doubt if anything will stem the tide which threatens to engulf us. But there is one thing his (Rimbaud's) coming did achieve — it transformed those of use who are still sentient, still alive to the future, into 'arrows of longing for the other shore'" (*Time of the Assassins*, 130).

The tone in *Time of the Assassins* manifests the pacifism later espoused in "Reflections on the Death of Yukio Mishima," and represents the opinions of a writer whose belief in literature has been shaken by the events of the Second World War and the increasing militarization of American society. It also represents a shift from Miller's view of the artist as inherently egomaniacal and apolitical in his pre-war writings, to a more critical view of the moral obligations of art. In order to do this, Miller structures *Time of the Assassins* so that two levels may function simultaneously: one is Miller's personal identification with Rimbaud, while the other is a polemic on the current state of affairs in America, in a creative as well as political context. In this sense, "the other shore" is a likely image of Europe; a way for Miller to use his previous explorations of European literature to criticize the current political situation in America, as well as a way to define a cultural experience he has left behind.

On another level, "the other shore" indicates a dual movement which embodies the search for death as either the elimination of creative responsibility — a decision which Miller ultimately rejects — and/or the search for the ultimate poetic gesture; a gesture which Miller sympathizes with. Between these two readings of Rimbaud, Miller posits the notion of a lost paradisiacal sphere for the artist, and death as the inevitable outcome of society's intrinsic hostility to that same artist. "What interests me extremely in Rimbaud is his vision of Paradise regained. Paradise earned . . . What defeats me is his life, which is at such utter variance with his vision. Whenever I read his life I feel that I too have failed" (*Time of the Assassins*, 109). The notion of a Paradise earned and regained is part of an American Puritan and Utopian work ethic, but it also refers back to the lost sphere of childhood and Rimbaud's role as the "boy" poet exiled from literary conventions and sexual morays.

According to Miller, Rimbaud broke the rules of artistic behavior in the most violent manner possible. He did not die and leave behind the works of a young poet cut down in the prime of life, but actually chose to stop writing voluntarily at the age of twenty-five. Rimbaud's choice to stop writing in favor of gun-running and other semi-legitimate business ventures in Africa, ensured him an outlaw persona not dissimilar to that of Yukio Mishima, and in both cases, the question emerges of whether death in real life is a failure or a heroic gesture without the actual work of the writers being taken much into consideration. In *Time of the Assassins*, Miller intends to show how this dichotomy is crucial for our understanding of the problems which besiege the artist, regardless of historical context. Claiming that "The abdication of Rimbaud is of another caliber from the self-liquidation of the contemporary poet," Miller, nevertheless, continuously connects the two.

Thus Miller is interested in a particular artistic behaviour, and in order to examine it, he distinguishes between the self-inflicted suffering of the surrealists and Rimbaud:

> They are writing not for a world which hangs on their every word but for one another. They justify their impotence by deliberately making themselves unintelligible. They are locked in their glorified little egos; they hold themselves aloof from the world for fear of being shattered at the first contact. They are not even personal, for if they were we might understand their torment and delirium. They have made themselves as abstract as the problems of the physicist. Theirs is a womblike yearning for a world of pure poetry in which the effort to communicate is reduced to zero. (*Time of the Assassins*, 59)

Miller's jab at surrealism is similar to that in "An Open Letter to Surrealists Everywhere," accusing "the modern poet" of turning "his back on his audience, as if he held it in contempt." Not only are the surrealists masking their fear of reality behind an elitist mentality, but they fail in representing the personal. They have forgotten that the modern poet "has a totally different function than those men who deal with the physical or the abstract world. . . . His language is not for the laboratory but for the recesses of the heart." The fact that the threat of scientism is linked to a form of emotional insensitivity which is defined as abstract, does not mean that Miller sees realism as the sole way to represent the personal. What he objects to is the reduction of communication in the form of an unintelligible symbolism, "an esoteric language understandable only to members of their own cult" (*Time of the Assassins*, 58). In this case, Miller stresses his own sense of individualism as indicative of an affinity with Rimbaud, but not with the surrealists.

Miller's stress on the personal, on the "interior" life of the poet, is ultimately what complicates his relationship to Rimbaud as well. As seen in his essay on Anais Nin, communication which is interior, personal, "womb-like," is also claustrophobic and menacing to the young male artist and it is this connection between femininity and a particular literary aesthetic which poses the greatest problem for Miller.

Throughout *Time of the Assassins*, the figure of the mother is singled out as the root-cause of Rimbaud's downfall, both in creative and psychological terms. In Miller's critique of surrealism, the link between poetic abstraction and the "womblike yearning for a world of pure poetry" is made obvious and rejected. The question remains though; how to escape from the threatening maternal figure, and yet continue to write from "the recesses of the heart." The voyage away from the mother has wider ramifications as well. Not only does it signal Miller's earlier escape from America, but now that he has returned, he must struggle to come to terms with an America he left behind and the "self-liquidation" of the writer he idolized, namely Rimbaud.

The image of the "womb" as a creative trap, as well as the inevitable starting point for the male artist, creates an ambiguous sense of nostalgia and fear, not unlike the emotional responses of the urban narrator in the surrealist romance. While Miller's representation of women focuses on the demonic aspect of the mother in *Time of the Assassins*, as opposed to the complex erotics of urban sexuality in the *Tropics*, similar anxieties appear to be present. One anxiety, in particular, has to do with the noticeably simplistic analysis, or rather lack of one, concerning Rimbaud's sexuality. While Miller criticized the surrealists for relying too much on stock Freudian imagery, his own representation in *Time of the Assassins* of the womb as representative of a return to a pre-natal state of security is alarmingly intertwined with that of the castrating female figure. The image of the "womb," symbolic of an emasculating mother, is also complicated by the added notion of childhood as an ideal sphere for the puerile voice. On the one hand, Rimbaud's role as child/poet embodies Bataille's "puerile existence," while on the other hand, the puerile voice is that of the writer who runs away from responsibility.[3] This makes it nearly impossible for the rebellious adolescent Rimbaud to survive, as he is caught between having to mature, and wanting to escape the responsibilities of adulthood:

> This refusal to mature . . . has a quality of pathetic grandeur. Mature into what? we can imagine him asking himself. Into a manhood which spells enslavement and emasculation? . . . Rimbaud had a glimpse of life in its splendor and fullness; he would not betray the vision by becoming a domesticated citizen of the world. . . . Alone and bereft, he carried his youth to the uttermost limits. (*Time of the Assassins*, 151)

This image of Rimbaud conveniently ignores his obsession with money and subsequent engagement in the slave-trade, both endeavors which go against the notion that he left France in search of artistic freedom. In addition, Miller stresses the inevitable stultification of the artist by describing maturity in terms of domesticity and emasculation, and in the process, sets himself up as a rare survivor of the mother and son struggle. In the introduction to *Time of the Assassins*, Miller breathes a sigh of relief: "But what I see most clearly is how I miraculously escaped suffering the same vile fate." While such misogyny is arguably dormant in Miller's earlier work, the focus on the mother — in this case — can be traced back to his friend and mentor Wallace Fowlie, a respected professor in French literature whose work on Rimbaud greatly influenced Miller. In a letter to Fowlie — one year prior to the completion of *Time of the Assassins* — Miller refers to the concept of the mother as an increasingly significant part of his own analysis: "I'm still on the Rimbaud. It's becoming a small book. And it's teaching me things — tremendous things! (For one, about my mother fixation.)"[4]

Fowlie's work on Rimbaud, with which Miller was familiar, was largely based on the idea of the poet as victim, both of his family and of society's antagonism towards his art: "The first childhood of Rimbaud . . . was spent without love and affection. . . . Only one person inhabited with him his child's cosmos, a single person who should have been his mother, but who was his enemy.[5] Fowlie's words are surprisingly close to those of

Miller, who also indicates that Rimbaud's mother failed in her maternal duties: "His revolt from her tyranny and stupidity converted him into a solitary. His effective nature completely maimed, he was forever incapable of receiving or giving love" (*Time of the Assassins*, 141).

> No wonder one is alienated from the mother. One does not notice her, except as an obstacle. One wants the comfort and security of her womb that darkness and ease. . . . Society is made up of closed doors, of taboos, laws, repressions and suppressions. One has no way of getting to grips with those elements which make up society and through which one must work if ever one is to establish a true society. It is a perpetual dance on the edge of the crater. (*Time of the Assassins*, 96)

While Miller's view of the "fearful" mother is placed tentatively within a larger societal frame work, Fowlie, instead, focuses on the inability to recognize "proper" gender roles:

> In the life of the man, the search for a mother (his real mother, his mistress, his wife) is the discovery of himself as a physical being; but the search for a father (his real father, his teacher, his friends) is the discovery of himself as a spiritual being. Paternity is a mystical state, whereas maternity is essentially a physical state. (*Rimbaud*, 15)

The stereotypical binary opposition of the physical, bodily defined female and the transcending philosophical male, clearly simplifies rather than explains Rimbaud's choices.[6] It also blatantly points to the sexual conservatism which makes it impossible for Miller and Fowlie to deal with the issue of Rimbaud's homosexuality (an inability Miller suffers from in "Reflections on the Death of Yukio Mishima" as well). While Miller simply does not mention it, Fowlie revealingly claims: "Almost everyone, in his youth, feels physically drawn to others of his own sex and worries that he is becoming homosexual and therefore different from the strong and central men of his race" (*Rimbaud*, 62). On a basic level, Fowlie's comments manifest certain personal sexual anxieties, but more importantly, they provide Miller with the critical leeway necessary to define Rimbaud as "perverted at the source," a perversion which consequently is again linked to the mother:

> But there is also a coldness about his acts, just as there was in his behavior as a poet. Even in his poetry there is this cold fire, this light without warmth. This is an element which his mother donated and which she aggravates by her attitude toward him. . . . No matter how he struggles to remove himself from the parental orbit, she is there like a lodestone pulling him back. (*Time of the Assassins*, 122)

Miller does not define how this "cold fire" actually manifests itself in the poetry. What seems more important is the fact that the mother conveniently functions as a scapegoat: "Like Rimbaud I hated the place I was born in." The fear of the womb, the controlling power of the matriarchal figure, thus becomes a fear of one's birthplace in a geographical sense as well. As Miller says in *Black Spring*: "Outside! Forever outside! Sitting on the doorstep of the mother's womb" (*Black Spring*, 199).

While *Time of the Assassins* promises a study of Rimbaud's "innocence, his hunger, his restlessness, his fanaticism, his intolerance, his absolutism," the book is also a convenient way for Miller to vent some of the anger he felt towards his own mother. This tendency, to unashamedly expose his personal traumas in relation to other writers, tends to undermine the value of Miller's literary criticism. But, more importantly, it points to the fact that Miller's chief project — the creation of self-identity through writing — has little to do with literary analysis, and more to do with what Miller calls "preserving intact the core of one's being" (*Time of the Assassins*, 75–77).

Nevertheless, this so-called "core" is less static and more fluid than the term implies. Fluctuating between a philosophy of a Bergsonian nature in which the individual is constantly undergoing change, and a more conservative one, in which it is assumed that all humans entail certain essential qualities, Miller's problem is precisely that he cannot define what such essential qualities might be. Assuming that this "core" is partly what Miller sets out to define in *Time of the Assassins*, rather than do so in terms of poetic or artistic traits, he opts to define the individual's "core" it in relation to what it seeks to escape: namely the influence of the mother. Perhaps Miller hopes that via Rimbaud he can both exorcise his psychological demons, i.e. his relationship to his mother and indeed women in general, and in the process illuminate the nature of artistic behavior.

In the introduction to the collected Henry Miller/ Wallace Fowlie Letters, "Miller and the French Writers," Fowlie describes Miller's initial contact with Rimbaud as a form of awakening: "he began reading about Rimbaud, and was struck, in his first contact with the poet's biography, by the endless parallels between Rimbaud's life, and his own." According to Fowlie, the "confirmation and emotions and illuminations" that Miller found in Rimbaud correspond to his own agenda:

> He began writing out phrases from Rimbaud on the walls of rooms where he lived. Thanks to the study of Rimbaud, the word "poet" took on a fuller meaning, as representing the man who dwells in the spirit and the imagination. He saw the poet Rimbaud also as the pa-

riah, as the anomaly, as the symbol of the disruptive forces now making themselves felt in the world. In Rimbaud, Henry rediscovered his
own plight in the world.

(*Henry Miller and Wallace Fowlie — Collected Letters*, 169)

Fowlie realized that Miller's fascination with Rimbaud stemmed from his
sense of artistic vocation, and crucially, that this vocation was intrinsically
linked to Miller's sense of being an "outsider." This image of the "outsider," the writer who sees the "disruptive forces" of contemporary society, is, as Fowlie acknowledges, a largely romantic image of the writer as
prophet and completely in accordance with how Miller will represent himself via Rimbaud. Nevertheless, in spite of being well-versed in Miller's
other writings, Fowlie fails to recognize that Miller's desire to construct
himself as a rebel-poet also serves an underlying political agenda. While
Fowlie focuses on Miller's self-confessed traumatic relationship to his
mother, Miller's exorcism of his own demons also includes a far more
complex issue, namely that of national and cultural alienation.

In *Time of the Assassins* Miller divorces himself from all cultural alliances, part of the outlook he maintains in the face of Western culture
after the Second World War. The post-war realization of the atrocities
committed during the holocaust, as well as the bombing of Hiroshima,
intensifies Miller's apocalyptic warnings:

> With the great event almost upon us the reading of the glyphs be-
> comes more than ever important, more than ever exciting. Soon, and
> most abruptly, we shall all be swimming breast to breast, the seer as
> well as the common man. A world totally new, a world awesome and
> forbidding, is at our door. . . . The poets and seers have been an-
> nouncing that new world for generations, but we have refused to be-
> lieve them. (*Time of the Assassins*, 54)

The poet-prophet, able to decipher the "glyphs" which announce the
coming of a new world, is also the holder of supreme knowledge; an inverted version, in a sense, of the heraldic poet of surrealism enthralled by
the Sphinx's riddle. As in surrealism, the link between poetic creation
and symbolism proves the ability language has to communicate a "spiritual" surplus. In this sense, Miller stands once again in opposition to
Bataille, for whom language is an ineffective, if necessary, mode of communication. The key relationship which Miller is at pains to describe, is
thus not only that of the poet and the reader, but that of language and
its representation of reality. As far as language is concerned: "The signs
and symbols which the poet employs are one of the surest proofs that
language is a means of dealing with the unutterable and the inscrutable."

Still, Miller — like Bataille — must in the end contradict himself by writing the unutterable. The suffering which the poet consequently encounters becomes proof of the authenticity of the poet's vision, a vision which partly explains why Rimbaud's "unique use of the symbol which is the warrant of his genius," also constitutes "a symbology forged in blood and anguish" (*Time of the Assassins*, 57). This celebration of a symbiotic relationship between annihilation and prophetic expectation may be difficult to take seriously, especially when Miller then paints an apocalyptic scenario in which "the seer" and the "common man" encounter the deluge "swimming breast to breast." In addition, it does not appear to bother Miller that he might belittle Rimbaud's artistic complexity by using "Après Le Déluge" in this way. Thus, while annihilation and destruction are made democratic, Miller's politics are still essentially pessimistic. To a large extent, Miller is also mimicking Fowlie's version of the Rimbaudian deluge: "After the fall of Adam the earth gradually became a sorry place of vice, and God sent the deluge to wipe away all traces of the decadence of the human race and to give a few chosen men the chance of starting afresh, in a world washed clean of sin and corruption" (*Rimbaud*, 216). What makes this description rather unnerving in political terms, is the fact that what is meant as a warning concerning the Second World War, actually echoes a pre-war 1930s fascist rhetoric. In this respect, the chosen title *Time of the Assassins*, is appropriately ambiguous as well. Are the assassins the "rebel-poets," the new super-powers, or as seen previously in Bataille, simply another denomination for an expenditure of heterogeneity through revolt and violence?[7]

Written just as the cold war begins Miller sees: "The spell of the millennium as being replaced by the thrall of utter annihilation," and Rimbaud as the poet who in "the symbolic language of the soul has described all that is now happening":

> Despite the denials of the men of science, the power we now have in our hands is radioactive, is permanently destructive. . . . There is nothing mysterious about the energies of the atom; the mystery is in men's hearts. The discovery of atomic energy is synchronous with the discovery that we can never trust one another again. There lies the fatality — in this hydra-headed fear which no bomb can destroy. The real renegade is the man who has lost faith in his fellow man. Today the loss of faith is universal. . . . We have put our faith in the bomb, and it is the bomb which will answer our prayers.
>
> (*Time of the Assassins*, 89)

Part anarchism, part pacifism, Miller's diatribe against militarization, although seemingly about Rimbaud, is really about Miller. When Miller faults Rimbaud for not being able to activate art politically and then links it with his failure as an expatriate in Africa, he could be talking about himself. "How ironical that the solitary poet who ran to the end of the world in order to eke out a miserable living should have to sit with hands folded and watch the big powers make a mess of things in his own garden" (*Time of the Assassins*, 84). Miller's mode of analysis obscures the real issue, namely the attempt to define his *own* creative processes. If the analogy between Miller and Rimbaud appears ill-defined in terms of shared stylistics and poetics, Miller's interest in his own mythical qualities seems more obvious. As Bertrand Mathieu puts it in *Orpheus in Brooklyn* (1976): "By recognizing the personal traits and outlook of the hero of a myth in his own personality, a writer acquires the power to instruct us in the urgencies and triumphs of that myth simply by telling us his own story."[8] Mathieu's book on Miller and Rimbaud is prefaced by none other than Wallace Fowlie, and it follows the optimistic premise that confessional writing, by nature, contains an instructive quality. However, while Miller uses Rimbaud's mythical qualities to prove his own much desired timeless qualities, it is not, as Mathieu writes, such a simple task. As Miller looks back on his past from the comfortable position of a writer confident in his ability to communicate, he sees Rimbaud as never having reached this stage: "It was as though, cut off in the prime of manhood, he was cheated of that final phase of development which permits a man to harmonize his warring selves." Miller seems to imply that had Rimbaud lived longer he would have returned, capable of uniting the urge to rebel with the urge to write. Thus, Miller, who has chosen the proper path can tell his fallen idol: "The only effort demanded of him (the poet) is that he open the eyes of his soul, that he gaze into the heart of reality and not flounder about in the realm of illusion and delusion" (*Time of the Assassins*, 92).

However, the confident rhetoric does not hide a fundamental problem, for in spite of Miller's self-assured position as a mature writer, he fails to question his own expatriatism in the process. On the one hand, Miller defines Rimbaud's move from France in tragic terms, while on the other, he acknowledges Rimbaud's craving for an ideal condition of freedom elsewhere: "I would rather die than be forced to spend the rest of my days in the place of my birth. I can only visualize myself going back to New York as utterly destitute, as a cripple, as a man who has given up the ghost" (*Time of the Assassins*, 105).

In the context of the first atom bomb, associating America with death is hardly an innovative move. More important is the way in which Miller connects political and artistic stasis with the figure of the mother, the "place of my birth." In trying to "harmonize his warring selves," as well as the American and European strands of his voice, the image of the mother becomes a form of displacement, a way for Miller to deal with something persistently American which he cannot get away from. In other words, the mother becomes symbolic of all the psychosexual and nationalistic baggage which Miller wants to leave behind.

In the first chapter of *Time of the Assassins*, subtitled "Analogies, Affinities, Correspondences and Repercussions," Miller tells us that he first encountered the name of Rimbaud when he was thirty-six and "in the depths of my own protracted Season in Hell." He explains that his season in hell was chiefly caused by an inability to write near his family in New York. It was not until his Paris Period during the 1930s, "the period of my Illuminations," that he became creatively confident. In this respect, the progression as a successful artist is measured in proportion to the distance from that artist's birth place.

Wallace Fowlie echoes these exact words in his essay on Miller and the French writers: "The parallels were there, but each had moved in an opposite direction: Rimbaud, from literature to life, and Miller from life to literature" — a phrase which reappears in *Time of the Assassins* — "Rimbaud turned from literature to life; I did the reverse." The comparison refers both to the fact that Rimbaud ended his career in order to become an expatriate while Miller started to write successfully only once he became one, and to the wider connection between art and life: "Rimbaud restored literature to life; I have endeavored to restore life to literature" (*Time of the Assassins*, 73).

To accentuate the personal connection between himself and Rimbaud, Miller also divorces Rimbaud from other creative alliances and movements: "He has nothing in common with the school of symbolists. Nor has he anything in common with the surrealists, as far as I can see. He is the father of many schools and the parent of none." Once again, Miller's individualism, and Rimbaud's ironically, is accentuated as masculine, fatherly, rather than feminine and maternal. According to Miller, if only Rimbaud had realized this, he would not have had to "surrender his calling because he has already evinced his despair, because he has already acknowledged his inability to communicate" (*Time of the Assassins*, 87–90).

Miller — by using Rimbaud's persona rather than his actual work — returns full circle to the critique originally leveled at the surrealists. The issue, while colored by sexual anxieties leveled at the mother figure, is basically the same: how to applaud an aesthetic which seeks to communicate the unutterable while pragmatically acknowledging that this is impossible. In this respect, Rimbaud's choice to stop writing is both heroic and lamentable. The situation ironically enough also reflects Miller's post-war situation in the United States, a position in which he finds himself paradoxically both nostalgic about French culture, and critical of Rimbaud's "Frenchness" and the ease with which he gave up his calling as a writer.

This paradox illustrates one of the fundamental differences between Miller's post-war and pre-war attitudes toward creativity as well. In *Time of the Assassins*, Miller seems to support a more pragmatic American idea about writing as a calling, a sort of job. The belief in man engaged in a spiritual quest in world is thus also the puritan's belief in finding one's own space and voice in the wilderness, a belief in redemption and new beginnings. Miller's voice, in this respect, is not new in *Time of the Assassins* but "old," presenting itself through an "Adamic" vision of man's intrinsic "Goodness" before the fall. In Bataille's terms, one could also say that Miller finally looses the puerile voice in favor of an adult one. This is one of the reasons why Miller's perspective on Rimbaud is more in tune with an American transcendental vision of human existence than it is with surrealism's fascination with Rimbaud as a forerunner of anarchy and decadence: "One has to establish the ultimate difference of his own peculiar being and doing so discover his kinship with all humanity, even the very lowest" (*Time of the Assassins*, 87). Miller's version of kinship is one of democratization, a utopian American belief in equality on a transcendental scale. Whereas Bataille's sociological definition of kinship was largely based on societal structures, with hierarchy as an essential element for heterogeneous expenditure, Miller's vision of paradise on earth is one of equals.

Such abstract theorization complicates Miller's analysis of Rimbaud. Unable to differentiate between his own struggle, taking place as it does within a twentieth-century American context, and the nineteenth-century European context for Rimbaud's life, Miller can do little but recognize his own ambiguous stance:

> Why could he not have compromised? Because compromise was not in his vocabulary. In all this I rediscover my own plight. I have never relinquished the struggle. But what a price I have paid! I have had to wage guerrilla warfare, that hopeless struggle which is born only of desperation. The work I set out to write has not yet been written, or

only partially. Just to raise my voice, to speak in my own fashion, I have had to fight every inch of the way. (*Time of the Assassins*, 56)

Through "guerrilla warfare," fighting and struggling, Miller can ultimately only set himself up as the rebel-poet. But while he needs the mythical persona of the rebel-poet, Miller — as Benjamin recognized in relation to the surrealists — is also weary of the mythical propensities which lie behind such a persona. In the *Colossus of Maroussi* (1941) (a precursor to *Time of the Assassins*), Miller writes:

> We forget in our enchantment with the myth, that it is born of reality and is fundamentally no different from any other form of creation, except that it has to do with the very quick of life. We too are creating myths, though we are perhaps not aware of it. But in our myths there is no place for the gods. We are building an abstract, dehumanized world out of the ashes of an illusory materialism.[9]

Together with "the thrall of annihilation," the twentieth century suffers from an "illusory materialism," the belief that the accumulation of worldly goods will suffice in a world where the divine, the gods, are neglected in favor of an aggrandizement of our own powers. Miller's definition of mythology is clearly different from, for example, the use of myth in Aragon's *Paris Peasant*, and in this sense, his vision of a "dehumanized world" almost appears as a somewhat simplistic version of Benjamin's critique of capitalist modes of production. But Miller is not writing from a European Marxist perspective and his critique of materialism and despiritualization is born out of a post-puritan and very American desire for a classless society. Nevertheless, if Miller's desire to "communicate" with even the "lowest" echoes the desire for a class less structure, it remains firmly within a spiritual and artistic realm rather than a political one.

In *Time of the Assassins*, any political agenda is usually overshadowed by a psycho-biographical perspective represented in the constant return to the mother figure. Nevertheless, it would be an oversimplification to equate Miller's association of the womb with a desire for wish fulfillment in a purely Freudian sense. And indeed Miller warns against the notion of a desired return to the womb as the end all of psychological angst: "The psychoanalysts have traced the poison back to the womb, but to what avail? In the light of this profound discovery, as I see it, we are given permission to step from one rotten egg into another." Miller's notebooks from Paris indicate how he feels about the issue of psychoanalysis:

> I should have told you before this, perhaps, that I am growing more and more contra psychoanalysis, that I have a manuscript at hand which

treats, in one or two chapters, of the increasing divergence of aim between the modern artist and the psychoanalyst. A manuscript which is
on ice, as it were, primarily because I have to clarify my ideas further.[10]

Time of the Assassins can partly be read as a case-study, an exercise in
Miller's attraction to and disgust with psychoanalysis. Although in-
trigued by a certain kind of Jungian self-analysis — as witnessed in his
essay on Nin — Miller's skepticism concerning psychoanalysis is partly
born out of his distrust of surrealist dogma. Thus, Miller uses Rimbaud
as a way to set up a schism between the scientific-inductive method of
psychoanalysis and what he considers the intuitive-sensual method of
art. Miller may feel that in trying to adjust the artist psychoanalytically
one appropriates his or her intention and emasculates that intention in
the process, but he cannot get away from the fact that he himself employs a pseudo psychoanalytical apparatus — albeit a bastardized version — in order to prove Rimbaud's mother fixation. Miller seems
aware of the bind he finds himself in, to avoid pat Freudian terminology while nevertheless expressing his anger against the mother figure.
In speaking of himself and Rimbaud, he writes: "They must come to
terms with the mother before they can rid themselves of the obsession
of fetters" (*Time of the Assassins*, 50). While the anger so demonstra-
tively put forth is of a more complex nature than Miller cares to admit,
at least he accepts that the flight away from the mother is always followed by a sense of guilt as well as freedom.

Of the nearly 100 pages which form *Time of the Assassins*, Miller de-
votes himself to a study which on its most basic level is about how to
survive creative alienation. One could criticize the book for not being
about Rimbaud per se, but the letters between Miller and Fowlie show
Miller obsessed with something quite different. In this book, the concept of the mother becomes a trope which signals a basic failure to
communicate: "He was incapable of learning from experience. . . . We
see him victimized by the illusion that freedom can be obtained by external means. We see him remaining the adolescent all his life, refusing
to accept suffering or give it meaning" (*Time of the Assassins*, 79).

Ultimately, the key issue is that of responsibility. Returning to
Miller's initial encounter with surrealism, the links between Miller and
Breton are located in the question of how to conscientiously use one's
abilities as a writer. For Miller, the answer lay in the self and in the
various means at his disposal to represent the self truly. While Miller
obtained the necessary freedom to write by leaving his family and
country, he remained acutely aware of the political and social reasons

for having done so. For, as he explains, these are, as the myths which are built upon them, the realities which form the basis of writing itself. In political terms, the poet who is not actively working relinquishes far more than a "divine mission," he gives up his raison d'être: "He is a traitor at heart because he fears the humanity in him which would unite him with his fellow man" (*Time of the Assassins*, 97). Such a notion presupposes an enormous responsibility inherent in the capacity for creation. To be true to one's experiences can take a life time of struggling, and to transmute these experiences into a language which captures the mystical as well as the political is practically impossible.

As usual, Miller provides no answers, but returns to the fear which prompted him to re-examine Rimbaud in the light of post-war apathy and destruction. The reader is left with a pessimistic vision of a future, but it is one in which Rimbaud's vocabulary of subversion has a place:

> The foundations of politics, morals, economics and art tremble. The air is full of warnings and prophecies of the debacle to come — and in the twentieth century it comes! Already two wars and a promise of more before the century is out. Have we touched bottom? Not yet. The moral crisis of the nineteenth century has merely given way to the spiritual bankruptcy of the twentieth. It is "time of the assassins," and no mistaking it. (*Time of the Assassins*, 152)

Miller's conclusion stresses the representation of "the foundations of politics, morals, economics, and art," the self-same issues in Miller which this book has examined in a European context. Rimbaud, in this context, functions as a marker for the emotional impetus that Miller sought in his own writing, but he also signals an acute fear of a feminization configured in both sexual and geographical terms. In 1946, Miller's so-called Americanism must have been hard to pin-point, and in this respect, his work represents an almost impossible move from the American vernacular of the street-wise womanizer, to the inspired voice of the surrealist poet. For Miller, he and Rimbaud are those "who have their roots in that very future which disturbs us so profoundly. They have two rhythms, two faces, two interpretations. They are integrated to transition, to flux. Wise in a new way, their language seems cryptic to us, if not foolish or contradictory" (*Time of the Assassins*, 46). Miller's good fortune was that he saw the contradictory aspect of his own persona and work as an intrinsic part of the demons which made him a writer in the first place. Quoting Whitman, Miller would say: "Do I contradict myself? Very well, I contradict myself."[11]

The contradictory aspect of Miller lies then, not only in his critique of psychoanalysis and subsequent use of it, nor in his fondness for criticizing as well as glorifying the surrealists, but in the underlying premise of his narrative and critical voice. The extent to which this contradictory aspect is self-made is ultimately impossible to pin-point. At times, an almost schizophrenic voice appears in Miller's more experimental work; such as "Last Will and Testament" and large segments of *Black Spring*, but the dual if not multiple nature of the protagonist/narrator is always integrated into the very premise of the writing itself. In some cases, this "duologue of author with Author," as Miller calls it in *Time of the Assassins*, could be seen as an excuse for a perhaps unnecessarily self-centered vision of creativity. However, in the *Tropics* ideas are presented through an improvisatory dialogue with the reader, and the success of the limited story line often relies on whether one feels absorbed by Miller as story-teller. In the essays, this principle of construction is not present and the so-called "duologue" takes over. Miller does not want the role of a sophisticated literary critic, but he still has to elevate the position of his first person narrator in order for the criticism to remain interesting. Writing under these circumstances becomes, as Bataille put it, nearly impossible. As Miller strives to combine the surrealist inspired voice of the poet, with more American concerns such as a democratization of the transcendental experience, he flounders in a rhetoric which is indeed "cryptic" rather than immediately understandable.

Miller's tendency to theorize on a wholly personal level is ultimately what *Time of the Assassins* is about. And in this respect, Miller's abilities as literary critic are intimately bound up with his own sense of the writer as prophet. On the whole, after *Time of the Assassins* the inspired voice of Miller's Paris work was gone. Occasionally, as seen in the essay on Yukio Mishima, Miller would apply his perspective as an outsider to other writers ill-considered or neglected by their contemporaries, a welcome respite from the unfortunate re-hashing of the *Tropics* in his later fiction. Miller's inability to continue the level of critical and fictional work of his Paris years is perhaps too easily blamed on the stultification he felt in America, but the fact is that the post-war return to the United States left Miller feeling like an "outsider" in literary terms. This sense of "outsiderness" and alienation is never directly articulated in *Time of the Assassins*. Nevertheless, the criticism leveled at Rimbaud — often obviously self-directed — seems to indicate if not an outright sense of failure then an unease with what he Miller has accomplished. Paradoxically, the self-aggrandizement which permits Miller to raise himself to

Rimbaud's level as a writer simultaneously serves as a scathing indictment of a Miller's own obsession with the self:

> The liberty he demanded was freedom for his ego to assert itself unrestrained. That is not freedom. Under this illusion one can, if one lives long enough, play out every facet of one's being and still find cause to complain, ground to rebel. It is a kind of liberty which grants one the right to object, to secede if necessary. It does not take into account other people's differences, only one's own. It will never aid one to find one's link, one's communion, with all mankind. One remains forever separate, forever isolate. (*Time of the Assassins*, 49)

Miller's critique of Rimbaud's "infantile" positioning of himself echoes not only Bataille's reading of Miller but indicates a rather bleak acknowledgment of the writer's intrinsically "separate, forever isolate" role. The question that remains is whether such a position paradoxically did not ensure Miller a literary "home"; a place where he — together with such luminaries as Rimbaud — retained the privilege to truly rebel. What is frustrating, in this respect, is that Miller has no answers in terms of how to forge a link with "all mankind." As witnessed in his distrust of surrealism's promise of automatism as the great democratizer in poetic terms, Miller prefers to leave the question open. As Rimbaud so perfectly illustrated for Miller, the writer is both blessed and cursed by choosing him or herself as the great inescapable topic:

> It is the fashion to speak of these demonic beings, these visionaries, as Romantics, to stress their subjectivity and to regard them as breaks, interruptions, stopgaps in the great stream of tradition, as though they were madmen whirling about the pivot of the self. Nothing could be more untrue. It is precisely these innovators who form the links in the great chain of creative literature. (*Time of the Assassins*, 87)

Notes

[1] Henry Miller, *Time of the Assassins* (New York: New Directions, 1962), 108. All subsequent quotes from this edition.

[2] Henry Miller, *The Air-Conditioned Nightmare* (New York: New Directions, 1945). In 1939, Miller was allegedly paid in advance to write a travel book on America whose patriotic message would stir the American GIs overseas. Instead he delivered a satirical account of small-town USA, the destruction of the South, and the inhumanity of America's increasing commercialization.

[3] In "Creative Writers and Day-dreaming" (1907), Freud links creative writing firmly within the sphere of childhood. The writer "does the same as the child at play. He creates a world of fantasy which he takes very seriously." Both Fowlie and Miller's definition of Rimbaud as a "puerile" writer can be seen in the light of Freud's notion that the purest "traces of imaginative activity" are to be found in childhood. From Sigmund Freud, *Art and Literature*, vol. 14 (London: Pelican Freud Library, 1985), 131–32.

[4] Henry Miller and Wallace Fowlie, *Letters of Henry Miller and Wallace Fowlie 1943–1972*, ed. by Wallace Fowlie (New York: Grove Press, 1975), 94. All subsequent quotes from this edition.

[5] Wallace Fowlie, *Rimbaud* (London: Dennis Dobson, 1946), 8. All subsequent quotes from this edition.

[6] In the same manner, Mary V. Dearborn in her book on Miller, *The Happiest Man Alive* (London: Simon and Schuster, 1991), sees Miller's problematic relationship to sexuality as primarily born out of his intrinsic hostility towards his own mother.

[7] "Time of the Assassins" is an original poem by Arthur Rimbaud in *Illuminations,* trans. by Louise Varèse (New York: New Directions, 1946), 43.

[8] Bertrand Mathieu, *Orpheus in Brooklyn — Orphism, Rimbaud, and Henry Miller*, pref. by Wallace Fowlie (Paris: Mouton, 1976), 12–13.

[9] Henry Miller, *The Colossus of Maroussi*, (London: Minerva, 1991), 237.

[10] Henry Miller, ms. notebooks (n.d.), (UCLA Special Collections).

[11] Walt Whitman, "Song of Myself," in *Leaves of Grass*, ed. by Harold W. Bloggett and Sculley Bradley (London: U of London P, 1965), verse 51, lines 1324–25, 88.

Conclusion

BEHIND THE EXAMINATION into Miller's engagement with surrealism lies another book; one on the American roots and traditions of Miller's transcendental voice. A strong case could be made for the fact that Miller's ability to assess and incorporate European aesthetics the way he did — that is to say without a sense of necessary political or artistic allegiance — in itself is a definably American characteristic. On the other hand, one then runs the risk of romanticizing Miller's individualistic ethos as something purer, less contaminated simply by nature of its nationality. Miller's acknowledgment of the large debt he owed the European artistic community of the 1930s was unique in the sense that he persisted in pursuing a creative ethos which in his mind was a-political, and strong enough to withstand mounting political pressures from both the left and right wing. Whether Miller succeeded in this endeavor is questionable, but one thing seems to be certain — that Miller's perspective on his contemporaries was formed and directed by an intense individualism — arrogant perhaps, but no less effective in its honest attempt to assess modernity as a problematic as well as fruitful force within the arts.

While the surrealists sought answers by combining a romanticized voice with a psychoanalytically informed notion of automatism, Bataille and Miller staked their claim in more radically politicized modes of communication — albeit using literature and fiction to back up their respective philosophical agendas. Within this context, Miller's shifts, between wanting the "irrationality" of the surrealist poetic voice and adopting a more pragmatic and sensible vision of individualism, ultimately leads to a reliance on past personal experiences in the Bergsonian mode, rather than a distinct political manifesto of creativity. The lack of any one ideology to explain Miller's use of obscenity is partly what causes such varying critical responses to his work. On the other hand, as this book has hopefully illustrated, to not focus on *one* ideology allows for an examination into the question of individualism (and thus also sexuality and gender) in relation to a variety of political ideologies, including fascism, and literary forms, including surrealist romances.

Above all, Miller's sexual aesthetics turn out to be infinitely more complex than previous Feminist critiques have indicated, a point supported by the various responses to Miller's work by writers whose agendas were not straightforward critiques or defenses of Miller himself. The "digression" into a literary debate on Bataille and the heterogeneous served a crucial purpose in this respect — namely to examine how literary theory of the period appropriated the idea of the obscene into the avant-garde. As a case-study of how French literary theorists of the 1930s and 1940s appropriated and used expatriate writers, Miller's "outsider" status was a remarkably useful way for these writers to examine their own political and philosophical agendas. Similarly, Miller's work on Yukio Mishima and Arthur Rimbaud is ultimately less about the two respective authors and more about Miller's attempts to delineate his own role as a writer. By pointing out literary and political traditions different than the American ones Miller came from, the question of how modernity is dealt with across the Atlantic comes to the forefront as well.

As Miller's fiction has re-emerged in print, a number of critical biographies have exemplified the problems of persistently analyzing him as either pornographer or prophet of sexual liberation. Such readings illustrate the value of more theoretical and philosophical approaches, but still, one cannot assume that Miller's use of an ambiguous authorial voice is necessarily complex enough to criticize, indirectly, the sexuality which it appears to espouse. In *Time of the Assassins*, Miller's misogynism, in an essay supposedly on the merits of on another writer, was decidedly more uncomfortable than similar sexual content would be in a fictional context. My focus on Miller's essays could be seen then as a convenient way to avoid the issue of misogyny in general. Hopefully, though, the preceding analysis has shown how Miller's level of intellectual engagement in the essays cannot be divorced from his actual fiction. In addition, to persistently look at Miller as a writer whose persona, above all, is intrinsically linked to the narrator of his fiction makes it tempting to provide simplistic psychoanalytical readings of Miller's life as an entry into his fiction. Nevertheless, by doing so one merely ends up repeating Kate Millett's original supposition that literary quality can be determined by taking Miller's polemics at face value.

The fact that one cannot take Miller's polemics at face value should be sufficiently illustrated by Miller himself. No doubt his eagerness to both work against the grain of established literary conventions, and participate in a tradition of avant-garde literature, brought with it an often muddled outlook on the nature of literary conservatism, the writer, and his politics. Miller thus emerges as a writer who does not fit into traditional literary demarcations, and whose attitude toward a collective sense of society was symptomatic of deeply personal as well as contemporary fears. Through automatism, where the unconscious takes precedence as an indisputable and scientifically grounded idea, the attempt to constitute a radical voice is both an anxious, deeply flawed and yet courageous attempt to invigorate literature in modern terms. From this perspective, Miller's link to surrealism is understandably both critical and sympathetic, as he both questions their originality and applauds their "newness."

Through the analysis of surrealism, and such writers as Benjamin and Breton, the interest in late nineteenth-century aesthetics manifested itself in the increasing concern with the psychological motivations of the writer, and more specifically, how these occur within the changing urban environment. In Henry Miller's work, the representation of the bohemian writer within the urban milieu links the image of the poet as a visionary in a mystical sense, with that of the socially conscious commentator, a commentator whose satirical and often hostile rhetoric strives to accentuate the political and sexual changes in contemporary society. In his multiple perspectives on the role of women within the urban environment, Miller differs from the surrealists and yet shares their eagerness in trying to appropriate the urban environment for a new kind of literature. This shared interest in the unconscious as a motivation behind experimental literature partly accounts for the temptation to fall into psycho-biography when it concerns an "explanation" for Miller's work. A great deal of fictional surrealist work, in particular Breton's romances, seem suited for the psycho-biographical approach, so much so that one wonders why the challenge of circumventing it is not taken more frequently.

Another problem, in critical terms, stems from two infamous pieces of Miller criticism: the radical Feminist stance in Kate Millett's *Sexual Politics* (1969) and Norman Mailer's *The Prisoner of Sex* (1971). These two texts served to radicalize later attempts at serious critical work on Miller by setting up the dichotomy between the male chauvinist protagonist, and his representation of obscenity and gender relations as valued according to political correctness rather than literary merit. While one might assume that an author is no longer judged within such a simplistic framework, many critics still, at least in Miller's case, value his literary accomplishment primarily in moral terms.

Oddly enough, this may have to do with the "modernness" of Miller's voice compared to some of his contemporaries. The surrealists, because of their more obvious nineteenth-century ancestry, are more likely to be forgiven politically incorrect transgressions whereas Miller — whose masculinist voice of the 1930s was taken up by writers

like Norman Mailer and Philip Roth in the 1950s, 1960s and beyond —
is cursed for being "ahead of his time." What such moralistic readings
do, apart from blame Miller for the writing he inspired, is skirt the issue
of how the obscenity in the novels is used on a political as well as historical level. If we take obscenity to mean more than simply graphic rendi-
tions of sexual activity, (Bataille's definition of a sordid obscenity for
example), then the psycho-biographical mode of analysis is increasingly
suspect. Miller's exaggerated descriptions of sexual activity in the *Tropics*
are deemed offensive because of his insertion of introspective philosophical passages in between them. The issue is evidently less about what is
being said than about the context in which it is being said.

This desire to claim consistency in Miller's narrative consciousness
says a great deal about literary theory as well. Always a useful catalyst
for discussions on what, why, and how we read literature in general,
such potentially post-modern concerns have also, unfortunately, put
Miller in a no-man's land of literary analysis. Put in simple terms, he is
too difficult for straightforward psychoanalytical readings and earlier
feminist readings seem outdated, their politics insensitive to the com-
plexities surrounding the literary persona and narrative voice within
Modernism. As an example, *Time of the Assassins* returns to the ambiguous positioning of the artist vis-à-vis his craft in Miller's early surrealist work, but the intervention of the Second World War shifts the
anarchical tone of the piece and makes it less self-assured in its rhetorical stance than say "An Open Letter to Surrealists Everywhere." On top
of this, far from being straightforwardly narcissistic or angry, *Time of
the Assassins* repeats some of the anarchical rhetoric from *Black Spring*,
although not in a critical mode.

Ironically, failure to take such inconsistencies into account is precisely what has created the type of criticism which put Miller on the literary map in the first place. For Millett, the entire issue of gender relied
on her ability to prove that Miller was consistently uninterested in understanding women as individuals in their own right. In doing so, she
described Miller's sexual angst as that of a victim of patriarchal ideals,
of a machismo described in Freudian terms, as though this in itself were
not a dubious practice in Feminist terms. Such analysis, still in existence, partly relies on a view which posits that within patriarchy men
are allowed a puerile and immature attitude towards women as objects
to be played with; a somewhat patronizing attitude which serves not
only to emasculate the male writer, but also in a sense lessens the fact
that he should have a sense of moral obligation toward his craft. By

casting him in the role of the disobedient boy who has no (conscious) sense to know better, the reader is given permission to be offended.[1]

Another problem is the underlying distance between Miller's fiction and espoused ideology, which seems to imply that one cannot be responsive to Miller's creative and artistic methods while being alienated by his intrinsically masculine ideology. In this respect, Miller is also a prime example of the incongruity between a feminist desire for liberation from the social conventions of patriarchy, i.e. sexual conformity, and its unfailingly prudish attitude which desires a "clean" and acceptable Miller. Having taken authorial control away from Miller via the insistence on deeper psychological motives as governing his texts, some critics also want him to be morally and politically correct. Because much of the work on Miller is troubled by the poetic intensity and complexity of his metaphysical introspections, when contrasted with the sexual and physical action, it seems a pity that psycho-biography and sloppy analysis are set to replace both the questions and answers which need to be stated. As shown, Miller's work on surrealism touches on the issue of how to aestheticize sexuality in new ways, as well as the dangers of making physiological theories abstract as a premise from which to do this. In this context, Miller's linking of a modern sensibility, seen markedly in his representations of the urban, both distances itself from a purely mythological representation of sexuality and comments on it at the same time. From a contemporary perspective Miller's interest in the stylistic as well as moral aspects of the avant-garde, and in particular in the links between political and sexual aesthetics, can thus be seen as the precursor of an ongoing debate on the importance of the relation of art to the body-politic in the twentieth century. Now that political and erotic discourses are inextricably linked, we are less adverse to fiction which overtly illustrates the interplay of gender and power.

In this respect, the setting up of the first person confessional voice can be seen to incorporate a description of sexual behavior as an ethical means of offering a social critique. For Miller, sexuality is a crucial factor in the progression of the narrative voice as it charts the author's love affairs on a physical as well as intellectual level, and, more importantly, the ways in which the two comment upon each other. As far as gender is concerned, Miller's use of women ties into this recognition that the urban is indeed more than just a mythical landscape born out of nineteenth-century romantic ideas of the bohemian writer. Instead the constant battle between the sexes is seen as an uncomfortable reminder of the nihilism which pervades Miller's own sexual revolution and which thus goes against the notion that he idealized a particular brand of male chauvinism.

If Miller is sentimental or romantic it is not in his exposition of himself as a male Don Juan but usually in his recollections of childhood before sexual maturity. As shown, this complicates Bataille's rather one-sided view of Miller as spokesman of a violent expulsion of heterogeneous energy. Miller wanted to expel a combination of his own anxieties about not succeeding as a writer and as an expatriate, not the radical re-arranging of society. This does not mean, however, as Orwell thought in 1938, that Miller was a traditionalist, reactionary writer whose views invalidate any efforts to be truly radical. Orwell fails to see that Miller's true goal is an exposition of the self — even in selfish terms — and that this search is complicated by the fact that he is permanently unsure of what constitutes his own voice.[2] One of the reasons why Miller's work from the 1930s may appear stronger and more focused than his later work is because Miller had an identity bestowed upon himself, however tenuous, by nature of his expatriatism. Miller nevertheless makes it difficult to opt for such a solution, since he was continuously defining his "Americanness" by incorporating bits and pieces of European aesthetics and then turning them to suit his own individualistic rather than nationalistic agenda. Miller's youth in America, rather than set him on course as a writer, becomes one of deliberate removal, as Miller sought a literary home in Europe. The fact that Miller would always remain an outsider in Europe partly explains his sense of ambiguity; an ambiguity born out of his desire to have a past in literary terms and yet remove himself from what he considered a dead end in 1930.

Miller's role as a transitional figure thus operates in two ways: on one hand, as someone who tried to incorporate a discourse of the erotic into a vision of what it means to write truthfully about the self, and on the other, as someone who strove to combine radically different influences of both an American and European nature into the representation of a first person confessional voice. As has been demonstrated, Miller was not only genuinely interested in engaging in an intellectual debate with his contemporaries but saw this engagement as crucial for his own progress as a writer. His permanent distrust of militarization in all of its forms pre-empts the later pacifist ethic to emerge in *Time of Assassins*, just as his distrust towards any collective sense of society becomes a way for Miller to assert his own art, which after all, was based on trying to purify an individual voice.

Although the focus on Miller, here, is within a European context, the discourse of the self, which must ultimately be Miller's overall project, clearly functions within the American autobiographical tradition as well. Miller's ethic of individual enterprise can be charted back to Benjamin Franklin, just as his poetic sense of the self owes a lot to Walt Whitman and Emerson. In more complex terms, Miller's sense of independence is undoubtedly grounded in American traditions while his need for dissent found its voice through a European tradition of obsessional writing wherein sexuality becomes the source of heroic power.

Without an understanding of these dual strands, Miller cannot be anything but misunderstood, which is why Miller's claim to identity as a writer in the U.S. for so long was tainted by his image as pornographer and male-chauvinist. In a roundabout manner, the knowledge that *what* he was writing was immensely provocative and obscene in its day, also meant that Miller had to see the *act of writing* itself as the point of origin for the writer's identity. A reoccurring misunderstanding about Miller, still exploited in current critical biographies, is to see Miller's fiction as an accurate rendition of Miller the man, instead of realizing that the self-referential consciousness gave him the means to convey the experience of writing itself rather than a true account of a writer's life.

Ultimately, Miller's use of sexuality must be seen as a discourse of a philosophical as well as physiological nature. The experimentation with language and obscenity, above all else, contains the means of liberation for the writer who strives to retain a humanity released from materialism and notions of what constitutes "proper" writing. In this sense, Miller, far from being a retrogressive writer, is a writer instrumental in defining a modern sensibility rooted in sexuality and self-exploration.

As far as surrealism was concerned, the attempted unification of the everyday and the transcendental is a fundamental strand in Miller's modernism because it seeks to restore integrity to actual experience without neglecting its spiritual qualities. For Miller, the autobiographical mode incorporated the ideal of personal growth as well the power of the prophetic rebel/poet, a notion influenced partly by Bergson's durée réelle and then incorporated into the icon of the male-chauvinist and street wise American which he then later was criticized as being. This dual nature of his work is partly what Bataille recognized as being within the sphere of the heterogeneous. Miller's greatest feat was to represent a consciousness always ready to question the givens of our culture, and in the process illuminate the contradictions of modern life without the need for resolutions. The erotic experience, the experience of the everyday as well as the sublime, is Miller's project and it is perhaps a testament to his enduring legacy that he is still volatile enough to be misunderstood.

Notes:

[1] Erica Jong, *The Devil at Large* (London: Chatto and Windus, 1993).

Jong's recent book is just one in a series of critical biographies that use psycho-biography as a determining factor in Miller's role as a writer: Mary V. Dearborn, *The Happiest Man Alive: Henry Miller, A Biography* (New York: Simon and Schuster, 1991). Robert Ferguson, *Henry Miller — A Life* (London: Hutchinson, 1991). For a review see: Caroline Blinder, "Henry Miller in No-Man's Land: A Review of Recent Critical Biographies," *New Formations* 22 (Spring 1994), 99–105.

[2] An acknowledgment and analysis of Miller's work as a constructed discourse of the self can be found in two earlier books: Leon Lewis, *Henry Miller — The Major Writings* (New York: Schocken Books, 1986).

Jane Nelson, *Form and Image in the Fiction of Henry Miller* (Detroit: Wayne State UP, 1970).

Works Cited

English translations of foreign works have been used wherever possible.

Adorno, Theodor W. "Looking Back on Surrealism." In *Notes to Literature,* ed. by Rolf Tiedemann, trans. by Shierry Weber Nicholson, 86-91. New York: Columbia UP, 1991.

Aragon, Louis. *Paris Peasant.* Trans. by Simon Watson Taylor. London: Jonathan Cape, 1971. Originally published as *Le Paysan de Paris.* Paris: Gallimard, 1926.

Bataille, Georges. *The Absence of Myth — Writings on Surrealism.* Trans. by Michael Richardson. London: Verso Books, 1994.

———. *The Accursed Share — An Essay on General Economy.* Vol. 1. Trans. by Robert Hurley. New York: Zone Books, 1988. Originally published as *La Part Maudite* (Paris: Éditions des Minuit, 1967).

———. *Eroticism.* Trans. by Mary Dalwood. London: Marion Boyars, 1987. Originally published as *L'erotisme* (Paris: Éditions des Minuit, 1957).

———. *Literature and Evil — Essays by Georges Bataille.* Trans. by Alastair Hamilton. London: Marion Boyars, 1990. Originally published as *La Littérature et le Mal.* Paris: Gallimard, 1957.

———. "The Psychological Structure of Fascism." In *Visions of Excess — Selected Writings, 1927–1939,* ed. and trans. by Allan Stoekl. Minneapolis: U of Minnesota P, 1987.

———. "La Morale de Miller." In *Oeuvres Complétes.* Vol. 7. Paris: Gallimard, 1971.

Benjamin, Walter. *Charles Baudelaire — A Lyric Poet in the Era of High Capitalism.* Trans. by Harry Zohn. London: Verso, 1983.

———. "Surrealism — The Last Snapshot of the European Intelligentsia." In *Reflections,* ed. by Peter Demetz. New York: Schocken Books, 1986.

———. "Theories of German Fascism." In *New German Critique* 17 (spring 1979): 120–28.

———. "The Writer as Producer." In *Reflections.* New York: Schocken Books, 1978.

Bergson, Henri. *Creative Evolution.* Trans. by Arthur Mitchell. London: Macmillan, 1964. Originally published as *L'évolution créatrice.* Paris: Felix Alcan, 1907.

——. *The Creative Mind — An Introduction to Metaphysics.* Trans. by Mabelle L. Andison. New York: Citadel Press, 1992.

Brassaï, *Henry Miller — The Paris Years.* Trans. by Timothy Bent. New York: Arcade Publishing, 1995. Originally published as *Henry Miller, grandeur nature* (Paris: Gallimard, 1975).

Breton, André. *Conversations: The Autobiography of Surrealism.* Trans. by Mark Polizzotti. New York: Paragon House, 1993. Originally published as *Entretiens* (Paris: Gallimard, 1962).

——. *The Immaculate Conception.* Trans. by John Graham. London: Atlas Press, 1990. Originally published as *L'Immaculée Conception* (Paris: Éditions Surréalistes, 1930).

——. *Mad Love.* Trans. by Mary Ann Caws. Lincoln: U of Nebraska P, 1987. Originally published as *L'Amour fou* (Paris: Gallimard, 1937).

——. *Manifestoes of Surrealism* Trans. by Richard Seaver and Helen R. Lane. Ann Arbor: U of Michigan P, 1972. Originally published as *Manifestes du Surréalisme* (Paris: Pauvert, 1962).

——. *Nadja.* Trans. by Richard Howard. New York: Grove Press, 1960. Originally published as *Nadja* (Paris: Gallimard, 1928).

——. *What is Surrealism? — Selected Writings.* Ed. by Franklin Rosemont. London: Pluto Press, 1978.

Caws, Mary Ann, Rudolf E. Kuenzli, and Gwen Raaberg, eds. *Surrealism and Women.* Cambridge: MIT Press, 1991.

Cendrars, Blaise. *Confessions of Dan Yack.* Trans. by Nina Rootes. London: Peter Owen, 1990.

Dearborn, Mary V. *Henry Miller — The Happiest Man Alive* (London: Simon and Schuster, 1991).

Eluard, Paul, and André Breton. *The Immaculate Conception.* Trans. by John Graham. London: Atlas Press, 1990.

Ferguson, Robert. *Henry Miller — A Life.* London: Hutchinson, 1991.

Foster, Hal. *Compulsive Beauty.* Cambridge: MIT Press, 1993.

Fowlie, Wallace. "Henry Miller." In *Little Reviews Anthology* 1946, ed. by Denys Val Baker. London: Eyre and Spottiswoode, 1946.

——. *Letters of Henry Miller and Wallace Fowlie — (1943–1972).* Ed. by Wallace Fowlie. New York: Grove Press, 1975.

——. *Rimbaud.* London: Dennis Dobson, 1946.

Freud, Sigmund. *Civilization and its Discontents.* Vol. 12. Pelican Freud Library. London: Penguin Books, 1985.

——. "Fetishism." In *On Sexuality*. Vol. 7. Pelican Freud Library. London: Penguin Books, 1977.

——. *Letters of Sigmund Freud*. New York: Basic Books, 1960.

——. "Creative Writers and Day-Dreaming." In *Art and Literature*. Vol. 14. Pelican Freud Library. London: Penguin Books, 1985.

Gillespie, Iris. "Mishima and the Archaic Mind." In *Adam — International Review*, nos. 487–92, 1988.

Habermas, Jürgen. "Between Eroticism and General Economics — Georges Bataille." In *The Philosophical Discourse of Modernity*, trans. by Frederick G. Lawrence. Cambridge: Polity Press, 1987.

Jong, Erica. *The Devil at Large — Erica Jong on Henry Miller*. London: Chatto and Windus, 1993.

Jung, Carl Gustav. *Archetypes of the Collective Unconscious*. London: Routledge, 1990.

Mauss, Marcel. *The Gift — The Form and Reason for Exchange in Archaic Societies*. Trans. by W. D. Halls. London: Routledge, 1990.

Mailer, Norman. *Genius and Lust — A Journey through the Major Writings of Henry Miller*. New York: Grove Press, 1976.

——. *The Prisoner of Sex*. New York: Primus, 1971.

Marcuse, Herbert. "The Struggle Against Liberalism in the Totalitarian View of the State." In *Negations*, trans. by Jeremy J. Shapiro. London: Penguin Press, 1968.

Matthews, J. II. *The Surrealist Mind*. London: Associated UP, 1991.

Miller, Henry. *The Air-Conditioned Nightmare*. New York: New Directions, 1945.

——. *Black Spring*. Paris: Obelisk P, 1936. Reprint, London: Grafton Books, 1988.

——. *The Colossus of Maroussi*. San Francisco: Colt P, 1941. Reprint, London: Minerva, 1991.

——. *The Cosmological Eye*. Norfolk: New Directions, 1939. Reprint, New York: New Directions, 1961.

——. *Letters to Emil*. Ed. by George Wickes. New York: New Directions, 1989. Reprint, London: Carcanet, 1990.

——. *Quiet Days in Clichy*. Paris: Olympia P, 1956. Reprint, London: Alison and Busby, 1988.

——. *Remember to Remember*. New York: New Directions, 1947.

——. *Sextet*. Santa Barbara: Capra P, 1977. Reprint, London: John Calder. 1980.

——. *Sunday after the War*. Connecticut: New Directions, 1944.

——. *Time of the Assassins*. New York: New Directions, 1946.

——. *Tropic of Cancer*. Paris: Obelisk, 1934. Reprint, New York: Grove Press, 1961.

——. *Tropic of Capricorn*. Paris: Obelisk, 1936. Reprint, New York: Grove Press, 1961.

——. *Wisdom of the Heart*. Connecticut: New Directions, 1941.

——. *The World of Sex*. Chicago: Ben Abramson, 1941. Reprint, London: Calder and Boyars, 1970

Millett, Kate. *Sexual Politics*. New York: Ballantine Books, 1978.

Mishima, Yukio. *Confessions of a Mask*. Trans. by Meredith Weatherby. London: Grafton Books, 1988.

——. *Death in Midsummer and Other Stories*. London: Penguin Books, 1971.

——. *On Hagakure — The Samurai Ethic and Modern Japan*. London: Penguin Books, 1987.

——. "Georges Bataille and Divinus Deus." In *My Mother, Madame Edwarda, the Dead Man*, ed. by Georges Bataille. London: Marion Boyars, 1989.

Nin, Anais. *Henry and June — From the Unexpurgated Diary of Anais Nin*. Ed. by Rupert Pole. New York: Harcourt Brace Jovanovich, 1986.

——. *The Novel of the Future*. New York: MacMillan, 1968. Reprint, Ohio: Swallow Press, 1986.

Pierre, José, ed. *Investigating Sex — Surrealist Discussions 1928–1932*. Trans. by Malcolm Imrie. London: Verso Books, 1992. Originally published as *Recherches sur la sexualité, janvier 1928 — aout 1932*. Paris: Gallimard, 1990.

Reich, Wilhelm. *The Mass Psychology of Fascism*. Ed. by Mary Higgins and Chester M. Raphael. London: Souvenir Press, 1972.

Rimbaud, Arthur. *Illuminations*. Trans. by Louise Varèse. New York: New Directions, 1946.

Sartre, Jean-Paul. "Un Nouveau Mystique." In *Situations I*. Paris: Gallimard, 1947.

Stoekl, Allan, ed. *On Bataille*. Yale French Studies, no. 78. New Haven: Yale UP, 1990.

Yourcenar, Marguerite. *Mishima ou La Vision du Vide*. Paris: Gallimard, 1980.

Index